The School Library
Media Center

LIBRARY SCIENCE TEXT SERIES

The Collection Program in Elementary and Middle Schools: Concepts, Practices, and Information Sources. By Phyllis J. Van Orden.

The Collection Program in High Schools: Concepts, Practices, and Information Sources. By Phyllis J. Van Orden.

Developing Library and Information Center Collections. 2d ed. By G. Edward Evans.

The Humanities: A Selective Guide to Information Sources. 2d ed. By A. Robert Rogers.

Immroth's Guide to the Library of Congress Classification. 3d ed. By Lois Mai Chan.

Introduction to AV for Technical Assistants. By Albert J. Casciero and Raymond G. Roney.

Introduction to Cataloging and Classification. By Bohdan S. Wynar. 7th edition by Arlene G. Taylor.

Introduction to Library Automation. By James Rice.

Introduction to Library Science: Basic Elements of Library Service. By Jesse H. Shera.

Introduction to Library Services for Library Technicians. By Barbara E. Chernik.

Introduction to Public Services for Library Technicians. 4th ed. By Marty Bloomberg.

Introduction to Technical Services for Library Technicians. 5th ed. By Marty Bloomberg and G. Edward Evans.

Introduction to United States Public Documents. 3d ed. By Joe Morehead.

The Library in Society. By A. Robert Rogers and Kathryn McChesney.

Library Instruction for Librarians. By Anne F. Roberts.

Library Management. 3d ed. By Robert D. Stueart and Barbara B. Moran.

Micrographics. 2d ed. By William Saffady.

Online Reference and Information Retrieval. By Roger C. Palmer.

Problems in Library Management. By A. J. Anderson.

The School Librarian as Educator. 2d ed. By Lillian Biermann Wehmeyer.

The School Library Media Center. 4th ed. By Emanuel T. Prostano and Joyce S. Prostano.

Science and Engineering Literature: A Guide to Reference Sources. 3d ed. By H. Robert Malinowsky and Jeanne M. Richardson.

The School Library Media Center

Fourth edition

Emanuel T. Prostano
and
Joyce S. Prostano

1987

LIBRARIES UNLIMITED, INC.
Littleton, Colorado

LIBRARIES UNLIMITED, INC.
P.O. Box 263
Littleton, Colorado 80160-0263

Library of Congress Cataloging-in-Publication Data

Prostano, Emanuel T.
    The school library media center / Emanuel T. Prostano and Joyce S.
Prostano. -- 4th ed.
    xiv, 257 p. 17x25 cm. -- (Library science text series)
    Includes bibliographies and index.
    ISBN 0-87287-568-7 : $28.50.   ISBN 0-87287-569-5 (pbk.) : $21.50
    1. School libraries. 2. Media programs (Education) I. Prostano,
Joyce S. II. Title. III. Series.
Z675.S3P758 1987
027.8--dc19   87-21174
                                                                    CIP

Libraries Unlimited books are bound with Type II nonwoven material that
meets and exceeds National Association of State Textbook Administrators'
Type II nonwoven material specifications Class A through E.

PREFACE

Through the 1960s and the early part of the 1970s, an extensive effort was made to improve education and to develop school library media centers. One reason propelling this extraordinary effort was a perceived need to improve education so that the nation could keep pace with and eventually exceed technological advances of the USSR. The first edition of this text, published in 1971, focused on the need to recognize the LMC as a vital and essential element in the educational process.

Succeeding editions of *SLMC* were published during a time when little external attention focused on education. There was a substantial decline in financial and other support as well as a rapid decline in student population. During this period, the editions of 1977 and 1982 dealt with refinements of the LMC as a unified system, the need to improve management practices, resource sharing, technological networks, and district-level activities.

Today, we appear to have come full circle. A wave of intense criticism has focused on the perceived failure of the educational system to prepare the nation to compete effectively with Japan and other nations in economic and technological endeavors.

The fourth edition of *SLMC* focuses on the purpose, structure, and function of the school library media center in the context of education. Emphasis is placed on the LMC as a system, the improvement of management practices, and expanding developments in the field.

Chapter 1 provides an overview of the condition of education and proposed plans to correct deficiencies. In chapter 2, an overview is provided of the LMC as a unified system of interrelated elements existing within and for the educational program of the school. The principal elements of the LMC system are defined as assets, activities, and achievements. Chapter 3 describes basic management activities—planning, organizing, leading, and controlling. An understanding of these activities or functions is essential if the LMC system is to become effective. What the LMC should achieve is the focus of chapter 4. Areas for achievement are guidance and consulting, instruction and in-service, the design and production of media, and curriculum development and improvement. In the remaining chapters, the assets of the LMC system are discussed—personnel, facilities, media, and budget.

This work is designed to be a guide to teaching and learning about school library media centers. For those seeking an overview of the field, students, practitioners, teachers, and school administrators, it presents a view of both the ideal and the reality of the modern LMC. Substantial independent investigation of the literature and field study are recommended supplements to the text.

CONTENTS

Preface v
Figures xiii

1 – THE SETTING 1
Objectives 1
Reforming Education 2
    Successful Schools 5
Library Media Contribution to Reforming Education 7
Reforming the Library Media Field 13
Summary 15
Activities 16
Notes 16
Bibliography 18

2 – THE LIBRARY MEDIA CENTER 20
Objectives 20
In the Context of Education 21
    External Factors: The School District 22
    Internal Factors: The Individual School 23
The Library Media Center 25
    Research 25
    Programming for the Individual School 28
    Teacher Needs 30
        Checklist of Teacher Needs 30
    Student Needs 31
        Checklist of Student Needs 32
The LMC as a System 33
    Assets of the LMC System 34
    Management Activities of the LMC System 34
    Achievements of the LMC System 35
The Extended System 35
LMC Facilities 37
Summary 39
Activities 39
Notes 40
Bibliography 41

3 – MANAGEMENT ACTIVITIES 43

Objectives 43
Current Management Ideas 43
Management Activities 46
   Planning 46
      Comprehensive Planning 47
      Decision Making 53
   Organizing 54
      Staffing Positions 57
      Assembling Resources 58
   Leading 59
      Motivation 59
      Leadership 60
      Communication 61
      Coordination 61
   Controlling 61
      Effectiveness and Efficiency 62
      Other Control Devices 64
Summary 69
Activities 70
Notes 70
Bibliography 72

4 – ACHIEVEMENTS 74

Objectives 74
Guidance and Consulting Services 75
   Guidance Services for Students 76
      Information Retrieval and Utilization 76
      Reading Guidance 77
      Communication 78
      Extracurricular Programs 78
   Consulting Services for Teachers 78
      Information Retrieval and Utilization 79
      Communication 79
      Professional Services 80
Instruction and In-Service 80
   Instruction 80
      Formal Programs 80
      Instructional Systems 87
      Small Groups 89
      Guidesheets 90
      Pathfinders 91
      Applications of Technology 92
   In-Service 92
      LMC-Initiated In-Service 93
      Library Media Specialists as Participants 94

4 — ACHIEVEMENTS — *continued*

Design and Production of Media 95
    Teachers 96
    Students 96
Curriculum Development and Improvement 96
    Curriculum Development 97
    Curriculum Implementation 99
Summary 100
Activities 101
Notes 101
Bibliography 102

5 — PERSONNEL 104

Objectives 104
School-Level Considerations 104
    School Administrators 104
    Service Approaches 106
Personnel Considerations 106
    Job Descriptions 107
    Position Classification 108
    Selection of Personnel 109
Staffing the LMC 110
    Library Media Specialists 115
        Certification 115
        Research 116
        State Guides 118
        Profile — The Library Media Specialist 122
    Support Staff 123
        Technician 123
        Aide 125
        Student Assistants and Volunteers 127
    Reality Staffing 127
    Deployment of Personnel 127
    Career Ladder 128
    Supervision 129
Summary 131
Activities 132
Notes 132
Bibliography 133

6—FACILITIES AND FURNITURE. 135
  Objectives. 135
  Factors in Planning. 135
    Rationale for Space. 135
    Role of the Head of the LMC. 137
    The Architect. 138
      Schematic Design Phase. 139
      Design Development Phase. 139
      Construction Documents Phase. 139
      Bidding or Negotiation Phase. 139
      Construction Phase. 139
    Alternatives in Facilities Organization. 140
      School as an LMC Concept. 140
      A Centralized LMC System. 141
      Centralized Divisional or Resource Center Schemes. 142
      A Decentralized LMC System. 144
  Location of the LMC. 145
    Relating Space to Program. 146
    Flexibility. 148
  Centralized Facilities. 149
    Primary Space. 150
    Support Space. 153
    Traffic Patterns. 157
    Internal Physical Environment. 158
      Temperature Control. 158
      Artificial Lighting. 159
      Ceilings. 159
      Acoustical Treatment. 160
      Flooring. 160
      Wall Treatment. 160
    Security. 160
  LMC Furniture. 161
    Seating. 161
      Carrels. 161
      Workstations. 161
    Other Furniture. 164
    Storing Media. 164
      Books. 165
      Pamphlets and Transparencies. 168
      Filmstrips and Films. 168
  Summary. 169
  Activities. 170
  Notes. 170
  Bibliography. 170

7—MEDIA AND EQUIPMENT................................172
Objectives..172
Media and Equipment.................................173
    Types of Media and Equipment....................179
        Still Pictures..............................179
        Motion Pictures.............................180
        Audio.......................................181
        Television..................................182
        Microcomputers..............................183
        Field Experience............................184
        Graphics....................................184
        Instructional Kits..........................185
        Realia......................................185
        Three-Dimensional Media.....................185
    Media Production................................185
Building Media Collections..........................185
    Media Collections in the New School.............185
    School Closings.................................187
    Balance in the Collection.......................187
    Resource Sharing................................187
Selection...188
    Media Policy....................................188
    Who Selects and Why.............................189
        LMC Professionals...........................189
        Teachers....................................190
        Students....................................190
        Parent and Community Groups.................190
        Other Specialists...........................190
    Organizing for Selection........................191
    District-Level Coordination.....................191
    Direct Evaluation...............................192
    Criteria for Selection..........................192
Technical Services..................................195
    Acquisitions....................................196
    Preparation and Organization....................196
    Circulation/Distribution........................196
    Maintenance of Media and Equipment..............199
    Inventory/Weeding...............................200
Summary...200
Activities..201
Notes...201
Bibliography..202

8—THE BUDGET...204

  Objectives...204
  Budget Preparation...204
    Background Information Needed..............................204
    Cost Estimates...209
  Budgeting Systems..211
    Line-Item Budgeting..211
    Formula Budgeting..212
    Performance Budgeting......................................212
    Program Budgeting..212
    Planning, Programming, Budgeting System (PPBS)............213
    Zero Base Budgeting (ZBB)..................................216
  Administering the Budget...218
  Summary..219
  Activities...220
  Notes..220
  Bibliography...220

Appendix A—Scope and Sequence................................222
Appendix B—Uses of Computers in Subject Areas...............228
Appendix C—Job Description...................................230
Appendix D—Performance Appraisal Instrument.................231
Appendix E—School Library Media Centers.....................235
Appendix F—School Library Bill of Rights....................239
Appendix G—Library and Classroom Use of Copyrighted
  Videotapes and Computer Software...........................242

Index..249

FIGURES

1.1   Recommendations for transforming American education...........8
1.2   Recommendations in response to *A Nation at Risk*.................9
2.1   Survey of "Recognition" school LMCs.........................27
2.2   The LMC system..33
2.3   The extended system.......................................36
2.4   Facilities of the LMC.....................................38
3.1   Key activities assigned to LMC personnel....................50
3.2   Performance standards and objectives.......................50
3.3   Plan to achieve objectives.................................51
3.4   Line organization in the school LMC........................55
3.5   District line organization.................................56
3.6   District line organization including supervisory level
           personnel...56
3.7   District line and staff organization........................57
3.8   District matrix organization...............................57
3.9   Feedback loop...62
3.10   Decision flow chart (teacher request for a specific book)...........65
4.1   Computer objective categories..............................85
4.2   Common instructional uses of computers.....................86
4.3   Learning activity package..................................88
4.4   Guidesheet—searching for information.......................90
4.5   Pathfinders..91
5.1   Generalized position classification scheme.....................109
5.2   Nevada—Staffing pattern...................................112
5.3   Illinois—*Recommended Standards for Educational Library
           Media Programs*...113
5.4   Ohio—Minimum standards...................................114
5.5   Achievements and competencies for managing school LMCs.......118
5.6   Job description, media coordinator..........................121
5.7   Recommended job description for media technician.............123
5.8   Recommended job description for media aide..................125
5.9   Career ladder...129
6.1   School as an LMC concept..................................141
6.2   A centralized LMC...142
6.3   Centralized divisional and resource center schemes.............143
6.4   Decentralized facilities....................................144

6.5 Space allotments, school of 1,000 students......................147
6.6 Relationship of spaces..148
6.7 Primary space structure...150
6.8 Support space structure...153
6.9 Relating primary and support space.............................157
6.10 Traffic patterns...158
6.11 Workstation 162
6.12 Carrels/workstations 163
6.13 Trapezoid tables...163
6.14 Counter height shelving..166
6.15 Record and periodical storage..................................167
6.16 Storage of filmstrips, audiotapes, 8mm films, and
      microforms 168
7.1 Ohio standards for media and equipment..........................174
7.2 Illinois standards for media and equipment......................176
7.3 Devices for the projection of still media.......................179
7.4 Microfilm/microfiche equipment.................................180
7.5 Motion picture projection equipment............................181
7.6 Audio and cross-media equipment................................182
7.7 Camera, recorder, and monitor.................................183
7.8 Microcomputer 183
7.9 Evaluation and selection process...............................192
7.10 Media evaluation form...193
7.11 Media cycle..197
8.1 Minimum standards—expenditures for Ohio and Illinois..........206
8.2 Summary of expenditure accounts...............................208
8.3 Annual contracted maintenance costs...........................210
8.4 Media required to meet stated goals (3 years)..................211
8.5 LMC budget summary...212
8.6 PPBS process...213
8.7 PPBS generalized program data sheet...........................215
8.8 ZBB process..216
8.9 ZBB generalized decision package..............................218

1

THE SETTING

OBJECTIVES

Identify economic, social, technological and political forces and cite their impact on education.

Compare various reports critical of education and cite similarities and differences in their recommendations.

Describe the attributes of successful elementary and secondary schools.

Describe the contribution the library media field can make to the improvement of education.

Identify areas in which the library media field is considered deficient.

Formal school library service can be traced to 1835, when the New York State Legislature passed a law allowing school districts to use their taxes to establish and maintain school libraries. Since that time, the school library, adapting to changing conditions, has evolved to become today's library media center (LMC). Functioning in the context of the educational system, the library media center has been subjected to the same economic, social, technological, and political forces that shape the schools and their communities.

Some of the forces that have shaken the nation in recent years have been international in scope and reflect in part the maturing of the industrial and technological capabilities of other nations. A significant related national problem has resulted in a shift in the United States from an industrial to a postindustrial society, based on a service economy, in only twenty years.

This shift has been described as the "Third Wave" by Alvin Toffler.[1] Taking issue with the concept—postindustrial society—John Naisbitt characterized the present era as the "Information Age," observing that the overwhelming majority of so-called service workers are involved in creating, processing and distributing information. According to Naisbitt:

> The problem is that our thinking, our attitudes and consequently our decision making have not caught up with the reality of things ... the level of change involved is so fundamental yet so subtle that we tend not to see it, or if we see it, we dismiss it as overly simplistic, and then we ignore it.[2]

It is obvious that dramatic changes have occurred in economic, social, technological, and political conditions, some resulting in severe dislocations. Responses have been broad based, typically beginning with a period of intense criticism and a search for easy answers: How? Why? What did we do wrong? Who's at fault? What must be done to correct the condition?

For example, the perceived failure of corporate management in the United States led to severe criticism followed by an intensive study of superior management practices of the Japanese. Somewhat later, a correction in the presumed total failure of United States corporate management was observed by Thomas Peters and Robert Waterman, who found salvation in the characteristics of excellent organizations in America.[3] These characteristics or attributes will provide a model for others.

There is a presumed direct relationship between the quality of education in America and the ability of the nation to lead the world in economic, social, technological and political endeavors. This relationship has made education at every level and in most fields a target for reform. The challenge for education in the second half of the 1980s is to move ahead to a period of steady growth and development in which excellence is the goal and innovation the means to achieve the goal.

REFORMING EDUCATION

Several reports have been written to shake up and shape up education in America. *A Nation at Risk: The Imperative for Educational Reform* called for dramatic efforts to improve education in the schools and education for teaching:

> If an unfriendly power had attempted to impose on America the mediocre educational performance that exists today, we might have viewed it as an act of war. As it stands we have allowed this to happen to ourselves. We have even squandered the gains in student achievement made in the wake of the Sputnik challenge. Moreover, we have dismantled essential support systems which helped make those gains possible. We have, in effect, been committing an act of unthinking, unilateral educational disarmament.[4]

Some facts cited to buttress recommendations for improvement included the following:

- Some twenty-three million American adults are functionally illiterate by the simplest tests of everyday reading, writing, and comprehension.

- About 13 percent of all seventeen-year-olds in the United States can be considered functionally illiterate. Functional illiteracy among minority youth may run as high as 40 percent.

- Average achievement of high school students on most standardized tests is now lower than twenty-six years ago when Sputnik was launched.

- The College Board's Scholastic Aptitude Tests demonstrate a virtually unbroken decline from 1963 to 1980.

- Many seventeen-year-olds do not possess the "higher order" intellectual skills we should expect from them. Nearly 40 percent cannot draw inferences from written material; only one-fifth can write a persuasive essay; and only one-third can solve a mathematics problem requiring several steps.

The major recommendations of the report focused on content, standards and expectations, time, and teaching:

Content
Content would be improved by strengthening high school graduation requirements for all students to include: 4 years English, 3 years mathematics, 3 years science, 1/2 year computer science, 3 years of social studies, 2 years of foreign language for college bound students.

Standards and Expectations
Schools, colleges and universities adopt more rigorous and measurable standards, and higher expectations for academic performance and student conduct. Also that four year colleges and universities should raise their requirements for admission.

Time
More time should be devoted to learning basics. Also, require a more effective use of the school day, a longer school day or longer school year. There should also be more homework requirements.

Teaching
Colleges and universities should improve the preparation of teachers and to make teaching a rewarding and respected profession.[5]

Tomorrow's Teachers: A Report of the Holmes Group was produced by the deans of several dozen research universities. The report outlined a program for reforming teacher education in America. Their recommendations included the following:

> Certification for teachers that would require teachers to have a strong liberal arts and disciplinary background.
>
> The elimination of the typical bachelor's degree program of teacher education.
>
> Graduate education and clinical experience should become the staples of professional preparation.
>
> University faculties should re-examine their contemporary offerings.[6]

Another work, *College: The Undergraduate Experience in America* was based on a study of twenty-nine colleges and universities and on separate surveys of 500 faculty, 5,000 college students, and 1,000 college-bound high school students.[7] In its findings, the report noted that the undergraduate college is a troubled institution. The points of tension are the transition from school to college, the goals and curriculum of education, the priorities of the faculty, the condition of teaching and learning, the quality of campus life, the governing of the college, measuring the outcome, and the connection between the campus and the world. A major recommendation focused on resources for learning, noting that the quality of education is measured by the resources on campus and the extent to which students become independent, self-directed learners:

> The college library must be viewed as a vital part of the undergraduate experience.
>
> Undergraduates should be given bibliographic instruction and should be encouraged to spend as much time in the library as they spend in class.
>
> A minimum of five percent of the total operating budget of the college should be available for library support.
>
> The college should work with schools and community libraries to strengthen holdings.
>
> The college should celebrate the book.
>
> The college should link technology to the library, to the classroom and to college goals.[8]

In *Schools of the Future,* the major recommendations of fourteen education reform reports were listed by Marvin Cetron.[9] These recommendations were brought together into three categories: curriculum standards, teaching, and organization. Reforms cited by 50 percent or more of the reports are listed below under the appropriate categories for public education K-12.

Curriculum Standards
    Revise curriculum

    Strengthen requirements: English, Math, Science, Social Studies, Technology/Computer Science

    Revise vocational/work courses

    Offer special help for slow learners

    Emphasize reasoning skills

    Expect more of students

    Test for promotion/graduation

Teaching
    Raise salaries

    Strengthen teacher education

    Provide more control/fewer administrative burdens

Organization
    Improve school leadership/management

    Increase business/community involvement

    Main federal role: funding specific projects

Successful Schools

While a great deal of attention has been directed to reports critical of the quality of education, the U.S. Department of Education has supported two projects designed to identify and recognize unusually successful elementary and secondary schools and to encourage their emulation.

The Elementary School Recognition Program for 1985-1986 identified 270 outstanding public and private elementary schools in the United States.[10] William J. Bennett, Secretary of Education pointed out that "These fine public and private schools are as diverse as America itself but they share a common attribute: they're good schools."[11] A comprehensive selection process was used that included nominations of schools by chief state school officers and two day site visits. Once a school's eligibility had been determined, the following criteria (Quality Indicators) guided the selection of schools for recognition:

1. Quality of school organization

2. Quality of building leadership

3. Quality of instructional program and curriculum, including character development

4. Quality of instruction

5. Quality of school climate

6. Quality of school community relations

7. Quality of efforts to make improvements to maintain high quality programs

8. Quality of student outcomes[12]

The Search for Successful Secondary Schools identified a total of 571 schools over a three-year period.[13] Again, the selection process included nominations of schools by chief state school officers and site visits. There were fourteen attributes of success, drawn from research on effective schools, used as criteria of quality. The attributes were:

1. Clear academic goals

2. High expectations for students

3. Order and discipline

4. Rewards and incentives for students

5. Regular and frequent monitoring of student progress

6. Opportunities for meaningful student responsibility and participation

7. Teacher efficiency

8. Rewards and incentives for teachers

9. Concentration on academic learning time

10. Positive school climate

11. Administrative leadership

12. Well-articulated curriculum

13. Evaluation of instructional improvement

14. Community support and involvement[14]

From the date collected in this study, a "powerful portrait" was developed of successful secondary schools. This "portrait" is described through nine themes. While in some ways these themes are similar to the attributes of success, they differ quantitatively in their focus on the importance of people and their talents, energies, and relationships.

• Clear goals and core values

• Leadership in action

• Control and discretion

• Good people and good environment

• Recognition and rewards for teaching

• Positive student-teacher relationships

• High expectations and recognition of achievement

• Solving problems and improving the schools

• Working in the community[15]

Survey information concerning school library media centers in elementary and secondary schools is provided in chapter 2.

LIBRARY MEDIA CONTRIBUTION
TO REFORMING EDUCATION

The library media field has responded in many ways to the criticism of education. Reports cited include two initiated by the U.S. Department of Education and one by the American Library Association.

"Transforming American Education: Reducing the Risk to the Nation" wwas produced by the National Task Force on Educational Technology at the request of the U.S. Secretary of Education.[16] The Task Force focused its first five recommendations on the immediate needs of the schools through 1990. It also made general suggestions about "steps schools can take now or plan for in their transformation in the 1990-2000 period."[17] The recommendations are listed in figure 1.1.

Recommendation: Planning

For the period through 1990, it was recommended that planning for the effective use of technology should take place at every level, that every educational decision-making group should participate, and that technology planning should be integrated with other aspects of planning, such as financing, teacher education, curriculum and instructional practice, evaluation, and dissemination. Specific references were made to the roles of schools, school districts, school boards, and state education agencies.

Recommendation: Financing

For the period through 1990, it was recommended "that the financing of technology-based education occupy a central and continuing place in the budgeting of education." Specific references were made to the roles of school districts and boards, parents, the federal government, and industry.

Recommendation: Teacher Education

For the period through 1990, it was recommended that those responsible for preservice and in-service education should design effective programs for teachers to learn how to use technology in instruction and for instructional management.

Recommendation: Curriculum and Instructional Practices

For the period through 1990, it was recommended "that schools use technology-based education to make learning more active and interactive for each student, including pacing at a rate appropriate for each student." Strategies were recommended for school districts and boards, state education agencies, and higher education. A recommendation for the schools noted that "the curriculum should include the application of information technology to acquire and process information for the diverse activities of that society and the development of higher-order skills of reasoning and analysis that successful accomplishment of such activities demand."

Recommendation: Research, Development, Evaluation, Dissemination

For the period through 1990, it was recommended that state education agencies, higher education, and the information industry should "cooperate to perform research and development to transform education through applications of technology, to evaluate the effectiveness of new methods and materials, and to disseminate successful practices to the field."

Recommendation: Demonstration Schools

It was recommended that each state establish one or more demonstration schools. It was suggested that the ideal situation would have a school at each level—elementary, junior high or middle school, and high school.

Fig. 1.1. Recommendations for transforming American education. From William Ridley and H. Hull McAllister, Jr., "Transforming American Education: Reducing the Risk to the Nation," *TechTrends* 31 (May/June 1986): 12-35.

The report, *Alliance for Excellence: Librarians Respond to "A Nation at Risk"* followed an intensive review of the role of libraries in a learning society and is considered to be the response of the nation's library community to *A Nation at Risk*. Two major parts of the report providing specific recommendations, "Libraries in Support of Education" and "Library Leadership in the Learning Society," are cited in figure 1.2.

"Libraries in Support of Education"

1. To Strengthen Content

Recommendation A

"We recommend that the elementary and secondary school curriculum be strengthened by teaching the effective use of information resources, including libraries."

Recommendation B

"We recommend that every elementary and secondary school have quality library services and resources."

(Fig. 1.2 continues on page 10.)

Fig. 1.2. — *Continued*

2. To Raise Standards and Expectations

Recommendation C
"We recommend that libraries, associations, state educational and library agencies, accrediting organizations adopt more rigorous and measurable standards for school library media services."

3. To Improve the Uses of Time

Recommendation D
"We recommend that school library media centers and public and academic libraries be open, to the fullest extent possible, to elementary and secondary school students and area residents. This policy would have the joint aims of expanding the time available for learning, while making more effective use of a community's library and information resources."

4. To Improve Teaching and Learning through Improved School Library Media Programs

Recommendation E
"We recommend that school library media centers and public and academic libraries develop the collections needed to inform educators and librarians about developments in education, and the library and information science field, and about new or expanded professional concepts and practices in those fields."

Recommendation F
"We recommend that candidates for the position of school library media specialist receive a broad general education that is geared to meet the challenge of the Information Age."

Recommendation G
"We recommend that school library media specialists be offered professionally competitive salaries and working conditions that are rewarding and satisfying."

Recommendation H
"We recommend that candidates for teacher or school administrator receive meaningful instruction in the role and activity of a school library media center."

"Library Leadership in the Learning Society"

1.   To Improve Service to People

Recommendation I
"We recommend that libraries accept their central role in the Learning Society as valid learning centers. Further, we recommend that these centers be staffed with user-oriented professionals who not only understand community needs but also know learning resources. These "learners" advisors would help patrons to gain the information and skills to function successfully in the Learning Society."

Recommendation J
"We recommend that libraries become active in adult literacy education programs at local, state, and national levels."

2.   To Strengthen Leadership through Research and Assessment

Recommendation K
"We recommend that the nation's school library media centers and public libraries be assessed for their ability to respond to the urgent proposals for excellence in education and lifelong learning."

3.   To Expand Linkages in Support of Lifelong Learning

Recommendation L
"We recommend that librarians at local, state, and national levels develop and implement plans to share the resources and services of their institution in support of education and lifelong learning. We also recommend that at the national level, leadership should be exerted to endorse, assist, and support, the states and local communities in 'their' efforts to share resources."

(Fig. 1.2 continues on page 12.)

Fig. 1.2. — *Continued*

4. To Refine Education for Library and Information Science

Recommendation M
    "We recommend that library and information science educators reform and refine the recruitment, preparation, and continuing education of librarians and information scientists. Further, we recommend that the entire library community hold higher education responsible for providing high quality education to equip professionals with special competencies to work effectively in libraries and information centers in the Learning Society."

Fig. 1.2. Recommendations in response to *A Nation at Risk*. From *Alliance for Excellence: Librarians Respond to "A Nation at Risk"* (Washington, D.C.: U.S. Department of Education, 1984).

Realities: Educational Reform in a Learning Society was also a response to *A Nation at Risk*.[18] It picked up a theme from that report, noting that proposals for educational reform must recognize the need for lifelong learning.

In *Realities*, the American Library Association (ALA) cited libraries as an essential part of lifelong learning and identified four realities for "effective educational reform within a learning society":

1. Learning begins before schooling.

2. Good schools require good libraries.

3. People in a learning society need libraries throughout their lives.

4. Public support of libraries is an investment in people and communities.[19]

The following actions were recommended:

1. State aid for public libraries must be increased so that library services are available to all people in the learning society.

2. State support for resources sharing must be increased, and additional aid must be provided to school and academic libraries to enable them to meet basic service needs and participate effectively in resource sharing.

3. Federal funds for library services must be increased through new initiatives in aid for elementary and secondary school libraries and through appropriations for the federal Library Services and Construction Act and the several library programs in the Higher Education Act.

4. Federal responsibilities for library statistical data and planning information must be assumed by the National Center for Education Statistics in cooperation with the state library agencies, state departments of education, and national organizations.

5. Local, state, and federal agencies developing human services and education programs — such as those concerned with the aging, public television, literacy improvement, day care centers, and the arts and humanities — should strengthen their programs by including librarians and libraries in their planning and program development.

6. Librarians, library boards, Friends of Libraries, parents, and educators should consider the recommendations which resulted from the Libraries and the Learning Society seminars sponsored by the U.S. Department of Education, and they should implement those which are needed to reshape and improve library services.[20]

REFORMING THE LIBRARY MEDIA FIELD

The library media field has made an important contribution through its recommendations for improving education in general. However, a great deal of criticism has also been directed to the performance of library media personnel at every level and to the schools that prepared them. Two reports funded by the U.S. Department of Education are cited below.

Accreditation: A Way Ahead was a project undertaken by the American Library Association because a variety of professional and educational groups have been concerned about the quality of programs leading to degrees in library and information science.[21] As an outcome of the project, ALA and a wide range of other interested societies hoped to accomplish a number of things:

1. Procedures and inter-organizational arrangements must be effected that will provide the basis for participation of multiple societies. These must provide means to deal with financial responsibilities, administration, and policy determination.

2. Guidelines must be established by which the specific interests and concerns of each participating interested society will be recognized in the accreditation process.

3. The 1972 *Standards for Accreditation*, which provide the current basis for evaluation of programs, may need to be revised to reflect the interests of the participating interested societies, beyond the extent guidelines may be able to satisfy.[22]

Recommendations of the report follow. Recommendation 1 is considered the major recommendation, while others are considered subsidiary, amplifying number 1.

Recommendation 1. The American Library Association should take immediate initiative to invite other interested professional societies to join it in the formation of an Inter-Association Advisory Committee on Accreditation.

Recommendation 2. The American Library Association should commit sufficient funds, estimated at $25,000, as an augmentation of the budget of the Committee on Accreditation, to cover the first year of operational expenses for the recommended Inter-Association Advisory Committee on Accreditation, with expectation that in subsequent years those costs would be shared equitably by the participating societies.

Recommendation 3. The Inter-Association Advisory Committee on Accreditation should be charged with the following responsibilities:

— To review the Final Report on this project, to evaluate the several recommendations embodied in the reports of the Working Groups incorporated in it, and to select those which should be implemented.

— To identify the continuing costs involved in the implementation of the selected recommendations, including the costs of the Inter-Association Advisory Committee itself.

— To identify the appropriate formula for sharing of the costs of the Inter-Association Advisory Committee among the participating societies in subsequent years.

— To identify potential sources for funding one-time costs involved in implementing other selected recommendations and to work with the Committee on Accreditation in developing and submitting proposals to those agencies.

— To cooperate with the Committee on Accreditation in the implementation of selected recommendations and advise the participating societies on the progress in implementation.

— To identify the appropriate formula for sharing of the continuing costs of accreditation among the participating societies.

Recommendation 4. It is recommended that, for the foreseeable future, accreditation should be focused on the first professional degree at the master's level.

Recommendation 5. It is recommended that the Inter-Association Advisory Committee on Accreditation should work closely with each of the participating professional societies in the development of policy statements and appropriate documents that identify the educational requirements, for both general and society-specific objectives, in forms that will assist the process of evaluation of programs for accreditation.

Recommendation 6. It is recommended that the 1972 *Standards for Accreditation* and associated or related guidelines continue to serve as the basis for accreditation, but that the Inter-Association Advisory Committee on Accreditation should establish, in cooperation with the Committee on Accreditation, a review process aimed at identifying the needs for additional guidelines and perhaps eventual replacement of the 1972 *Standards.*[23]

New Directions in Library and Information Science Education, a research study funded by the U.S. Department of Education, sought to achieve

- the listing, description and validation of the competencies required at several professional levels and within the several areas of professionalization in the library and information science field; and

- the discussion and examination of present and future education requirements necessary to achieve the discrete levels of competencies by professional level and specialty.[24]

Information professional competencies were identified and validated. The competencies — knowledge, skills, and attitudes — were organized by work setting, function performed, and professional level. Although the report is considered only a beginning, it has the potential for relating more directly what is taught in schools offering professional education and the functions performed by professionals in the field. Competencies relating to school library media specialists are considered in chapter 5.

SUMMARY

- The school library media center functions in the context of the school and school district. Economic, social, technological, and political forces have an impact upon the educational system and the LMC.

- We have entered a period of educational criticism and reform. *A Nation at Risk* was one of several important reports that aimed to improve the condition of education.

- The Elementary and Secondary School Recognition Programs identified successful schools that could be emulated.

- The library media field offers, through its resources and services, a means for the improvement of education and lifelong learning.

- Library media personnel at every level and the schools that prepare them have received a full share of criticism.

ACTIVITIES

1. Complete a research report in which you respond fully to one or more of the objectives cited for this chapter.

2. Use the attributes cited for successful elementary or secondary schools as the basis for an analysis of a selected school.

3. Compare *Realities* and *Alliance for Excellence*.

4. Compare the competencies listed in *New Directions* to requirements for various school library media positions.

NOTES

[1]Alvin Toffler, *The Third Wave* (New York: Morrow, 1980).

[2]John Naisbitt, *Megatrends: Ten New Directions Transforming Our Lives* (New York: Warner Books, 1982).

[3]Thomas Peters and Robert Waterman, *In Search of Excellence: Lessons from America's Best-Run Companies* (New York: Harper & Row, 1982).

[4]National Commission on Excellence in Education, "A Nation at Risk: The Imperative for Education Reform," *Chronicle of Higher Education* 26 (4 May 1983):11.

[5]Ibid., 12-16.

[6]The Holmes Group, "Tomorrow's Teachers: A Report of the Holmes Group," *Chronicle of Higher Education* 33 (26 November 1986):15.

[7]Carnegie Foundation for the Advancement of Teaching, "College: The Undergraduate Experience in America," *Chronicle of Higher Education* 33 (5 November 1986):16.

[8]Ibid., 21.

[9]Marvin Cetron, *Schools of the Future: Education into the 21st Century* (New York: McGraw-Hill, 1985).

[10]*Elementary School Recognition Program* (Washington, D.C.: U.S. Department of Education, 30 June 1986). (News release).

[11]Ibid.

[12]*Elementary School Recognition Program: Selection Criteria* (Washington, D.C.: U.S. Department of Education, n.d.), 1.

[13]*The Search for Successful Secondary Schools: The First Three Years of the Secondary Schools Recognition Program* (Philadelphia, Pa.: Research for Better Schools, 1985). (Draft).

[14]Ibid., 11.

[15]Ibid., 55-94.

[16]William Ridley and H. Hull McAllister, Jr., "Transforming American Education: Reducing the Risk to the Nation," *TechTrends* 31 (May/June 1986): 12-35.

[17]Ibid., 19-35.

[18]*Realities: Educational Reform in a Learning Society* (Chicago: Task Force on Excellence in Education, American Library Association, 1984).

[19]Ibid., 1.

[20]Ibid., 12.

[21]*Accreditation: A Way Ahead* (Chicago: Committee on Accreditation, American Library Association, 1986).

[22]Ibid., 1.

[23]Ibid., 2-3.

[24]José-Marie Griffiths and Donald King, *New Directions in Library and Information Science Education* (White Plains, N.Y.: Knowledge Industry, 1986).

BIBLIOGRAPHY

Academic Preparation for College: What Students Need to Know and Be Able to Do. New York: The College Board, Office of Academic Affairs, 1984.

Accreditation: A Way Ahead. Chicago: Committee on Accreditation, American Library Association, 1986.

Action for Excellence: A Comprehensive Plan to Improve Our Nation's Schools. Denver, Colo.: Education Commission of the States, 1983.

Adler, Mortimer. *The Paideia Proposal.* New York: Macmillan, 1982.

Alliance for Excellence: Librarians Respond to "A Nation at Risk." Washington, D.C.: U.S. Department of Education, 1984.

Boyer, Ernest. *High School: A Report on Secondary Education in America.* New York: Harper & Row, 1983.

Carnegie Foundation for the Advancement of Education. "College: The Undergraduate Experience in America." *Chronicle of Higher Education* 33 (5 November 1986): 16-22.

Cetron, Marvin. *Schools of the Future: Education into the 21st Century.* New York: McGraw-Hill, 1985.

Educating Americans for the 21st Century. National Science Board, National Science Foundation, 1983.

Education for Tomorrow's Jobs. National Academy Press, 1983.

Elementary School Recognition Program. Washington, D.C.: U.S. Department of Education, 30 June 1986. (News Release).

Elementary School Recognition Program: Selection Criteria. Washington, D.C.: U.S. Department of Education, n.d.

First Lessons: A Report on Elementary Education. Washington, D.C.: Government Printing Office, 1986.

Goodlad, John. *A Place Called School.* New York: McGraw-Hill, 1984.

Griffiths, José-Marie, and Donald King. *New Directions in Library and Information Science Education.* White Plains, N.Y.: Knowledge Industry, 1986.

High Schools and the Changing Workplace. Washington, D.C.: National Academy Press, 1984.

The Holmes Group. "Tomorrow's Teachers: A Report of the Holmes Group." *Chronicle of Higher Education* 33 (26 November 1986): 15.

Making the Grade. New York: The Twentieth Century Fund, 1983.

Naisbitt, John. *Megatrends: Ten New Directions Transforming Our Lives.* New York: Warner Books, 1982.

National Commission on Excellence in Education. "A Nation at Risk: The Imperative for Educational Reform." *Chronicle of Higher Education* 26 (4 May 1983):11-16.

An Open Letter to America on Schools, Students, and Tomorrow. Washington, D.C.: National Education Association, 1984.

Peters, Thomas, and Robert Waterman. *In Search of Excellence: Lessons from America's Best-Run Companies.* New York: Harper & Row, 1982.

Realities: Educational Reform in a Learning Society. Chicago: Task Force on Excellence in Education, American Library Association, 1984.

Ridley, William, and McAllister Hull, Jr. "Transforming American Education: Reducing the Risk to the Nation." *TechTrends* 31 (May/June 1986): 12-35.

The Search for Successful Secondary Schools: The First Three Years of the Secondary School Recognition Program (draft). Philadelphia, Pa.: Research for Better Schools, 1985.

Sizer, Theodore. *Horace's Compromise: The Dilemma of the American High School.* Boston: Houghton Mifflin, 1984.

Toffler, Alvin. *The Third Wave.* New York: Morrow, 1980.

2

THE LIBRARY MEDIA CENTER

OBJECTIVES

Identify and describe research relating to the school library media center.

Identify and describe various standards and guidelines that affect the development of the library media center (LMC).

State the philosophy and describe the elements of the school LMC system.

Identify and describe system elements beyond the individual school that can enhance and supplement the school LMC.

The school library has evolved since its formal beginning in 1835 to become the modern library media center. It has demonstrated the ability to adapt to changing conditions while maintaining continuity in its central purpose — to provide resources and services for the improvement of teaching and learning.

The years between 1960 and 1975 represented a period of unprecedented growth for school libraries in the United States. Although a multitude of factors influenced this growth, three precipitated the changes. The first was the publication of national standards and guidelines in 1960, 1969, and 1975, which set the stage for the development of the modern library media center.[1] The second was funding by the Knapp Foundation of two national projects. One project demonstrated effective school library service, while the second was directed toward improving the effectiveness of personnel.[2] The third factor was the Elementary and Secondary Education Act of 1965, which provided funds for library and audiovisual resources, personnel, facilities, and equipment. Each of these factors caused related activity at state and local levels, bringing about the following significant changes: the rapid growth of library media centers in areas that formerly lacked even modest school libraries, the employment of large numbers of school library and audiovisual personnel as well as the subsequent retraining of professional and support staff for new roles, the expansion and integration of media collections to include all forms of printed and audiovisual resources, and the focus on school library media centers as important components of education. The idea of integrating all learning resources into one organization within the schools was not new; conditions were right for fundamental changes.

During this period, the school library became a unified library media system (though not uniformly so). *Unified* implied the joining or integration of traditional library and audiovisual components into a single administrative configuration. *Media* implied that the LMC would accommodate existing printed and audiovisual forms and that LMC personnel would become involved in the production of new forms. The term *system* used in this context implied a multifaceted operation, having diverse elements but sharing a common purpose.

A basic, recurring problem associated with changes and improvements in the field was a proliferation of new terminology. For example, the terms *learning center, resource center, instructional media center*, and *media center* had been cited as appropriate names for the modern LMC. The efforts of the 1969 Standards and 1975 Guidelines to identify terminology (*media center, media specialist*) have not been successful.[3] *Library media center*, the term chosen by the authors and others, provides a bridge between the long tradition of a library and the use of newer terms intended to explain what has transpired in the field.

The period between 1975 and 1985 witnessed a leveling, and in some areas a substantial decline, in the base of support for continued growth and development of school LMCs and education in general. At the same time, there continued to be new and expanded developments in technology-related activity, in the preparation and certification of school library media professionals, and in efforts to develop more effective and efficient methods of delivering essential library media services.

IN THE CONTEXT OF EDUCATION

The school library media center functions within the context of the educational system. In order to function effectively in this milieu, the library media specialist should know how the schools are organized to cope with changing conditions in order to carry out a viable educational program.

Provided on the following pages is a checklist of external and internal factors relating to the school district. *External* refers to factors outside of the individual school that have a bearing on how the school's educational program is carried on; *internal* refers to those factors within the school which act in concert with or independent of factors outside of the school. These factors should be carefully analyzed, since they provide the insight needed to be effective on the job. Checklist items range from general facts about the community, district, and school to items which focus on the power structure within the district, including those persons in leadership positions. These factors may be viewed in relation to the characteristics of successful elementary and secondary schools cited in chapter 1 — ten quality indicators for elementary schools; fourteen attributes/nine themes for secondary schools.

External Factors: The School District

- The Community

    Socioeconomic and ethnic composition.

    Political structure and community power structure.

    School board organization: members elected or appointed, positions taken on vital issues, relations with central administrative staff, community involvement in the board's operation.

- School District Organization

    Town, city country, regional district.

    Organizational structure of the school district: central headquarters and individual schools, a district divided into distinct regions for day-to-day operations, other patterns.

    The graded structure of schools: **grade** levels, school attendance boundaries fixed or changing to integrate schools, school closings.

    Regional or state cooperative educational services providing direct or indirect benefits to the district.

    District budget: average percent of increase, constraints, participants in the budget-making process, administration of budgets, allocation of funds, special funding sources.

- The Administrative Hierarchy

    A strong central administrative organization, authority decentralized on a regional or individual school level, action people in the administrative hierarchy.

    Curriculum development: responsibility vested in one individual or dispersed, projects currently underway or planned, who participates.

    Development of federal and state funded projects: planners and participants.

    Staff development activities.

- District Library Media Services

    History of library media service in the district.

    Districtwide administration, district center functions, what functions are coordinated.

- Regional and Networking Services

    Source of support.

    Membership requirements, fees, contracts.

- Teacher Organizations

    Teacher power structure in the district.

    Representation of professional viewpoints.

    Leadership of the organization.

    Support for educational improvement.

- Priorities and Constraints

    Programs receiving priority for development.

    Factors influencing priorities.

    Constraints imposed by priorities.

    Constraints on LMC development for other reasons.

Internal Factors: The Individual School

- School Organization

    Grade organization and class size.

    Scheduling: rigid or flexible.

    Staff organization: departments, team structure.

- Curriculum

  Subject matter and articulation.

  Changes or modifications planned.

  Instructional methodologies employed by individuals or groups: traditional, innovative.

- Administrative Structure

  Philosophy, experience, educational background and interests of administrators.

  Leadership role in the school: innovative instructional practices, assist teachers and others in their work.

  Commitments to districtwide and community-oriented activities: budget planning, project writing and implementation, policy making, community action program.

- Professional and Other Staff

  Experience, educational background, and department structure.

  Teacher power structure: leadership, advisory council to principal and administrative staff.

  Elements of cooperation and team action.

  Attitudes toward and use of the LMC.

- Special Programs

  Programs funded by special federal or state grants.

  Innovative programs for the gifted, curricular areas, technology, individualization.

  Organization of special projects.

- Staff Development Activities

  Organization at school level: the plan, release time from teaching provided.

  Teachers' participation in planning and implementation at school and district level.

  School and districtwide in-service training related to media utilization.

- Priorities and Constraints

    Administrative, community, and teacher priorities relating to curriculum and student needs.

    Constraints on library media development.

- Students

    Age, grade levels.

    Socioeconomic and ethnic makeup.

    Interests and abilities.

    Social, emotional, psychological and physical development.

    Interest in social and political action.

- Physical Plant

    Organization of space.

    Design: traditional or flexible to accommodate creative programming.

    LMC design compared to program potential.

THE LIBRARY MEDIA CENTER

The elements of the modern library media center are drawn primarily from the fields of library science and instructional technology. Both fields have similar goals, such as concern with management of an organization. Both fields focus on similar functions: research and evaluation; the process of acquiring, organizing, and disseminating media; the relationship of professionals and media to users; and the design and production of media.

Information science, another interdisciplinary field dealing with the information transfer process, has also made a contribution through its concern with information theory, information technology, and service-oriented functions. Of the three fields, library science has provided the basic philosophy and structure. In the modern LMC, there is a meshing of all three fields into a unified system.

Research

A considerable amount of effort has gone into research designed both to justify the existence of the LMC and to determine specific contributions of the LMC to education in general and to student learning in particular.[4]

Two recent studies focused on the elementary and secondary schools cited in chapter 1 as those recognized as exemplary by the U.S. Department of Education project. These studies give a picture of the current state of library media programs across the country.

The first study, conducted by Loertscher, Ho, and Bowie[5] investigated the LMC programs in 209 elementary schools recognized as exemplary. Their survey probed both staffing patterns and the types of services provided by these schools. Staffing patterns were as follows:

- 43 percent had full-time professionals and clerks

- 26 percent had full-time professionals with no clericals

- 16 percent had part-time professionals with clerks

- 3 percent had part-time professionals with no clericals

- 12 percent had no professionals but did have clericals

- 1 school did not have an LMC

The services probed by the study included instructional development, other services to teachers, services to students, and the state of collections. The authors concluded that "there seems to be a staffing threshold at which the elementary library media program begins to pay the kinds of dividends expected for the investment made in it."[6] This threshold is a full-time professional and a full-time clerical. Library media centers without adequate staff are caught in the web of the warehousing function rather than being able to carry out instructional services.

The study of services provided in the exemplary elementary schools with fully staffed LMCs showed that activities designed to build enjoyment of literature and to promote reading were the bedrock services of the LMC program. Individualized attention to students, the teaching of library skills, and the provision of an atmosphere conducive to media interaction were also major program components. Fully staffed LMCs provided significantly more cooperative teaching and instructional development services than did understaffed programs.

The authors conducted a survey of LMCs in secondary schools recognized by the government in 1985.[7] A random sample of the 571 recognized schools produced seventy-four usable responses. A questionnaire was constructed which matched the criteria for which the schools were judged for excellence. The questions follow:

1. Do library media specialists perceive that their roles and functions are adequately integrated into the regular school program? How?

2. Do the library media specialists feel they have ample opportunity for communication with subject area teachers, building administrators, support staff, and parents?

3. How do library media specialists see their programs and projects contributing to the overall success of the school?

The responses of library media specialists are shown in figure 2.1. Library media specialists in 74 percent of the schools believed that to a great extent their functions were integrated into the regular school programs; 76 percent believed they had an opportunity to communicate with teachers and other groups; 77 percent believed that the LMC contributes greatly to the success of the school. One of the key factors of success of the LMC program is its personalized service to individual students. Library media specialists felt that budgets to provide resources were too small.

Total Responses = 74 Note: Only 73 responses to items 3, 4, 6, 9	To a Great Extent %	To Some Extent %	To No Extent %
TO WHAT EXTENT:			
1. ... are your functions integrated into the regular school program?	74	26	
2. ... do you have the opportunity to communicate with teachers, administrators, support staff, parents?	76	24	
3. ... does your program contribute to the overall success of the school?	77	23	
4. ... does your budget provide for needed resources and services?	45	51	4
5. ... does your facility meet the needs of students and faculty?	70	30	
6. ... do your resources meet the needs of students?	63	37	
7. ... do your resources meet the needs of teachers?	64	36	
8. ... does your instructional program contribute to the success of students?	64	36	

(Fig. 2.1 continues on page 28.)

Fig. 2.1. — *Continued*

9.	... does personalized service to individual students contribute to their success?	85	15
10.	... does your assistance to teachers contribute to their success?	70	30
11.	... does the administration of the school foster use of the LMC?	64	35
12.	... do teachers foster use of the LMC?	68	32

Fig. 2.1. Survey of "Recognition" school LMCs.

Programming for the Individual School

Within the individual school and district, the LMC program reflects both educational philosophy and programming. However, it should be recognized that each LMC has a unique philosophy and service focus of its own. Three related concepts — individualization, inquiry, and independent study — provide the rationale and basis for the operation. Though compatible with the most fundamental purposes of education, the LMC must be reconciled with conditions in the school.

The modern LMC developed over a period of years. Its development has been based, at least in part, on an analysis of the curriculum of the school, teacher needs in conducting the instructional program, and the needs of students in the learning process. Various authorities provide insight into the system. The North Carolina Department of Public Instruction offers the following statement about the LMC:

The school library/media program is designed to support the educational goals of a school, and to serve all students and teachers. Its two main functions are:

• to teach information skills within the framework of the school's curriculum, [and]

• to provide materials and services that support the instructional program.

The school library/media program is designed to assist students in locating, evaluating, and using information, so that they may function more effectively as individuals and participate successfully in society. Quality media programs serve students by:

- providing a well-chosen collection of media appropriate to different levels of maturity, ability, and interests;

- providing guidance in the location, selection, evaluation, and use of these resources;

- contributing to the development of reading, viewing, listening, evaluating, and community skills; [and]

- teaching students techniques for fully using the resources within the school's own media collection, as well as locating and properly using information sources outside the school.

An effective school media program depends upon the support of the school board, the superintendent, the school principal, and requires a mutually supportive partnership between teachers and media personnel. Teachers, as members of this instructional team, inform media coordinators about curricula, content, and assignments. Teachers also participate in the planning of information skills instruction, evaluation of learning resources, motivating students towards media use, and implementing the media program within the context of curricular areas. A learner-centered approach to instruction focuses attention on the school media center as the main instructional force which supports, complements, and expands classroom learning.[8]

The 1975 AASL/AECT guidelines, due to be revised in 1988, endeavored to provide some assistance by offering the following definition of the library media program: "Patterns of interfacings among program components, e.g., people, materials, machines, facilities, and environments, managed by media professionals who establish and maintain relationships between or among the components."[9] The guidelines also cited specific user activities:

- Finding needed information on an appropriate level and in an acceptable format.

- Selecting and using appropriate means for retrieval of information in all media formats.

- Obtaining resources from the media center, district center, local agencies, and networks.

- Communicating in many modes, demonstrating an understanding of the structure and language of each mode.

- Utilizing instructional sequences of tested effectiveness to reach personal and program objectives.

- Designing and producing materials to achieve specific objectives, as well as using materials designed and produced for them by the media staff.

Teacher Needs

Teacher needs for an LMC are perhaps greater than those of students. In the past, when the pattern of service in the schools was divided between separate school library and audiovisual departments, libraries focused primarily on student needs; audiovisual departments directed their attention exclusively to teacher requirements. Today's unified approach should allow library media specialists to correct any imbalances of the past.

A focus on teacher needs is required for two reasons. First, reaching the teacher guarantees that student needs will be clarified and provided for adequately. Second, as a director of student learning experiences, the teacher is expected to diagnose individual student needs and prescribe the types of experiences required for the student to perform. This is no easy task. Without the LMC, the job probably cannot be accomplished effectively.

Teachers will rely on the LMC for two kinds of service: service related to the curriculum and their students' needs, and service related to their own professional needs. But they will rely on the LMC only if it has demonstrated the capacity to meet their needs.

Checklist of Teacher Needs

- A need for *curriculum development* assistance in structuring innovative, educational experiences for students. School and district adoption of textbooks, curriculum guides, and curricular change can occur more smoothly if the library media specialist is involved early so that the appropriate resources, facilities, and equipment are in place when the change occurs.
- A need for *instructional planning assistance* on a continuing basis. Teachers require the assistance of the library media professional on a day-to-day basis in determining methods, activities, and media to employ in specific teaching-learning situations.
- A need for *cooperative teaching*. Team teaching may be structured to include library media specialists as idea sources, as materials specialists, as activity generators, and as coteachers using media effectively.

• A need to *create and modify media* related to the improvement of instruction. This means the creation of original media forms such as tapes, slides, filmstrips, transparencies, videotapes, microcomputer programs, and various graphic representations needed in teaching and learning. Also, if teachers are to individualize instruction, media may be modified. An example is the development of a simple worksheet to accompany a filmstrip. Creation and modification may be accomplished by teachers individually or in groups, with or without assistance from the library media staff.

• A need for *production services*, specifically in the reproduction and duplication of media.

• A need to *improve knowledge and skills* in order to operate effectively in an extensive media approach to learning. Teachers need to learn more about the organization and potential of LMC services. Ordinarily, this requires considerable assistance from a competent LMC staff.

• A need for *information* about media, service, utilization, and students. Also included here is the need for information about educational opportunities and newer concepts and approaches in education.

• A need for *assistance in selection of media* to be used in teaching and learning. The previewing, evaluation, and selection of media related to instruction are particularly critical areas of need in the school situation.

• A need for *interaction* with media, students, associates, and library media specialists on a continuing basis.

• A need for *assurance* that their expectations for students are being met. Teachers expect students to learn to use the LMC efficiently, to receive guidance needed to learn to work independently, and to locate and use media suited to their abilities and interests.

• A need for the *opportunity* to be creative and effective in their work. This opportunity is found in a comprehensive LMC.

Student Needs

Student needs for an LMC are of two kinds: those related to the curriculum of the school and those related to individual and personal needs. Each need brings into focus interrelated aspects of the LMC.

• Employing a variety of media to find, evaluate, use, and generate information.

• Enjoying the communication arts and gaining inspiration from them.

• Receiving assistance, both formally and informally, in the production of learning resources.

• Functioning in learning environments that reflect their developmental level as well as the tasks at hand.

• Locating space in which to accomplish a variety of activities responding to curricular and personal needs.

• Participating in the formulation and implementation of both general and specific media program policies.[10]

The development of an effective LMC must also take into account the age, grade, sex, interests, and intellectual capacities of students. One other important consideration is that students and teachers may not be able to articulate their needs. In fact, they may not be aware of the range of opportunities open to them through the LMC. The knowledgeable and experienced administrator or library media specialist will both anticipate their needs and create new or expanded needs through demonstrated effective services.

Checklist of Student Needs

• A need to *read* from a variety of printed media such as books, periodicals, and pamphlets. These printed resources may be located in the library media center, the classroom, the public library, and the home. These materials are fluid rather than rigid, meaning they flow back and forth from classrooms, libraries, and homes as needed by the student.

• A need to *view* media such as filmstrips, films, television, transparencies, and pictures.

• A need to *listen* to audiovisual media such as records, tapes, and compact disks.

• A need to *use various combinations* of media such as a filmstrip and record, a tape and slides, or simply to use many media forms to glean information and ideas.

• A need to *interact* with computer media in their many forms.

• A need to *practice skills* related to various types of machine use such as typewriters, adding machines, calculators, and microcomputers. Location of the activity may be confined to specialized areas in the library media center where assistance is available.

• A need to *create* media such as tapes, slides, transparencies, filmstrips, and videotapes. Location of this activity is ordinarily confined to specialized areas in the LMC. The media created may become a part of the collection.

• A need for *instruction* in the efficient use of the library media center and of the various services available in the program. Some basic instructional needs include orientation to the program, care and use of media, and investigation and study methods. This may be accomplished in a variety of ways. Location of the activity may be partially confined to the LMC.

• A need for *guidance* in selecting media for reading, viewing, listening, and writing.

• A need for *information* about media relating to the various areas of the curriculum or areas of personal interest, to academic and vocational programs, and to school and community activities and services. The kinds of information required by students appear to have no limits.

• A need to *interact* with peers, with teachers, with LMC personnel, or with other adult specialists on an individual or small group basis in relation to media. Location of the activity may be confined to specialized areas in the LMC.

• A need for the *opportunity to function* as an individual who initially may be totally dependent, then partially independent, and ultimately completely independent, functioning competently in the LMC.

THE LMC AS A SYSTEM

The LMC should be viewed as a unified media system designed for the improvement of teaching and learning. Using the term *system* to describe the LMC program requires an explanation of the term as it applies to libraries in general. Edward Chapman defined six basic library systems: acquisitions, cataloging, circulation, reference, serials, and administration and planning which together comprise a total library system.[11] Each of these six systems is composed of subsystems. For example, the acquisitions subsystem is composed of order, preorder search, accounting and reporting, and receiving and checking. In the context of this work, the system is "a complex unity formed of many often diverse parts subject to a common purpose."[12] This definition is commonly applied also to school systems, public library systems, and so on.

The LMC system may be referred to as the triple A or 3A System — "Assets," "Activities," "Achievements" (see figure 2.2). These components are mutually dependent. The proper mix can be determined by extensive planning. Viewed as a systems model, "Assets" are the essential resources (input) available to the LMC; "Achievements" are the goals (output) intended for the LMC; "Activities" are the functions of management needed to create an effective organization by relating assets to intended achievements.

Assets		Activities		Achievements	
Personnel	Facilities	Planning	Organizing	Guidance and Consulting Services	Instruction and In-Service
Media	Budget	Leading	Controlling	Design and Production of Media	Curriculum Development and Improvement

Fig. 2.2. The LMC system.

Assets of the LMC System

The assets of the LMC system are (1) personnel, (2) facilities, (3) media, and (4) budget. In previous editions of this work, assets were called *foundation elements*—the fundamental or basic resources needed to build an effective system.

1. *Personnel.* Professionals, technicians, and aides required to operate the system, assisting students and teachers in the educational process.

2. *Facilities.* LMC spaces and furniture, suited to the needs of students and teachers.

3. *Media.* A comprehensive and unified collection of printed and audiovisual sources and their accompanying technology. Quality media in sufficient quantity are needed at varying levels of interest and understanding for an extensive approach to learning.

4. *Budget.* Adequate financial support to provide the wherewithal to achieve the goals and objectives of the LMC system and school.

Management Activities of the LMC System

The management activities of the LMC system are (1) planning, (2) organizing, (3) leading, and (4) controlling. In previous editions, activities were referred to as *support elements*—management functions required to balance and coordinate assets and achievements.

1. *Planning.* The selection of courses of action for the LMC.

2. *Organizing.* Identifying and defining the work to be done to meet goals and objectives; grouping work activities to structure jobs; delegating authority to carry out jobs; and coordinating authority and informational relationships.

3. *Leading.* Maintaining and extending activities by guiding and leading personnel, clarifying assignments, and improving performance.

4. *Controlling.* Knowing what is actually happening within the organization by monitoring performance to correct deviations from standards and objectives.

Achievements of the LMC System

Achievements of the LMC system refer to the goals or intended output of the system: (1) guidance and consulting services, (2) instruction and in-service, (3) design and production of media, and (4) curriculum development and improvement. In previous editions, achievements were referred to as *primary elements*—the most important services of the LMC system. These are inter-related and, therefore, often defy clear definition.

1. *Guidance and consulting services.* Individualized services to students and teachers. Guidance covers a broad range of individual and group services to students, while consulting services are those provided to teachers.

2. *Instruction and in-service.* Instructional activities to improve the student's ability to function effectively in the LMC and to use media and equipment efficiently in the learning process. In-service activities to prepare teachers to utilize media and equipment in the teaching-learning process and to foster LMC utilization by students.

3. *Design and production of media.* The creation of new media or modification of existing media for teaching-learning purposes.

4. *Curriculum development and improvement.* The involvement of LMC personnel in curriculum, from the inception of a specialized program through the modifications and refinements made in the school on a continuing basis.

THE EXTENDED SYSTEM

The school LMC may be considered one subsystem in a total library media system for the school district. A district-level LMC would be considered another subsystem of the system. In general, a district-level LMC may provide the following:

1. Service elements too costly for individual school LMCs, but necessary for comprehensive media services.

2. Service elements requiring specialized equipment and personnel.

3. Services having a broad districtwide or regionwide application.

4. Services requiring a large amount of space.

Some examples of these resources and services are technical services; television studios; preview and evaluation collections; professional media collections; comprehensive production services, including printing and duplicating; graphics and photographic departments; in-service training programs; online access to computerized databases; and consulting services.

Beyond the district LMC system, which has articulated components and clearly defined levels of authority and responsibility, there are other organizations (systems) in the community, region, state, and nation that can greatly enhance the services and level of performance of the school LMC (see figure 2.3). Resources and services available from museums, art galleries, nature centers, and other educational, cultural, and recreational centers should be investigated for their value to the educational program of the school. Public television, cable, and other systems also provide options for effective educational programming. Library cooperatives, both single-type, such as a grouping of public libraries, and multitype, including academic, public, school, and special libraries, offer a wide range of possibilities for access to resources and services. In some cases, the opportunity for direct participation in the governance of the operation and the development of services is possible.

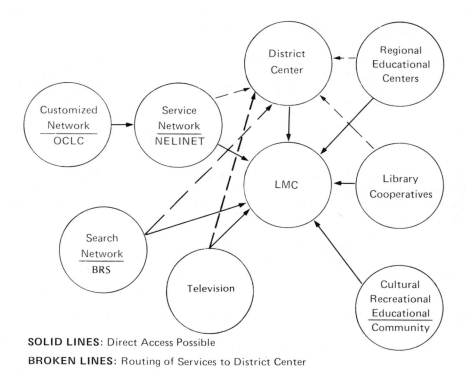

SOLID LINES: Direct Access Possible

BROKEN LINES: Routing of Services to District Center

Fig. 2.3. The extended system.

Online networks providing access to computerized databases can also enhance and extend the LMC system. Search service networks, such as Dialog and BRS, provide access to bibliographic records and text particularly useful for in-depth reference services. A customized service network such as OCLC provides shared cataloging, interlibrary loan information, and other information and services for users. Search service networks may be accessed directly from a school LMC, a district LMC, or through services provided by a library cooperative. Customized service networks are typically accessed through a service center network such as the New England Library Network (NELINET), which acts as a broker. Again, this may be accomplished through the school LMC, district LMC, or a cooperative.

Expanding the school LMC system beyond the district level requires at least the following:

1. An examination of LMC objectives and needs. Also, consideration of what the LMC has to offer another system (where appropriate).

2. An examination of various systems and organizations in the region, state, and nation to determine their potential in meeting the needs of the LMC and its users.

3. A determination of the cost-benefit of services available.

4. Selection of services and development of a strategy for the implementation of these services, including appropriate school and district approvals and the signing of agreements or contracts if required.

LMC FACILITIES

The LMC may be a centralized facility having a service system that reaches out into the school and beyond. The facility may also be decentralized, having satellite centers located throughout the school. Another alternative is an integrated system which loses its physical identity in an open space school (see figure 2.4). Regardless of the physical arrangement, the LMC system is unified by its management structure.

Centralized Media System

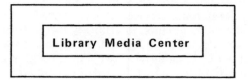

Decentralized Media System (Satellites)

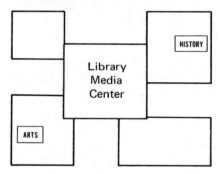

Integrated Media System

Fig. 2.4. Facilities of the LMC may be centralized, decentralized, or a totally integrated media system.

SUMMARY

- The school LMC functions in the context of the educational program of the school and the district.

- The LMC must be responsive to the educational and personal needs of students and teachers. The comprehensive LMC system develops, in large measure, from an assessment of these needs.

- Standards, guidelines, and research influence the development and operation of the LMC.

- The LMC system consists of assets, activities, and achievements which must be balanced to provide effective services. The resulting system extends to students and teachers wherever they work — in the school, in the field, or at home.

- The LMC may be considered a subsystem of a total system for the school district. LMC resources and services may be extended and enhanced through appropriate arrangements with external systems and organizations.

ACTIVITIES

1. Trace the history of school library and audiovisual program development and cite areas of overlap, merging, and major cooperative efforts.

2. Compare school library media center guidelines with guidelines for academic and public libraries.

3. Review the activities of national and state professional organizations directed toward the development of unified school LMCs.

4. For a selected school and district, cite external and internal factors that have an impact upon the LMC; identify external LMC system elements available to supplement the school LMC.

5. Investigate one or more of the following topics: (1) networks, (2) selected technological developments in school LMCs, (3) national and state legislation dealing with school LMCs, and (4) research relating to LMC services.

NOTES

[1]American Association of School Librarians, *Standards for School Library Programs* (Chicago: American Library Association, 1960); American Association of School Librarians and Department of Audiovisual Instruction, *Standards for School Media Programs* (Chicago: American Library Association and National Educational Association, 1969); American Association of School Librarians and Association for Educational Communications and Technology, *Media Programs: District and School* (Chicago and Washington, D.C.: American Library Association and Association for Educational Communications and Technology, 1975).

[2]American Association of School Librarians, *Realization* (Chicago: American Library Association, 1968); American Association of School Librarians, School Library Manpower Project, *School Library Personnel Task Analysis Survey* (Chicago: American Library Association, 1969); *Occupational Definitions for School Library Media Personnel* (Chicago: American Library Association, 1971); *Behavioral Requirements Analysis Checklist* (Chicago: American Library Association, 1973); *Curriculum Alternatives: Experiments in School Library Media Education* (Chicago: American Library Association, 1974).

[3]American Association of School Librarians and Department of Audiovisual Instruction, *Standards for School Media Programs*; American Association of School Librarians and Association for Educational Communications and Technology, *Media Programs*.

[4]Jacqueline Mancall, "An Overview of Research on the Impact of School Library Media Programs on Student Achievement," *School Library Media Quarterly* 14 (Fall 1985): 33-36.

[5]David V. Loertscher, Melvin Bowie, and May Lein Ho, "Library Media Center Programs in Exemplary Elementary Schools," *School Library Media Quarterly* (Spring 1987): in press.

[6]Ibid.

[7]Emanuel Prostano and Joyce Prostano, unpublished research, Fall 1986.

[8]*Media Program Recommendations: Guidelines for School Media Programs* (Raleigh, N.C.: Department of Public Instruction, 1986), I-1.

[9]American Association of School Librarians and Association for Educational Communications and Technology, *Media Programs.*

[10]Ibid., 5-6.

[11]Edward Chapman, Paul St. Pierre, and John Lubans, *Library Systems Analysis Guidelines* (New York: Wiley-Interscience, 1970), 11-14.

[12]*Webster's Third New International Dictionary* (Springfield, Mass.: G. & C. Merriam Co., 1986), 2322.

BIBLIOGRAPHY

American Association of School Librarians. *Realization.* Chicago: American Library Association, 1968.

American Association of School Librarians. *The Role of the School Media Programs in Networks and Interlibrary Cooperation.* Chicago: American Library Association, 1978.

American Association of School Librarians. *Standards for School Library Programs.* Chicago: American Library Association, 1960.

American Association of School Librarians and Department of Audiovisual Instruction. *Standards for School Media Programs.* Chicago and Washington, D.C.: American Library Association and National Educational Association, 1969.

American Association of School Librarians and Association for Educational Communications and Technology. *Media Programs: District and School.* Chicago and Washington, D.C.: American Library Association and Association for Educational Communications and Technology, 1975.

American Association of School Librarians, School Library Manpower Project. *School Library Personnel Task Analysis Survey* (1969); *Occupational Definitions for School Library Media Personnel* (1971); *Behavioral Requirements Analysis Checklist* (1973); *Curriculum Alternatives: Experiments in School Library Media Education* (1974). Chicago: American Library Association.

Bender, David. "Networking and School Library Media Programs." *School Library Journal* 26 (November 1979):29-32.

Chapman, Edward, Paul St. Pierre, and John Lubans. *Library Systems Analysis Guidelines.* New York: Wiley-Interscience, 1970.

Day, Bettie. "Standards: Targets for Excellence." *Catholic Library World* 55 (May/June 1984):452-54.

Hannigan, Jane. "School Media Standards." *Library Trends* 31 (Summer 1982):49-63.

Jones, Milbrey. "School Library Media Standards: Changing to Suit the Times." *Journal of Research and Development in Education* 16 (Fall 1982):13-18.

Keck, Jack. "Regional Educational Media Centers." *Catholic Library World* 55 (March 1984):343-45.

Liesener, James. "Learning at Risk: School Library Media Programs in an Information World." *School Library Media Quarterly* 14 (Fall 1985): 11-20.

Mahar, Mary. "Office of Education Support of School Media Programs." *Journal of Research and Development in Education* 16 (Fall 1982):19-25.

_____. "The World Bank and School Library Services." *School Library Journal* 30 (March 1984):113-17.

Mancall, Jacqueline. "An Overview of Research on the Impact of School Library Media Programs on Student Achievement." *School Library Media Quarterly* 14 (Fall 1985):33-36.

"On the Role of Libraries in the Process of Education." *International Library Review* 14 (July 1982):335-41.

3

MANAGEMENT ACTIVITIES

OBJECTIVES

Identify and describe management activities needed for the effective and efficient operation of a school LMC or district LMC.

Describe systems which can be effectively used in planning and controlling school LMCs or district programs.

Design the organizational structure for a school LMC or district LMC system.

Management activities are used to design, maintain, and expand an environment suited to the needs of the LMC system and school. The assets (input) available to the system are manipulated or transformed to effect specific achievements (output).

CURRENT MANAGEMENT IDEAS

Concepts from the field of management may be applied to the LMC since management is considered a universal that is applicable to any organization. "Management is a discipline, an organized body of knowledge which is continually evolving ... management is also a type of work and as such it has its own skills, its own tools, its own techniques."[1] The field of management has advocates for various approaches to success. It also has its critics. Knowingly or not, school library media specialists are managers.

There are many definitions of management; including the following:

Both the people responsible for running an organization and the running process itself .... A *top manager* is one of those who makes policy for, and is responsible for the overall success of the organization. A *middle manager* is responsible for the execution and interpretation of top management policies and for the operation of various departments. A *supervisory manager* is responsible for the final implementation of policies by rank and file employees.[2]

Working with and through individuals and groups to accomplish organizational goals.[3]

What has been described as a new consensus for the direction and improvement of management is referred to as the 7S framework:

Strategy	—	Plan of action leading to the allocation of resources to achieve goals
Structure	—	The way the enterprise is organized
Systems	—	How information moves around the organization
Staff	—	Types of people—demographic characteristics
Skills	—	What the organization and key people do well
Style	—	How top managers behave in achieving goals
Superordinate Goals	—	Significant meanings or guiding concepts that an organization imbues in its members[4]

In general, taking into account the 7S framework, managers perform four or five important functions. Peter Drucker, for example, listed five operations which form the basis for what managers do:

1. setting objectives

2. organizing

3. motivating and communicating

4. measuring

5. developing people, including themselves[5]

Another common approach, the operational system, has focused on five basic interrelated functions:

1. planning

2. organizing

3. staffing

4. leading

5. controlling

There are also variations that either expand or reduce the total number of major functions. One alternative, citing the major functions as planning, organizing, motivating, and controlling, reduces the number of functions but includes all required activities. Two additional important functions — assembling resources and coordinating — are either treated as separate elements or integrated with the major functions wherever appropriate.

Management and *administration* are frequently used as synonymous terms both in the literature and in an operational sense, because persons known as managers and administrators frequently perform similar functions. Where differentiated, administration is seen to have a more restricted focus, relating to organizing, staffing, and leading functions, whereas the primary focus of management is planning for and controlling the organization.

The term *style* applied to management or leadership refers to consistent patterns of behavior exhibited by individuals when they are working with and through other people (as perceived by these people). George Odiorne listed ten elements of a management style for the 1980s:

1. Old shoe will be in (human, down-to-earth)

2. Management will be more systematic

3. Managers will be more developmental centered (personnel training and development)

4. There will be an increase in situational management

5. Management by commitment will increase

6. There will be a rapid spread of achievement motivation

7. There will be more and better uses of group management processes

8. There will be more due process in personnel decisions

9. There will be more management by information

10. The physical aspects of the workplace will change[6]

In the effective organization, the functions of management should be buttressed by specific assumptions about how the organization will attempt to conduct its day-to-day affairs. When these assumptions are acted on, positively or negatively, they become the visible attributes of the organization. The assumptions/attributes are as follows:

- *Excellent performance* means that people within the organization accept and articulate the idea that they strive to be the "best" — that excellence is a valid goal. This assumption/attribute also touches on each person's need for recognition.

- The *importance of people* means that all members of the organization accept the fact that people are important as individuals and that each should be respected. Beyond their worth as individuals, it is understood that individually and collectively people are the organization and they have the ability to be leaders and innovators.

- *Informality* means that relationships will be characterized by a down-to-earth style. This applies to the style of managers in their interactions with each other and with others in the organization.

- *Superior service* relates directly to excellent performance and implies that resources and services provided to constituents will be of superior quality. It implies also that members of the organization will pay attention to the details which make their resources and services superior.

MANAGEMENT ACTIVITIES

Taking into account the many suggested ways of structuring management action, the authors have divided the entire scheme into four major interrelated activities or functions of management of importance to the library media specialist: (1) planning, (2) organizing, (3) leading, and (4) controlling.

Other important activities such as assembling resources, staffing, and coordinating, have been integrated into the model. Each part of the model is further divided into four components and an overview is provided for each. In succeeding chapters, an effort is made to relate these activities to the assets (input) and achievements (output) of the LMC.

Planning

Planning is concerned with the selection of courses of action for the school LMC. It is the initial management activity; it incorporates other management activities; it is a process used in other management activities.

Planning is used to determine which goals and objectives to pursue and when they will be achieved, what resources are needed and how they will be utilized, what services are needed and how these services will be delivered, when and who will perform the activities needed to deliver the services, and how performance will be measured.

Planning is a process which may result in a formal document such as a long-range plan for the LMC program, or a yearly plan of action. Comprehensive planning is also known as strategic, long-range, integrated, and managerial planning. Planning also relates to making plans for the implementation of large goals that have been determined by comprehensive planning and relatively brief day-to-day plans for instruction and other services. At some point, comprehensive planning is needed to provide the basis for future activities.

Comprehensive Planning

Whenever comprehensive planning occurs, at least the following activities take place:

1. Determining mission and goals

2. Analyzing and making judgments about the present condition of the LMC or district library media services system.

   a. External and internal constraints and their potential impact

   b. Needs of users

   c. Comparison of the existing LMC system

      (1) to a predetermined standard (such as national or state guidelines)

      (2) to external and internal constraints

      (3) to needs assessment data

      (4) to cost data

3. Determining alternative programs for the LMC or the district based on findings. Each containing goals and objectives, content or context, strategies for achieving objectives, resources and budget requirements, control-evaluation processes.

4. Analysis and comparison of programs

5. Selection of programs and approvals

6. Implementation of approved program

Comprehensive planning may be accomplished in many ways. It may follow the formal guidelines of established systems such as PPBS (Planning, Programming, Budgeting System) or ZBB (Zero Base Budgeting), which provide both a philosophical and operational approach to integrating program and budget development. It may also be accomplished through the use of MBO (Management by Objectives).

Originated by the Rand Corporation, *PPBS* received its major impetus in the U.S. Department of Defense in the early 1960s and was established as the budgetary process for federal agencies in 1965. PPBS brings together all aspects of the operation by identifying and clarifying objectives, increasing communication among different levels of management, measuring the effectiveness of each program in qualitative and quantitative terms by considering the long-range impact of each program, providing alternative programs for reaching objectives, and evaluating alternative levels of funding for each program.

Originated at Texas Instruments Corporation in 1970, *ZBB* can be traced back to PPBS, and like PPBS it has been used in business, industry, government, education, and libraries. ZBB differs from PPBS and other budgetary approaches in that it requires the development of a budget without reference to what has happened in the past — there is, theoretically, no carry-over of funding from previous years. What is important about PPBS and ZBB, at this point, is the emphasis that both integrated systems give to the planning phase of the entire process and their focus on objectives and output.

MBO is an accepted system for managing the total organization, or specific elements of the organization. This system may also be used for the implementation phase of comprehensive planning. MBO emphasizes the need for the manager to become more effective by achieving the output requirements of the position. William Reddin noted that, in addition to the emphasis on managerial effectiveness, MBO also emphasizes: (1) effectiveness areas, (2) effectiveness standards, and (3) objectives.[7] These may also be termed *key activities*, *performance standards*, and *objectives*. The relationship of these elements is as follows:

1. Key activities represent general output requirements for the organization and an assigned managerial position such as the head of the LMC. An example of a key activity would be *training and developing media personnel.*

2. Performance standards are the output requirements and the measurement criteria of a managerial position. An example, related to the key activity above, would be that *media aides must be 80 percent accurate and efficient in the performance of all work.*

3. Objectives are very specific statements about what is to be accomplished. (1) Objectives should be attainable — meaning due consideration is given to the capabilities of those performing the task, the availability of resources and time, and unusual occurrences. (2) Objectives should be measurable in order to determine whether or not they have been accomplished. (3) Objectives should have associated activities which are observable so that a control system may be used to correct problems. (4) Objectives must be clear and understandable. (5) Objectives may incorporate the standard set for the key activity. An example of an objective related to the key activity, and incorporating the performance standard would be *to train new media aides through orientation, demonstration, and practice to perform assigned tasks at 80 percent accuracy and efficiency levels within two weeks from the date of employment.*

A more ambitious objective, oriented toward the improvement of both accuracy and efficiency, might be stated in the following manner: To reduce the training time for new media aides to one week, and to increase accuracy and efficiency levels by 10 percent.

The forms in figures 3.1-3.3 may be used in this planning approach. The form in figure 3.1 is designed both to identify key activities and to assign these activities to various LMC personnel in the school district. In figure 3.2, a form is provided which enables each manager, in cooperation with a district director, to set performance standards and objectives for the key activities. Figure 3.3 represents a form to be used by a manager in creating a plan designed to achieve a stated objective. Space is provided for the key activity, performance standard, and objective, as well as the specific sequence of activities required to achieve the objective. The form also provides for the control of activities, since specific steps can be reviewed in advance by the district director, or head of the LMC, and the progress can be monitored.

Since the form in figure 3.2 may be used as the basis for the development of output-oriented job descriptions, and the form in figure 3.3 can be used to measure the effectiveness of performance, the basis for a performance appraisal of personnel has also, in large measure, been covered.

Key Activities	District Director	District Supervisors	Head of District LMC*	Head of School LMC's
Management Activities 1. 2. 3. Assets (Input) 1. 2. 3. 4. Achievements (Output) 1. 2. 3. 4.				

*If other than district director

Fig. 3.1. Key activities assigned to LMC personnel.

Key Activities	Performance Standards	Objectives
— Training and developing media personnel	— Media Aides must be 80% accurate and efficient in the performance of all work	— To train new Media Aides through orientation, demonstration, and practice to perform assigned tasks at 80% accuracy and efficiency levels within two weeks from the date of appointment

Fig. 3.2. Performance standards and objectives.

Key Activities:	Training and developing media personnel
Standard:	Media Aides must be 80% accurate and efficient in the performance of all work
Objective:	To train new Media Aides through orientation, demonstration, and practice to perform assigned tasks at 80% accuracy and efficiency levels within two weeks from the date of appointment

Program of Activities:	Dates
1.	
2.	
3.	
4.	

Evaluation:	*The extent to which both trainer and aides achieved the object.*

Fig. 3.3. Plan to achieve objectives.

A formal planning system designed by Liesener specifically for school LMCs is outlined below to provide a view of a process that is oriented to both LMC personnel and LMC end users. Steps in the prescribed process are:

1. *Definition of Program Output Alternatives.* This step requires the use of a survey instrument called the "Inventory of School Library Media Center Services" and provides for a comprehensive list of potential services under broad service categories: access to Materials, Equipment, and Space; Reference; Production; Instruction; Consultation; and Public Relations.

2. *Survey of Perceptions of Current Services.* The "Inventory" is used as a basis for surveying users' perceptions of services, for increasing the awareness of potential services, and for stimulating user involvement in the total operation of the media system.

3. *Determination of Service Preferences and Priorities in Relation to Local Needs.* This step requires the use of a form called "Form for Determining Preferences for School Library Media Center Services." The process involves representative participation in determining service preferences and priorities. The instrument is essentially an abbreviated outline of the inventory. Output is a statement of priorities that may best serve the needs of users.

4. *Assessment of Resources and Operational Requirements of Services.* This step uses an instrument called the "School Library Media Center Data Collection Guide." The intent is to gather data in such a manner as to be able to identify the specific resources and staff time required for providing user services at a given level.

5. *Determination of Costs of Preferred Services and/or Current Services.* An instrument called the "School Media Program Costing Matrix" is used. Data collected in step four are used with salary and materials cost figures to determine the expenditures for current service offerings as well as estimated cost of preferred services at a given level.

6. *Calculation of a Program Capability.* The process requires comparing current available resources with resource costs of preferred services, and calculating the range and level of preferred services presently feasible with resources available. The results of these calculations will reflect how many and to what extent preferred services can be provided with available resources. A picture of additional resources needed to improve service offerings is also given.

7. *Communication of Preferred Services Currently Feasible to Total Client Group.* This step is used to inform users and administrators which of the preferred services can be provided within the constraints of existing resources.

8. *Reallocation of Resources and Implementation of Changes in Operations to Provide the Range and Level of Services Selected.* In this step, judgments are made about the reallocation of resources to preferred services where possible. Also, an effort is made to provide recommendations specifying the changes needed in standard budgetary procedures in order to accommodate change.

9. *Periodic Evaluation of Services Offered and Documentation of Changing Needs.* The process is never entirely closed since implementation and evaluation lead naturally to renewed systematic planning and modification.[8]

Some plans are complex and require that they be written in great detail while other plans are neither complex nor do they require significant elaboration. Plans developed as the result of a planning or decision-making process will include objectives, policies and procedures, strategies, rules, programs, budget, and control processes relating to objectives.

Where there is a district director, comprehensive planning should be initiated and coordinated by that office. Planning may be done by an individual, such as the district director or head of the LMC, to provide an efficient mode of operating; however, in situations where activities relate to users or those who must carry out specific activities, it is desirable to solicit formal or informal input into the process from those who are to be affected. Where significant changes are contemplated, it is both desirable and advisable to involve those who are to be affected.

Decision Making

An important aspect of the planning process is decision making, which is usually defined as a process in which one selects from two or more choices. Steps in the decision-making process vary, but, in general, focus on the following:

1. Identify or define the problem

2. Determine factors/facts related to the problem

3. Develop alternative solutions to the problem

4. Analyze alternatives and consequences

5. Select the best solution

6. Take action

Strategies employed in the decision-making process include optimizing and satisficing.[9] The optimizing strategy is a process of selecting the course of action having the highest payoff or likelihood of success. It takes into account a large number of requirements or objectives, requires a thorough search to find good alternatives using repeated examination and comparative judgments, and takes into account all the pros and cons with due regard for their relative importance. Since an optimizing strategy ordinarily requires the gathering of a great deal of information, the manipulation of data, frequently by a computer, and may require more time, money, and effort than is available, the more common strategy of satisficing is usually employed. Satisficing, a concept developed by Herbert Simon, is a course of action that is good enough—that is, it meets a minimal set of criteria. In this strategy, alternative courses of action are considered sequentially until one that is good enough is found. Alternatives are usually tested only once, and perhaps in a haphazard fashion, until one meets minimal requirements.

It has been found that the same strategy is not used for all types of decisions. For example, it is common for a simple satisficing strategy to be used for relatively unimportant decisions, and an optimizing approach for more important ones. Also, decision makers may use a mixed approach, incorporating both optimizing and satisficing elements. Conflict and emergency situations which bring into play psychological stress due to the risk involved create a new set of conditions which can influence the decision-making process.

Decisions are also frequently guided by values rather than by rationally determined facts. For example, in the corporate structure, judgments about company image often outweigh profit considerations, traditions and past policies receive considerable weight, and decisions are not always made for the long-range good of the organization since bureaucratic politics are a major consideration.

Organizing

Organizing is the activity concerned with identifying and defining work to be done to meet goals and objectives. It involves (1) defining work to be done, (2) grouping work activities to structure positions and departments, establishing authority and informational relationships, (3) staffing positions, and (4) defining and providing (assembling) resources.

Determining the organizational structure for the LMC system at the school and district level is accomplished through the planning process. The MBO approach to sorting out key activities can facilitate the process. It provides a basis for defining work to be done and the nature of positions and departments needed.

Two factors which form the basis for the organizational structure are authority and departmentation. Authority is the right, inherent in a position, to set and achieve objectives. District directors and the heads of LMCs are delegated such authority. Authority also provides a basis for coordination within the organization. The grouping of employees to carry out activities is referred to as departmentation, a system used to continually expand organizations.

Basic organizational structures, based on authority and departmentation, are the line organization and line and staff organization. In line authority, a superior (manager) exercises direct supervision over a subordinate. Where there is a line and staff organization, the staff person ordinarily functions in an advisory capacity to a line manager. A matrix organization is a third structure, which overlays a typical line or line and staff structure. This structure may be used for special programs and projects at a school LMC or district level.

Departmentation appropriate for a school LMC having a multiple staffing pattern may include organizing by function, such as reference or technical services; territory, such as physically decentralized satellite centers; process or equipment, such as television or media production; subject, such as the humanities and social sciences; form (format), such as periodicals and maps; and a mixed situation such as a department structured along functional lines but including both subject and form elements. The school district which has a district-level LMC will have departmentation options at two levels. Departmentation at a district level may be quite dissimilar because the resources and services offered at that level are ordinarily not available in the school LMCs.

Organization charts provide the means of illustrating lines of authority and departmentation. In figures 3.4-3.8, alternatives are provided for the school LMC and district structure. Figure 3.4 depicts a line organization in a school LMC which has two departments organized along functional lines. Authority flows downward from the head of the LMC to two department heads.

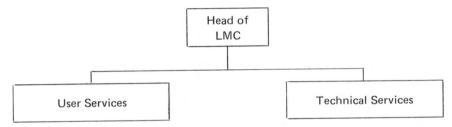

Fig. 3.4. Line organization in the school LMC.

Figure 3.5 shows a line organization at the district level, with authority flowing downward to the heads of various school LMCs. Implied in the chart is the absence of a district LMC as well as a departmental structure in school LMCs. Figure 3.6 depicts a possible structure for a large school district. Below the level of director, the structure accommodates a level of supervisory personnel to coordinate media activities in elementary and secondary schools. An alternative structure for the same district could focus on a regional structure for supervisory personnel with each region including both elementary and secondary schools. This structure implies that authority flows downward from the director, to supervisors, and then to school LMCs. Since the structure imposes a level between the director and school LMC heads which increases the cost of the overall operation, the need for personnel at the supervisory level must be clearly determined. It is noted that the structure of the school district would, in large measure, determine or influence the configuration of the media system.

A line and staff organization at the district level is shown in figure 3.7. This somewhat more complex structure shows line authority flowing from the district director to supervisory personnel for elementary and secondary schools, a district LMC and a staff position. The district center may have various departments organized to provide services to the entire district. The staff person works in an advisory capacity to the director and ordinarily has no authority over line supervisors. Although it is not usually advisable to do so, this office may be assigned functional authority over specific activities, such as data gathering or project development. The matrix structure shown in figure

3.8 is used for special projects or task force groupings which operate on a short- or long-term basis outside of the standard line or line and staff organization. In this case, the project director reports to the district director. Although new personnel may be employed for this project, the shifting of personnel from existing departments to the project is not uncommon. Since the special project group will ordinarily require access to resources and services of the line organization, or will need to provide a service to the line organization, the careful delineation of authority is needed to avoid misunderstanding or conflict.

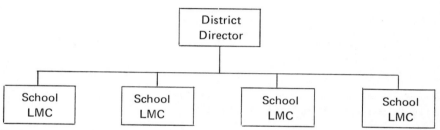

Fig. 3.5. District line organization.

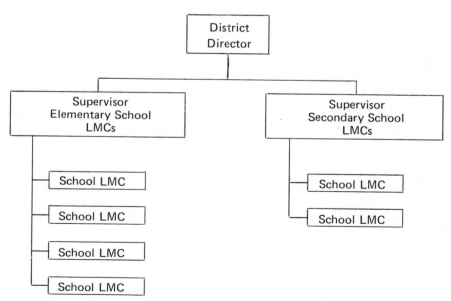

Fig. 3.6. District line organization including supervisory level personnel.

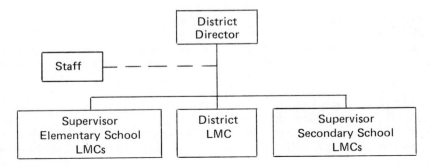

Fig. 3.7. District line and staff organization.

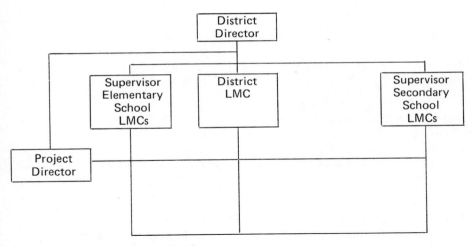

Fig. 3.8. District matrix organization.

Staffing Positions

Staffing is concerned with securing qualified personnel for various positions, and training and developing personnel to perform essential tasks for the organization. Associated with staffing is a personnel planning process which includes job analyses and skills inventories, personnel forecasting, recruitment, selection, employee development, as well as promotions, transfers, and separations.

The job analysis is a process of determining, through observation and study, pertinent information relating to the nature of a specific job; while the skills inventory provides basic information on all employees in an organization, including personal history, skills and education, salary and job information, health and related information, and job preferences. By combining the job analysis with the skills inventory, the organization can determine its present position relative to its human resources.

Personnel forecasting is an attempt to determine the future personnel needs of the organization. Some variables to be considered are the composition of the present staff, potential new or expanded service requirements, student enrollment projections, and the status of existing or potential funding sources.

Recruitment involves various activities associated with seeking qualified candidates for job vacancies. The selection process includes affirmative action and related activities, screening and interviewing, reference checking, testing when appropriate, and personal judgment. A search committee structure is also possible.

Employee development is concerned with the improvement and growth of individuals and groups within the organization. Its purpose is to facilitate the achievement of organizational objectives. Included in the process are the determination of needs, training and development programs, performance reviews, and counseling.

The final step in the personnel planning process involves promotions, transfers, and separations. Promotion involves moving an employee to a job requiring a higher level of performance, such as a supervisory position, involving higher pay and higher status. Transfer involves moving an employee to another job at approximately the same level, with the same pay, performance requirements, and status. Separation denotes either voluntary or involuntary termination of an employee. Union or association contracts with the school district usually govern processes associated with transfers and separation, which are of considerable concern to public school employees in the 1980s.

The head of the school LMC should provide input into the various personnel planning processes. A district director should play a major role in all personnel activities involving or relating to LMC personnel. In the large school district in which most personnel activities may be directed by a specialized department, the district director may function as a consultant to this department in all areas affecting the LMC system.

Assembling Resources

Personnel, facilities, media, and budgets are the resources or assets of the LMC. The availability and allocation of assets determine the extent to which the LMC is effective.

Leading

The activity called leading is designed to maintain and extend the activities of the organization by guiding and leading personnel, clarifying assignments, and improving the performance of personnel. It is the interpersonal aspect of managing and is intended to lead personnel to understand and contribute to the achievement of objectives. The assumptions/attributes cited earlier are of concern here—excellent performance, importance of people, informality, and superior service.

The major elements of leading are (1) motivation, (2) leadership, (3) communication, and (4) coordination.

Motivation

If personnel are to perform effectively, a motivating environment must be created and maintained. Much of what we know about motivation in any environment is based on the work of Mazlow.[10] People are different not only in their ability to do things but also in their will or motivation to do things. Motivation depends on the strength of people's motives at a particular time—needs, wants, drives, impulses. The hierarchy of needs is a framework into which human motivations (needs) arrange themselves.

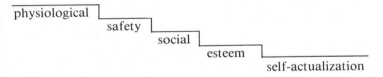

physiological

safety

social

esteem

self-actualization

- Physiological needs are most strong until somewhat satisfied.

- Once physiological needs are somewhat satisfied, safety needs predominate.

- Once physiological and safety needs are somewhat satisfied, social concerns become important.

- Once social concerns (to belong) have been satisfied, people need esteem (self-esteem and recognition from others).

- Once esteem needs are close to being satisfied, self-actualization (maximizing one's potential) takes over.

Under different conditions, the strength of the individual's motivation will change. Gerard Nierenberg has used the hierarchy as the basis for negotiation—knowing one's own motivation and the motivation of another leads to the satisfaction of the need of one or both parties.[11] Negotiation, using motivation as a basis, is seen by some to be an effective way to deal with people under any circumstances.

Leadership

Leadership has been defined as "the art or process of influencing people so that they will strive willingly toward the achievement of group goals."[12] It is also defined in a manner similar to management, in that leadership is believed to be a process or style used in working with and through individuals and groups to accomplish stated goals. The primary difference is that management focuses on the accomplishment of organizational goals. In brief, a manager may be a leader, but a leader need not be a manager. A manager may be a leader most of the time but defer to another, voluntarily or otherwise, in a situation in which superior knowledge of skill held by that person is recognized as essential to the solution of a problem.

For many years, investigators have attempted to determine effective leadership styles by observing successful leaders carrying out their activities. Studies have related concerns for tasks to be accomplished to concerns about people, and to what has been learned about motivation. Findings have often suggested that the most appropriate leadership style combines both factors — a high concern for getting the job done well and a high concern for people. At one point, a democratic style of leadership, which implies a high level of participation by workers in all facets of the operation, was deemed appropriate for all situations. However, research has demonstrated that other styles of leadership can be more effective in certain situations, and that performance can be affected by changing either the leader's style or the situation.

Situational leadership, the model for the 1980s, focuses on the behavior of leaders and their followers (members of a group) and various situations. The leader must be able to diagnose the behavior of a follower in the context of a given situation and then apply an appropriate leadership style to that condition. In simplistic terms, the key is "Different strokes for different folks."[13] In the context of two basic leadership behaviors — directive and supportive — there are four leadership styles which may be applied.

1. Directing: The leader provides specific instructions and closely supervises task accomplishment

2. Coaching: The leader continues to direct and closely supervise task accomplishment, but also explains decisions, solicits suggestions, and supports progress.

3. Supporting: The leader facilitates and supports subordinates' efforts toward task accomplishment and shares responsibility for decision making with them.

4. Delegating: The leader turns over responsibility for decision making and problem solving to subordinates.[14]

Leadership in a group situation requires a sensitivity to three concerns: the task of the group, the individuality of each person in the group, and the need to have the group work together in an effective manner. The task of the group, either assigned or group selected, is clearly objective-oriented, and it is often assumed that motivation will exist to accomplish this task. Since each individual in the group also has a fundamental concern about self-image, all must guard against any damage which may be inflicted on this self-image through the group process. Also, if the task is to be accomplished, and all are to emerge from the meeting with images intact and with a sense of accomplishment, the unity of the group must be maintained by reconciling differences, helping individuals to participate, compromising, and testing possible decisions. Consensus is frequently cited as an objective for decision making in the group process.

Communication

If LMC objectives are to be achieved, a communications network having both horizontal and vertical dimensions must be in place. Communication is the process used to reach a common understanding with another person or group by the sharing of information, ideas, or attitudes. One-way communication, as with a memo, presents many hazards to successful communication because the receiver must respond or act on the basis of the perceived message. Two-way communication, which permits feedback, increases both the communicator's and the receiver's confidence in a common understanding of the message. This idea becomes the basis for meaningful personal interaction or for the design of other feedback mechanisms which would ensure the accuracy of communications.

Concerns about motivation, leadership, and communication are significant within the LMC system. These concerns also extend to other relationships of media personnel with students, teachers, or administrators.

Coordination

Coordination applies to the creation of harmonious relations in the design and operation of the LMC. It is the means by which the assets, activities, and achievements of the LMC system are kept on target and in balance.

Controlling

Controlling means knowing what is actually happening within the organization. The process of control includes the establishment of standards and objectives which are used as a point of reference. Controlling includes (1) a comparison to objectives and standards, (2) determining the causes of deviations from objectives and standards, (3) correcting deviations, and (4) adjusting control processes.

When MBO or a similar systems approach is employed, the elements of control are established through the process of determining key activities, performance standards, and objectives which incorporate a feedback mechanism (see figure 3.9).

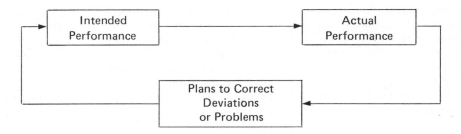

Fig. 3.9. Feedback loop.

Effectiveness and Efficiency

The term *effectiveness* is commonly used in the field of management and is related to the evaluative aspects of the control activity. Effectiveness may be judged in terms of specific criteria or in terms of a particular set of values. It may also be judged in terms of user and LMC staff attitudes and behavior. For example, the following questions, relating to effectiveness, require fairly definitive answers.

- User Attitudes

  How do students and teachers feel about the resources and services provided?

  What are their beliefs about the contribution of the LMC to the teaching-learning process?

- User Behavior

  Do students and teachers use the LMC?

  Do students and teachers rely on the LMC to accomplish teaching-learning objectives?

  Has teacher performance in instruction improved as a result of utilizing the LMC's resources?

  Has there been growth and improvement in the knowledge and skills of students as a result of utilizing LMC resources?

- LMC Staff Attitudes

  Do staff members feel that their efforts have been successful?

- LMC Staff Behavior

  Do staff members relate their efforts to satisfying needs of users?

  Do they meet or exceed the objectives and standards established for effective service?

A determination of effectiveness is also made by school district officials when they maintain, increase, or decrease funding for the LMC system. Although other constraints, such as the availability of funds, have an impact upon such decision making, there is a concern about the degree to which the LMC system contributes to the educational goals of the school district.

Drucker, in his work on executive effectiveness, noted five important concerns for managers which can be applied to most LMC personnel:

1. You must know where your time is spent. Time is always in short supply, and there are many pressures toward unproductive and wasteful time. Since time lost cannot be retrieved, the focus must be on accomplishing tasks which make a contribution.

2. You must focus your attention on outward contribution. The focus on contribution is the key to effectiveness. A basic question to be answered is—What can I contribute that will significantly affect the performance and results of the institution? Another question might be—What results are expected of me?

3. You must build on strengths—your own, the strengths of superiors, colleagues, and subordinates—rather than weaknesses. It is probably true that no one is strong in every area. "Know thyself" is aptly applied here.

4. You must concentrate on the few major areas where superior performance will produce outstanding results. There are always more important contributions to be made than time available to make them. Priorities must be set. To do "first things first," to concentrate on major opportunities gets results.

5. You must make effective decisions. This is a matter of system—the right steps in the right sequence. What is needed is fewer, but fundamental decisions.[15]

Beyond effectiveness, there is a concern about the means and costs of being effective. *Efficiency* deals with the relationship between output and its costs. Efficiency is often referred to as cost-effectiveness. Although cost in terms of dollars or man-hours is a real concern of any organization, it is not the only measure of efficiency. The term can also be applied to the system that operates without waste, that is well coordinated, and that has clearly defined lines of authority and jobs.

In terms of efficiency or cost-effectiveness of the organization, there is a real concern to either hold constant or reduce the amount of money allocated for any endeavor. Questions such as the following must be answered:

- Is it possible to maintain a given quantity and quality of service if there is a significant reduction in funds for input?

- Is it possible to increase output while maintaining the same level of funding?

- Is it possible to maintain or increase a given quantity and quality of service if there is a significant reduction in funds by means of altering the services rendered?

Other Control Devices

There are many other devices used to control various aspects of the organization. These devices include both budgetary and nonbudgetary controls. Traditional nonbudgetary controls include statistical data, special reports and analyses, personal observation, and the internal audit which is an independent appraisal of various operations. All controls should be related to the planning process.

Budgets are probably the most widely used control devices since they provide a statement of expected results or requirements in financial terms.

Flow charting is used as both a planning and control mechanism since charting illustrates graphically the sequential flow of work and information through a system (see figure 3.10). When there are clearly defined objectives, charting can be extremely useful. The principal advantage of this process is that it allows one to temporarily halt for scrutiny operations that may be difficult to understand because of their complexity, or because of the relationships that exist within a system. This does not imply that only complex operations can or should be charted. Flow charting is especially useful in either the initial organization or the comprehensive revision of a total system. Another practical and realistic use of charting is to interpret and help others to understand various elements of a system or the total system itself. An IBM flowchart template is commonly used in the development of program and system flowcharts.

Various types of charting procedures are used for different purposes. For example, a block diagram is a simple graphic representation of a process or collection of processes. It may be used alone as a generalized explanatory device or as the first step in charting the improvement of a given situation.

Figure 3.10 illustrates a decision chart which is a means of representing work flows that include yes and no decisions. This type of chart is generally considered best for analyzing complicated work flows requiring many decisions.

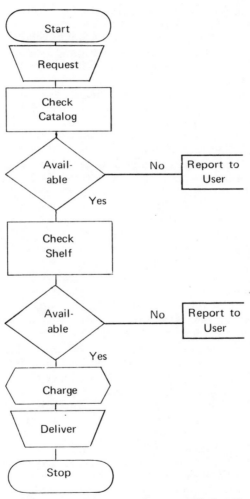

Fig. 3.10. Decision flow chart (teacher request for a specific book).

In developing the flow chart, flow or progression may be vertical (top to bottom) or horizontal (left to right). All charts should follow the same procedure. The main flow, referred to as the trunk, consists of processes and decisions that are expected to occur. Usually, "yes" decisions follow the main trunk. Exceptions, as noted by "no" decisions, are represented by branch flows, which set up a deviant pattern. Symbols used are connected by directional lines, while arrows represent an exit or entry from one symbol to another in a direction that deviates from the flow direction. Start and stop points are clearly defined. Several consecutive pages may be used for related segments of the flow chart to avoid crowding and to clarify the total picture. A general recommendation is to keep information, product, and personnel chartings separate. The type of charting that will best suit the purpose should be chosen as early as possible.

The application of flow charting to such LMC processes as the technical services area can do much to streamline procedures, aid in the training of personnel, and generally clarify service patterns.

Reports. Work expands to fill the amount of time available. This statement applies especially well to data gathering and report writing. Collecting circulation and other statistics may be a waste of time unless special use of the gathered statistics is intended. The purpose should be clear, a standard for comparison should be used, and the reports generated as the result of data gathering should be meaningfully expressed. Reports should be as brief as possible. Focusing on the concept of brevity, Riaz Khadem and Robert Lorber discussed three one-page reports: (1) the focus report, (2) the feedback report, and (3) the management report.[16] These reports highlight the fact that when a person is drowning in a sea of information, a screening system is needed.

An annual report can be an effective informational piece as well as a major public relations document. The report should do three things: (1) report concisely and informatively on significant happenings during the past year, (2) provide recommendations for program improvement, and (3) provide a forecast of expectations for the following year. This report should be used in conjunction with the annual budget request. If the budget follows PPBS or some modification of it, program objectives are stated. The annual report then highlights significant achievements in terms of meeting the stated objectives. As a need for new program input is seen, recommendations for improvement develop naturally. The forecast of expectations deals with anticipated new or additional output or, conversely, with a decrease in existing levels of performance.

The task of coordinating LMC reports for use outside the individual school would be assumed by a district director. Before release, a review of internal reports may also be required. In the absence of a district director, the heads of school LMCs should work together to coordinate reporting systems.

Public relations consist of the total LMC image projected to its public, that is, the community, the school staff, and the students. *Publicity* is the method used to inform the LMC's public about what is being done, how it is being done, and the degree of success that is achieved.

The LMC staff is principally responsible for the public relations program. Anyone who comes in contact with the LMC may develop an attitude (favorable or unfavorable) toward the program. An effective program is constructed from a careful analysis of the LMC system and an evaluation of the needs of its public. Some activities that will contribute to success in this area follow:

1. Students, teachers, and administrators are involved in the preview, evaluation, and selection of media as well as the establishment of policy guidelines that set the pattern of LMC service for the school.

2. Students are involved in special programs emanating from the LMC. They receive, as needed, guidance in research, reading, and the design and production of media. Service and facilities are available to accommodate special interest groups.

3. Teachers are satisfied that the LMC is meeting the media and service needs of their students. Teachers are offered assistance, as needed, through structured in-service programs or individual consultation on curriculum planning and implementation, and through the design or modification of media for instructional purposes. Their requirements for professional media and information are satisfied.

4. School administrators and the central administrative staff receive reports as needed. They are provided with both planning and operational assistance as new programs are developed and implemented and they receive, on a continuing basis, professional information of interest to them and to the total school staff.

5. As for other agencies encompassed by the system, there is a planned exchange of information, and there are clearly defined levels of cooperation which can be advertised. Where applicable, the writing of projects for the development of externally funded programs is carried out cooperatively.

6. The community is kept informed of school activities and of the special contributions of the LMC through commercial news media, through publicity hand-outs carried home by students, and, indirectly, by students who provide visible evidence of assistance.

7. The school board, representing the attitudes and opinions of the public, receives news releases that pertain to the school LMC. LMC bulletins, reports, and special displays of media and equipment, as well as media productions, are provided as needed.

As with reports, public relations and publicity for the LMC should be coordinated at a district level whenever possible. In a large school district, having both a director of library media services and a district LMC, a department within the center may be assigned the duty of initiating and coordinating this important activity.

Evaluation. When we wish to evaluate something or someone, our intent is "to examine and judge concerning the worth, quality, significance, amount, degree or condition of" whatever is to be evaluated.[17] In order to do this, some norm or standard must be applied, against which to gauge the subject for evaluation. However, as soon as the term *standard* is mentioned, there appears to be some confusion of meanings. Hence, it becomes necessary to supply another definition. A standard is "something established by authority, custom, or general consent as a model or example to be followed—a definite level or degree of quality that is adequate and proper for a specific purpose." There are many types of standards, including accreditation and personnel standards. Of particular interest to the library media specialist are diagnostic standards and projective standards.

Diagnostic or benchmark standards are based on a model of conditions existing in LMCs that have programs of superior quality. These standards become practical to use because they represent conditions as they exist. One major problem with diagnostic standards is that they frequently fall short of what we believe should be the pattern of conditions in a given situation. They do not satisfy one's desire for optimum conditions.

Projective standards are directed to conditions as they ought to be. They are guidelines for the development of programming. Because projective standards cannot be easily realized, however, they become controversial. A typical administrative reaction to national school media standards has been simply to challenge the credibility of the recommendations. Nevertheless, these standards do meet many of our needs, serving as a basis for comparison with existing conditions and goals for long- or short-range planning for educational improvement.

LMC standards are part of a larger field of educational standards and the overall question of standardization in education. Quantitative and qualitative factors are usually considered in educational standards, though it is not imperative that the standards include both factors.

Quantitative standards provide numerical measurements and detailed requirements for resources and services. Standards stated in numerical terms and applied to a given situation make measurement, evaluation, and, where applicable, enforcement relatively easy. However, if quantitative standards are used as the only criterion, there is no way to judge the results of the quantitative inputs against an educational output. They require continuous monitoring and evaluation.

Qualitative standards, on the other hand, represent an attempt to express in functional terms the same ideal requirements as quantitative standards, encouraging a level of service that is adequate for each school in terms of its own needs. Because they are not expressed in exact quantitative amounts, they are difficult to measure or to enforce. Standards that reflect some coordination of quantitative and qualitative factors are most desirable.

There are many ways to evaluate school LMCs. Using projective national standards and/or diagnostic standards as a basis for comparison is a common method. Regional, state, and local standards, where available, are additional tools.

Evaluative criteria, designed specifically for the evaluation of elementary, middle, and senior high schools, are commonly used to relate the LMC to the instructional program of the school.[18] Some schools or school districts use consultants, paid or voluntary, as another means of determining the worth or quality of the LMC system. The professional consultant, besides using various standards available for comparison, usually brings several years of experience to the task of evaluation.

There is a special need to evaluate the LMC, since LMC personnel devote themselves philosophically and operationally to a particular vehicle for educational improvement. Evaluation is needed to prove the system. This is more important now than at any other time, because taxpayers and educators want the educational system improved and want to achieve the maximum benefit at the lowest costs. Any alternative approach that can guarantee a reasonable degree of success will be considered very carefully.

The LMC's value to a quality educational program is not necessarily known and appreciated, and an adequately funded LMC is not an insignificant budget item. Costing-out a comprehensive LMC program and comparing its cost with that of other programs provides an idea of how program priorities are established. A fair estimate of cost may be arrived at by computing staff costs, media inventory costs, furnishings and equipment costs, and the square foot cost of space occupied. For a more complete picture, the cost of custodial service, electricity, heat, and telephone can be prorated and added to the previous total. An investment is made in the LMC because it is believed that this system will make a contribution to a sound educational program. Evaluation is the process used to determine to what extent this is actually happening.

SUMMARY

- The management activities of the LMC system are planning, organizing, leading, and controlling.

- Definitions of management vary. Two have been provided.

  1. Management is "both the people responsible for running an organization and the running process itself."

  2. "Working with and through people to accomplish organizational goals."

- Systems which can be effectively used in planning and controlling LMC or district programs include PPBS, ZBB, and MBO. MBO can be used in conjunction with PPBS, ZBB, or the operational approach to managing.

ACTIVITIES

1. For a selected school LMC having a multiple staffing pattern, complete the forms provided in figures 3.4-3.6 (adapting forms as needed). Complete the same process for a school district having both school LMCs and a district director.

2. For a selected school LMC having a multiple staffing pattern, prepare an organization chart depicting lines of authority and departmentation. Complete the same process for a school district having both school LMCs and a district director.

3. Describe the relationship between school LMCs and the district LMC.

4. Describe the relationship between management activities and assets/achievements.

5. Investigate one or more of the following topics: (1) management, (2) Management by Objectives, (3) motivation, (4) leadership, or (5) communication.

NOTES

[1]Peter Drucker, *Management: Tasks, Responsibilities, Practices* (New York: Harper & Row, 1974), x.

[2]Daniel Oran and Jay Shafritz, *MBA's Dictionary* (Reston, Va.: Reston Publishing, 1983), 251, 253.

[3]Paul Hersey and Kenneth Blanchard, *Management of Organizational Behavior* (Englewood Cliffs, N.J.: Prentice-Hall, 1982), 3.

[4]Richard Pascale and Anthony Athos, *The Art of Japanese Management* (New York: Warner Books, 1981), 125; Thomas Peters and Robert Waterman, *In Search of Excellence* (New York: Harper & Row, 1982), 9-10.

[5]Drucker, *Management*, 400.

[6]George Odiorne, *MBO II: A System of Managerial Leadership for the 80's* (Belmont Calif.: Pitman Learning, 1979), 21-28.

[7]William Reddin, *Effective Management by Objectives* (New York: McGraw-Hill, 1971), 23.

[8]James Liesener, "The Development of a Planning Process for Media Programs," *School Media Quarterly* 1 (Summer 1973): 278-87.

[9]Irving Janis and Leon Mann, *Decision Making* (New York: Free Press, 1977), 21-41.

[10]Abraham Mazlow, *Motivation and Personality* (New York: Harper & Row, 1954).

[11]Gerard Nierenberg, *The Art of Negotiation* (New York: Simon and Schuster, 1981).

[12]Harold Koontz and Cyril O'Donnell, *Essentials of Management* (New York: McGraw-Hill, 1978), 439.

[13]Kenneth Blanchard, and others, *Leadership and the One Minute Manager* (New York: Morrow, 1985), 19.

[14]Ibid., 30.

[15]Peter Drucker, *The Effective Executive* (New York: Harper & Row, 1967), 23-24.

[16]Riaz Khadem and Robert Lorber, *One Page Management: How to Use Information to Achieve Your Goals* (New York: Morrow, 1986), 44.

[17]*Webster's Third New International Dictionary* (Springfield, Mass.: G. & C. Merriam, 1986), 786.

[18]National Study of School Evaluation, *Elementary/Middle/Senior High School Evaluative Criteria*. Washington, D.C.: American Council on Education, n.d.

BIBLIOGRAPHY

Anderson, Eric. "The Amazing Library Computer." *Electronic Learning* 2 (March 1983): 68-71.

Barrow, Evelyn. "How're We Doing." *School Library Journal* 29 (September 1982): 49.

Bernard, Keith. "Computer Applications in Library Media Center: An Introduction to Electronic Spreadsheets." *School Library Media Quarterly* 12 (Spring 1984): 222-26.

Blanchard, Kenneth, and others. *Leadership and the One Minute Manager.* New York: Morrow, 1985.

Blanchard, Kenneth, and Spencer Johnson. *The One Minute Manager.* New York: Morrow, 1982.

Blanchard, Kenneth, and Robert Lorber. *Putting the One Minute Manager to Work.* New York: Morrow, 1984.

Callison, Daniel. "Justification for Action in Future School Library Media Programs." *School Library Media Quarterly* 12 (Spring 1984): 205-11.

Drucker, Peter. *The Effective Executive.* New York: Harper & Row, 1967.

Drucker, Peter. *Management: Tasks, Responsibilities, Practices.* New York: Harper & Row, 1974.

Graham, Judy. "My Micro Chased the Blues Away." *School Library Journal* 29 (February 1983): 23-26.

Hersey, Paul, and Kenneth Blanchard. *Management of Organizational Behavior.* Englewood Cliffs, N.J.: Prentice-Hall, 1982.

Immroth, Barbara. "Technology and Network Participation." *Drexel Library Quarterly* 20 (Winter 1984): 27-38.

Janis, Irving, and Leo Mann. *Decision Making.* New York: Free Press, 1977.

Johnson, David. "Wave the Computer Wand, and Remake School Libraries." *American School Board Journal* 172 (May 1985): 40.

Khadem, Riaz, and Robert Lorber. *One Page Management: How to Use Information to Achieve Your Goals.* New York: Morrow, 1986.

Koontz, Harold, and Cyril O'Donnell. *Essentials of Management*. New York: McGraw-Hill, 1978.

Liesener, James. "The Development of a Planning Process for Media Programs." *School Media Quarterly* 1 (Summer 1973): 278-87.

Mazlow, Abraham. *Motivation and Personality*. New York: Harper & Row, 1954.

National Study of School Evaluation. *Elementary/Middle/Senior High School Criteria*. Washington, D.C.: American Council on Education, n.d.

Nierenberg, Gerard. *The Art of Negotiation*. New York: Simon and Schuster, 1981.

Odiorne, George. *MBO II: A System of Managerial Leadership for the 80s*. Belmont, Calif.: Fearon Pitman, 1979.

Oran, Daniel, and Jay Shafritz. *MBA's Dictionary*. Reston, Va.: Reston Publishing, 1983.

Ouchi, William. *Theory Z*. New York: Avon, 1981.

Pascale, Richard, and Anthony Athos. *The Art of Japanese Management*. New York: Warner Books, 1981.

Peters, Thomas, and Robert Waterman. *In Search of Excellence*. New York: Harper & Row, 1982.

Reddin, William. *Effective Management by Objectives*. New York: McGraw-Hill, 1971.

Smith, Lotsee. "Microcomputers in School Library Media Centers." *Drexel Library Quarterly* 20 (Winter 1984): 7-15.

Tarkington, Fran. *Playing to Win*. New York: Harper & Row, 1984.

Yerkey, A. Neil. "Small Business Microcomputer Programs: Tools for Library Media Center Management." *School Library Media Quarterly* 12 (Spring 1984): 212-16.

4

ACHIEVEMENTS

OBJECTIVES

Describe the achievements component of the LMC system.

Describe the relationship between assets and achievements.

Design plans for the achievements component of the LMC for a selected school.

What the LMC seeks to achieve should be visible. The services should make a difference in what teachers teach, the way they teach, and the way students learn. Achievements are the most important goals, the essential output to which activities and assets are devoted. Specific areas of achievement are guidance and consulting services, instruction and in-service, design and production of media, and curriculum development and improvement. All are associated with the school LMC and are supported by the resources and services of a district LMC and an extended library media system.

Achievements represent a system in and of themselves—a group of inter-related and interlocking elements. This is the primary domain of the library media specialist, supported by other staff of the LMC.

1. *Guidance and Consulting Services.* A continuing individualized, personalized service to students and teachers. For students, guidance relates to their individual learning and personal needs. For teachers, consulting relates to their teaching needs and professional improvement.

2. *Instruction and In-Service.* A formal system for improving teaching and learning capabilities. For students, instruction in LMC research and the extensive use of media for learning. For teachers, in-service relating to the use of the LMC to improve instruction and for professional improvement.

3. *Design and Production of Media.* A service to students and teachers providing for the creation of new or modified forms of media.

4. *Curriculum Development and Improvement.* The involvement of library media specialists and LMC staff in the design of new programs through implementation on a day-to-day basis.

These elements do not represent the total array of opportunities afforded users of the LMC. They represent the most significant services. Through these achievements, the LMC helps students and teachers achieve their learning and instructional goals.

A fundamental question to be answered for each LMC and school is "To what extent or degree do we want to achieve in these areas?" In the study of successful schools conducted by the authors (see chapter 2, figure 2.1), library media specialists were asked to what extent they perceived the LMC as contributing to the success of the school. In 85 percent of the schools (item 9), they believed that personalized services to individual students (guidance) contributed to their success. In 64 percent of the schools (item 8), they believed that their instructional program (instruction) contributed to the success of students. In 70 percent of schools (item 10), they believed that their assistance to teachers (consulting) contributed to their success. Does "to a great extent" the scale rating used, mean they have a 90 percent success rate in meeting the needs of students and teachers? Or a 75 percent success rate? Or a 60 percent success rate?

Priorities, objectives, and measurable standards of performance should be included in the planning process, defining areas of emphasis as well as levels of service to be provided. Objectives and standards provide the basis for implementation and the evaluation of performance.

GUIDANCE AND CONSULTING SERVICES

These are dual, personalized, interactive services to students and teachers. To provide for differentiated service patterns, guidance is defined as a range of specialized services for students which may vary in intensity with grade levels, orientation of the curriculum, and student needs; consulting services are designed to assist teachers in their instructional work on a continuing basis and to aid in professional improvement.

Guidance and consulting services:

1. directly support the efforts of students and teachers to learn on their own,

2. integrate and individualize efforts in instruction/in-service, design/production, and curriculum development/improvement, and

3. epitomize the interpersonal one-on-one relationship that is at the heart of teaching and learning, facilitating individualization, inquiry, and independent study.

Guidance Services for Students

The LMC has the potential for an almost unlimited range of direct services to students. Decisions must be made as to what services are most useful and significant. A few are highlighted here:

Information Retrieval and Utilization

Students who are required to do research or investigative work are of three types: those who are well versed in the mechanics of using the LMC, are familiar with the resources available, and are able to function independently; those who have some knowledge of the workings of the LMC but may or may not be familiar with their topics and therefore are semi-independent; and those students who are totally dependent because they have neither learned how to use the LMC nor are aware of the resources available.

The purpose of this service is to provide each student with as much assistance as is needed to complete the work effectively and efficiently. When the student presents a problem, the library media specialist helps clarify the research needed, and determines whether the student can proceed independently or to what degree assistance is needed.

The first phase of direct assistance to students is usually complete after the range of resources has been surveyed and selection has been decided. In some cases, this is where professional assistance ends. When necessary, the reference-research cycle should go beyond investigation: to the evaluation of information sources, to the organization of information, and to the presentation mode to be used by the student.

Requests for location of media in the LMC and directions for the use of a particular audiovisual device are tasks that can be performed by a media technician or aide who has received training in this area. The professional role is to analyze the questions posed by students and to decide how and who should be involved in solving the problem.

The library media specialist should know students well enough to determine which ones require little assistance and which need comprehensive guidance. This knowledge also allows the professional to provide feedback to LMC staff and teachers about individual students, whether the assignments made are reasonable, and whether the existing collections can meet the instructional and personal needs of students. As a guide to providing effective service in the future, exceptional and difficult search problems and their solutions should be recorded.

The information retrieval and utilization service is critical. It is related to both the instructional program of the school and to the LMC and requires a major focus for development. Guidance in this area is individualized and extends to satisfying the personal interests of students. The student should know what service is available and whom to seek out for assistance. The student should also feel confident that help will be provided.

Different types and levels of service require varying amounts of time, effort, and resources (the assets of the LMC). Decisions are needed as part of the planning process to differentiate types and levels of service which can be provided given specific levels of input. Since we expect to tap the resources and services of a district LMC and the extended media system, including online information retrieval from remote databases, research is needed to determine whether the library media specialist should perform all information searching for students, allowing them to devote their time to analysis, synthesis, and presentation activities.

Reading Guidance

In an age when technology is making significant strides in education, reading has become even more important than before. The focus on reading in the schools has a twofold purpose: improving the skills required to read, and fostering the desire to read in students. The traditional role of the LMC in reading should be enlarged and strengthened.

Reading is the responsibility of all members of the school's professional staff. Those who should be most involved are teachers, reading personnel, and LMC professionals. A first step toward improving a school reading program should be to allow these groups to exchange information about their existing roles in the school. A continuing dialog should focus the attention of this group on the reading needs of students.

The purpose and objectives of the reading program for the school should be clearly stated, alternative program components provided for, and adequate data from which to build should be available. This approach allows consideration of a broad range of alternative means of reaching the program objectives. Professional participants in the school reading program should assume constructive roles that are not too far removed from their existing roles. The reading specialist should play a leading role in selecting and coordinating the use of skill-building media. The teacher should develop teaching strategies that accommodate information input from varied sources rather than "pat" answers from a text. Library media specialists should coordinate the selection of media in all areas to accommodate student differences, and should be aware of the needs of individual students and groups. This implies being in touch with students as they select media to satisfy instructional requirements, and it also demands a continuing assessment of the depth and diversity of selections. Although reading is the thrust, media (in any form) should be regarded in the same way.

At the elementary school level, as part of the LMC instructional program the library media specialist often is assigned, or elects, the responsibility for storytelling and picture book hours, book fairs, assembly programs, literary clubs, and other activities designed to stimulate an interest in reading. The time and effort involved must be weighed against the benefits of these activities as compared to each other and to other services. The consideration of alternative ways to deliver vital services is also important.

At the secondary level, similar specialized activities may be sponsored by the library media specialist. The benefit to students and the school should be weighed against the use of time, energy, resources, and creativity devoted to providing other services.

Communication

Various schemes can be used to provide students with information about the LMC. Although this aspect of the LMC may seem less important than other program elements, a good public relations program is essential.

The need to inform students about policies, procedures, and services of the LMC can be met through the use of a handbook for students and teachers or through a periodic bulletin. If students are willing and capable, a student information series can be developed to disseminate information by radio, television, tapes, or direct student contact in the classroom. The same array of media can be used to inform students of school programs, activities outside the school, and various LMC-sponsored activities. Given the opportunity and a degree of responsibility, student response to this type of experience is generally very positive.

Extracurricular Programs

Recreational programs in the school may be extensive. In the ranking of guidance services, support of such activities probably receives the lowest priority. However, if included in the planning process, services beyond-the-ordinary should be provided. These services extend to providing professional staff as sponsors and coordinators of extracurricular activities and providing space for activities. Also included are the initiation of projects for special interest groups and design/production services required by these groups in carrying out their programs.

Consulting Services for Teachers

Consulting services are the individualized activities and services provided by the professional LMC staff to assist teachers in their work. Curriculum development and improvement, design and production, and in-service activities may be incorporated in this service. Also, the range of guidance services to students is directed to helping teachers do a more effective job. Service to teachers will become more important and significant as educational reform activities are initiated in the schools.

Information Retrieval and Utilization

Closely related to the library media specialists responsibility in curriculum development and improvement is the information service to teachers. A teacher request for information related to an instructional unit should bring forth a range of activities. Through the consultative dialog, the LMC professional ascertains the number of students to be involved, determines which students will have problems in dealing with the subject, judges the space needed to accommodate users, ascertains the types of activities to be programmed, and determines the need for instructional and production services. The need for specialized resources may require, in addition to in-house research, contact with a district LMC or the extended media system.

Another principal consultative function of the LMC professional relates to the development of instructional systems. Unlike the usual exploratory or inquiry process, which is free flowing, the instructional system is rooted in behavioral objectives and is a step-by-step, sequential learning process for the student or students. Each medium employed in the system is evaluated for informational input, and specific direction for use is provided. The system is controlled by purpose and performance based on predetermined objectives.

Communication

Teachers should be informed about policy and procedures for operation of the LMC; new services, equipment, and media; special activities of the LMC; reviews of new media; and national, state, and local events, whether television or radio broadcasts or special programs of the local museum or art gallery. The same medium used to inform students about special activities of the school and events outside may also be employed for teacher information. Teachers may be provided with a looseleaf notebook, appropriately labeled *LMC*, into which may be filed bibliographies and bulletins.

A high priority should be placed on feedback to teachers about student performance. A guidance department in the school would also benefit from this information. If a well-developed reading guidance program is in operation, feedback to faculty is important. The progress of students in an individualized, independent learning program must be carefully assessed. Independent investigation carried on by students requires two responses: first, direct assistance to the student as needed; and second, feedback to the teacher on problems encountered by students and on their general progress.

Effective interaction with teachers is facilitated when the library media specialist has developed a means of working successfully with teachers on a continuing basis. Examples include membership on a principal's advisory council or working through an LMC committee of teachers, a media selection committee, a reading guidance committee, or a school curriculum committee.

Professional Services

These services require the development of professional resources and services to support teacher professional development activities. A low priority was assigned to these activities in the past because many school districts did not accept professional development as a district responsibility. However, the national and state drive to improve teacher competence through continuing education and other activities will stimulate significant activity in this area. For many school districts, professional services will be assigned to a district-level or a regional center. Because of a general lack of school and district resources to satisfy the range of needs, extensive contact with the extended media system can be anticipated.

Library media specialists can play a significant role in professional services which, in large measure, relate to information retrieval services. Where district or school activities, in the area of professional development, have not been initiated, library media specialists can take a leadership role in development.

INSTRUCTION AND IN-SERVICE

It has been said that "the library will function as the teacher of that neglected half of knowledge — 'the knowledge of where to find it' — and as the interdisciplinary synthesizer which establishes interrelations among various fields of knowledge."[1] Such an achievement relates to helping students and teachers learn how better to use the LMC system in the learning and teaching process. For some time to come, this will be an imperative, and planning will have to accommodate a formal and structured approach.

Instruction is the term selected for aspects relating to students. *In-service* is the term used to denote formalized aspects of teaching teachers to become more effective professionals.

Instruction

Formal Programs

The LMC program of instruction may be limited to media utilization, research methods, and the design and production of media. Or it may be considerably more extensive, involving a comprehensive approach to the understanding and appreciation of literature in all its forms as well as the intensive study of such forms of media as film, television, and microcomputers. The back-to-basics emphasis of the schools and the trend toward competency-based instruction and testing will influence the nature of the LMC curriculum. Decisions about the specific content of the LMC curriculum should be made as part of the planning process. The curriculum should generally be applied districtwide, with adaptations made at the individual school level. To whatever extent possible, the LMC program should be integrated into the general curriculum of the schools; that is, subject matter (for example, social studies) becomes the content and context for LMC program applications.

The library media specialist assumes responsibility for teaching the skills students need to eventually work independently in the school LMC, other libraries, and information centers. They also teach the skills needed for online information retrieval from remote computerized databases.

Many state departments of education have, through a broad committee structure, produced guidelines and recommended instructional programs for the schools. A common pattern has emerged, although significant variations exist. The common pattern usually provides a basic list of core objectives (or continuums) intended to be generalized enough to cover K-12 activities. The core is then followed either by a grade-by-grade list of skills and activities or by a level-by-level approach (e.g., K-3, 4-6). Various approaches are discussed below; an example of a scope and sequence chart is provided in appendix A.

The program for Virginia provides a listing of core objectives, cited here. Objectives and activities for each grade are keyed to objectives in language arts and social studies. Core objectives are essential at each grade level. These skills should be emphasized each year after being introduced in kindergarten. (There is no correlation between core number and grade level.):

Core 1   The student will demonstrate responsible use of the library/information center.
Descriptive Statement: Emphasis is on citizenship, care of materials, and policies/procedures.

Core 2   The student will select recreational and informational sources appropriate to his level.
Descriptive Statement: Emphasis is on choosing materials appropriate to ability, interest, and need.

Core 3   The student will participate in a variety of experiences to increase appreciation of literature.
Descriptive Statement: Emphasis is on a variety of literary forms and formats, which are introduced at appropriate grade levels.

Core 4   The student will use appropriate questioning skills to retrieve information.
Descriptive Statement: Emphasis is on the development of questioning skills.

Core 5 The student will recognize the availability of information from a variety of community resources.
Descriptive Statement: Emphasis is on public, academic, and special libraries as well as other institutions, agencies, and individuals.

Core 6 The student will demonstrate an understanding of the ownership of ideas.
Descriptive Statement: Emphasis is on respecting copyright regulations and crediting sources.

Core 7 The student will participate in a variety of media production activities.
Descriptive Statement: Emphasis is on the development of student creativity through various enrichment experiences.[2]

North Carolina provides a list of six "information skill competencies," cited here. They serve as a basis for identifying desired learning outcomes:

- *Orientation and organization*—the learner will demonstrate a working knowledge of the media center's organization, and of the procedures required to use the center and its collections.

- *Selection and utilization*—the learner will select and use materials and equipment appropriate to personal needs and classroom assignments.

- *Comprehension and application*—the learner will identify concepts presented in media, interpret and organize information, and develop evaluative skills for understanding media at school and elsewhere.

- *Production and presentation*—the learner will design, produce, and/or select a variety of media formats to present information.

- *Enrichment*—the learner will expand reading, listening, and viewing interests by using a variety of media for personal growth, vocational pursuits, and recreation.

- *Computer awareness*—the learner will demonstrate an understanding of computers, their operation, and their possible application to solving relevant problems.[3]

South Dakota's guide places emphasis on four categories of library and information skills, cited here. Each category is broken down into specific skills for each grade level:

I.   Orientation

The student will become familiar with the unique features of the library/media center (LMC).
A.   The student will recognize the roles of LMC staff.
B.   The students will know where various information formats are located within the LMC.
C.   The student will follow LMC rules.
D.   The student will demonstrate appropriate behavior for various LMC activities.
E.   The student will identify services available from the LMC.

II. Reference and research

The student will become familiar with the methods for organizing information in the school and community.
A.   The student will know that information is available in subject categories and in a variety of media formats.
B.   The student will distinguish between different types of information sources.
C.   The student will use appropriate organizational and indexing systems to locate information.
D.   The student will select material based on content, level of difficulty, and preferred learning style.

III. Production

The student will design, produce, present, and evaluate the presentation of information in a variety of formats.
A.   The student will handle, set up, use, and care for equipment appropriately.
B.   The student will develop independence in planning, producing, presenting, and evaluating media presentations in a variety of formats.

IV. Reading promotion and appreciation

The student will value, use and enjoy print and nonprint media for educational, personal, vocational and recreational purposes.
A.   The student will develop a positive attitude toward books, reading, and library media centers.
B.   The student will develop critical reading, thinking, viewing, and listening skills.[4]

The guide for Connecticut divides library media skills instruction into four general competencies, cited here. Specific skills are listed under these four competencies for each grade level.

Competency I   Students should demonstrate a working know-ledge of library media center organization, facilities, personnel and procedures.

Competency II   Students should select and use materials appropriate to their level for curricular and leisure activities.

Competency III   Students should comprehend concepts presented in print and nonprint media in order to analyze, interpret, organize and evaluate information for curricular and personal applications.

Competency IV   Students should demonstrate the ability to communicate through oral, written and visual modes.[5]

Most schools and districts have accepted the challenge of *A Nation at Risk* and now consider the ability to use the computer a fourth basic skill. However, the rapid rise of computer use has caused significant and unique problems, since the same skills are being learned by elementary and senior high school students. What to teach, when to teach it, and who should teach it remains a problem for many schools. Some help is expected when the results of a national assessment become available. The National Assessment of Educational Progress is involved in a study of nine, thirteen, and seventeen-year-olds in the nation's schools.[6] The study will report on competencies in three areas: computer applications, computer science, and knowledge and attitudes (see figure 4.1). Exercises in the three categories of the assessment will be distributed among the following cognitive levels: knowledge, operation, and problem solving/design. "Knowledge refers to the recognition or recall of specific ideas, facts and procedures. Operation refers to routine manipulation of symbols and procedures required to complete specific tasks. Problem solving/design refers to more complex intellectual processes than those routinely involved in procedural skill application and elaboration of conceptual understanding."[7]

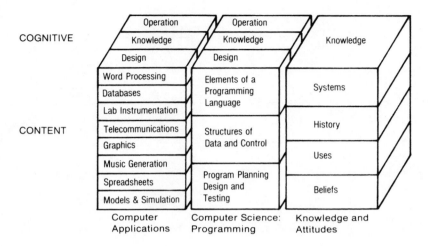

Fig. 4.1. Computer objective categories. Reprinted with permission from National Assessment of Educational Progress, *A Framework for Assessing Computer Competence: Defining Objectives* (Princeton, N.J.: Educational Testing Service, 1986), 7.

Connecticut's guide to the use of computers in education provides a view of common instructional uses of computers.[8] Two general categories are provided: the study of computers (literacy and computer science) and computer applications to other subjects (figure 4.2). A section on the uses of computers in subject areas is provided in appendix B.

Computer applications of various kinds fall naturally into the LMC instructional program. In many schools, the LMC will contain a microcomputer lab for general use by students and teachers. Also, in most schools, responsibility for this technology will be assigned to the LMC.

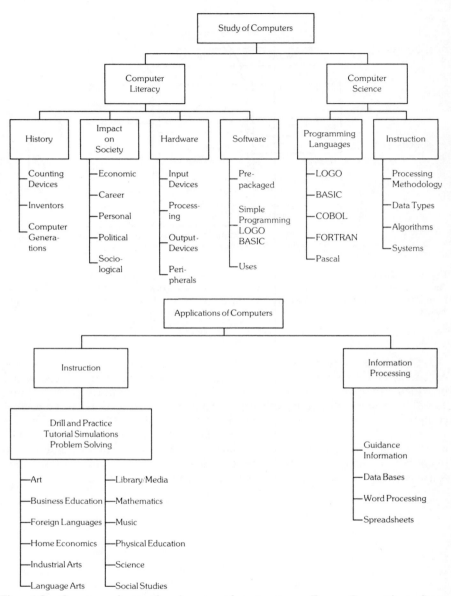

Fig. 4.2. Common instructional uses of computers. From Connecticut State Department of Education, "Instructional Uses of Computers in Connecticut Public Schools," 1983. Reprinted with permission of the Connecticut State Department of Education.

Instructional Systems

As an instructional system, the Learning Activity Package (L.A.P.) is presented to illustrate a viable alternative to, or component of, formal "classroom" instruction, and to describe the content and uses of the system. The L.A.P. was developed for the classroom as a means of establishing a nongraded or continuous progress program in the schools. As a practical and formalized means of teaching, the system is highly compatible with an LMC approach. It is both an effective and an efficient methodology.

Many alternative methods of application are possible using the L.A.P. structure. If scheduled class periods are required by administration, they can be offered as a structured sequence and still provide a refreshing alternative to group-paced instruction. At any grade level, when the need arises for a particular skill, L.A.P.s may be fed into the program for a particular class, group, or individual. Perhaps most important, individual users of the LMC can be given a self-instructional program that does not rely on any one teacher or any specific time schedule. Using this approach can free the library media specialist from a formal teaching schedule and at the same time ensure that each student will have the opportunity to learn these skills independently.

It is possible to develop an articulated sequence of L.A.P.s covering use of the catalog, reference tools, and so on, for elementary grades through high school. It is also possible to create one L.A.P. for a single topic (e.g., *Readers' Guide*), which would be suited to the needs of most senior high school students. Similarly, an analysis of school organization and curriculum will provide insight into the what, where, and how of creating basic skills packages in a given area.

The L.A.P. is intended to be a self-directed, self-pacing instrument, not a workbook. It is a program of objectives and activities that direct the learner to experiences through which he or she can become proficient in a given area of study. The structure is prescribed and the format is reasonably consistent, although the writer has considerable latitude in building in alternatives. A typical outline would include the elements shown in figure 4.3.

The primary idea for the package is specifically the subject or title of the package. Keyed to the primary idea is the rationale, which is a brief statement telling the student why he or she should learn about this primary idea or subject.

It should be possible to break the primary idea or subject down into three or four ideas or concepts. These become the secondary ideas for the L.A.P. and represent the basic learning areas required of students. Each part of the package containing secondary ideas is called a segment. Each segment is structured in precisely the same manner. The statement of the secondary idea is followed by three or four behavioral objectives. Behavioral objectives tell the student what must be done to demonstrate what has been learned, under what conditions the learning task must be performed, and to what extent it must be performed.

PRIMARY IDEA

(Reference Sources)

RATIONALE

    (Why students should learn about reference sources)

SECONDARY IDEA I - (Encyclopedias)

    Behavioral Objectives

    Pre-Test

    Activities
        - Multi-mode
            - content
            - activities
            - media

    Student Self-Assessment

    Evaluation

SECONDARY IDEA II - (Almanacs)

    Pattern Repeated

                    SELF-ASSESSMENT

                    EVALUATION OF PACKAGE

                    IN-DEPTH

Fig. 4.3. Learning activity package.

The pre-test is usually an optional item for the student. If he or she can pass the pre-test, competency has been demonstrated and the section may be omitted. If it is known that the L.A.P. material will be totally new to students, the development of a pre-test is unnecessary.

The activities built into the package provide a common core of understandings for all learners and enable them to fulfill the stated objectives. For each secondary idea or segment, the learner selects from many alternatives and works on activities of his or her choice. However, it is possible for the writer to specify completion of certain activities. Student options may include reading, writing, listening, viewing, conferences, group work, and other activities. The writer, in planning these activities, must accommodate varying student interests and abilities and must vary the mode, content, activities, and media employed. Media input may be both commercially available materials and teacher-produced materials. The most common teacher-produced materials are tapes, slides, transparencies, and worksheets of various types designed to be used in combination.

A self-assessment is a self-test that the student administers and corrects. The purpose of the self-assessment is to help the student decide whether he or she has successfully completed enough activities to pass a teacher evaluation. Usually, a student-teacher conference is scheduled after the self-assessment to discuss progress and to recycle the student if he or she has not been successful. Checkpoints for student-teacher conferences may also be built into the various segments if it seems desirable for the student to meet with the teacher. The teacher evaluation must be closely related to the stated behavioral objectives and self-assessment. It should not have unexpected elements built into it.

In-depth activities may comprise some 50 percent of student work in L.A.P.s prepared in specific curriculum content areas. Designed as activities for exploration and discovery, these cover the broad spectrum of student interests and abilities related to the subject. More than any other area of the package, these may be individualized activities. Some of the principal benefits of this approach are that:

1. It is geared to a media approach to learning. The media orientation and unique individualized and independent style are suited to a library media center approach.

2. The student functions as an individual and has both a broad selection of alternative experiences and a variety of media to suit his or her personal learning style.

3. The LMC professional may greatly reduce reliance on formal presentations. While students are working independently, the library media specialist can work with other students and teachers as needed.

4. For the school administrator who views an LMC program as 99 percent skills teaching, this approach ensures that students will learn media skills on an individual and independent basis.

5. The library media specialist becomes skilled at developing individualized learning programs for students.

6. The library media specialist may apply this knowledge and experience as a consultant to teachers in the content areas, whether in the development of L.A.P.s or merely in the structuring of individualized and independent programming.

Small Groups

An alternative to the formal class structure or an instructional system is the use of small groups (five to ten students) for directed learning experiences. Because of the size of the group, each student receives a fair share of individual attention, and teaching and learning are accomplished in an effective manner. Where group patterns are used in elementary and secondary classrooms, this process can work very efficiently. A flexible school schedule enhances the possibilities for individualized or small group work in the LMC.

Guidesheets

The use of various types of "hand-out" materials may be of value to students (and faculty) as they work independently in the LMC. For example, guidesheets should be available which detail the specific steps to be followed in using various pieces of equipment, or steps in a particular process. Figure 4.4 shows a generalized guidesheet (secondary level) listing appropriate questions to be asked when an information search is to be conducted.

SEARCHING FOR INFORMATION

This guide provides a list of questions to ask yourself when you are going to conduct an information search.

1. Do I know what I want and what I will do with the information that I collect?

2. What information do I already have about the subject? Are there leads or clues in this information that will save me time when I begin my search?

3. Have I developed a subject (topic) list of key words that are most likely to get me to the information I need?

4. How soon do I need the information? If I have a limited amount of time, will I have to limit my search to one or two search tools (sources)?

5. What time period must I cover? Is it important to start with up-to-date information and then trace the subject back for several years?

6. What search tools (sources) appear to be good choices for information? Can I list these in the order in which I would use them?

7. Are these search tools readily available? Do I know how to use them?

8. Do I need a record of my progress, such as a card file of sources I looked at and the information found?

9. Do I know when to stop searching for additional information?

10. Do I know when to ASK A LIBRARY MEDIA SPECIALIST FOR ASSISTANCE?

Fig. 4.4. Guidesheet — searching for information.

Pathfinders

A pathfinder is a modified instructional system that can be used to introduce an LMC user to basic information sources on a specific topic. It can be used as a tool in teaching investigative skills in subject areas, integrated into a L.A.P., given to teachers to use, or merely made available to interested students. Pathfinders can be produced as the need arises or as part of a curriculum development project. Format and content may be modified as needed to suit a given situation. They are not bibliographies or exhaustive subject guides, and they ordinarily assume some prerequisite LMC knowledge and skill on the part of users. Typically, the pathfinder will follow a set format similar to a search strategy used by a reference librarian (see figure 4.5).

TOPIC

SCOPE

(Brief overview of the topic)

INTRODUCTORY SOURCE

(Cite an appropriate beginning source of information such as an encyclopedia article)

SUBJECT HEADINGS

(Appropriate subject headings to be searched in the catalog)

CALL NUMBERS

(Numbers associated with related materials for browsing)

HANDBOOKS, ENCYCLOPEDIAS, DICTIONARIES

(Specific citations provided)

SUBJECT HEADINGS

(Appropriate subject headings to be searched in specific periodical indexes)

PERIODICALS

(Those frequently containing articles on the topic)

Fig. 4.5. Pathfinders.

Applications of Technology

The full range of technology should be integrated into segments of LMC instruction—as the medium of instruction and as the content of instruction. Computer, video, and telecommunications technologies offer challenging opportunities for extending LMC and other programs to remote locations in the school, district, and beyond.

In-Service

In-service is a component of employee training and development and a part of the broader concept of continuing education—"a general term that usually refers to graduate or undergraduate course work undertaken on a part-time basis in order to keep up to date on new developments in one's field, or contribute to one's general education."[9] In-service and continuing education are as important to educational improvement as are curriculum development and improvement. The range of criticism directed to the perceived lack of competence of the nation's teachers has raised these elements to a new level of importance.

In-service activities may be formal or informal. Formal activities include attending college for extension course work, sabbatical leave for study, travel, teacher exchanges, participation in research and curriculum revision, and school and district workshops. Informal activities include an array of potentially valuable experiences, among them attending professional association conferences and faculty and department meetings in schools and school districts. Although all too frequently faculty and department meetings are devoted to administrative detail, the possibilities for professionally beneficial experiences are broad. Some areas suitable for exploration include reviewing the school program of studies, articulation of the program through the grades, reviewing procedures for individualization opportunities, evaluation of student performance, policy and procedures for day-to-day operations, and demonstrations of potentially successful teaching-learning experiences.

The library media specialist has the opportunity and responsibility to participate in various types of in-service programming: as a catalyst to improve instructional practices in all content areas through the use of media, to publicize the benefits of using the LMC, to contribute new information about research in the content areas, and to develop new competencies. A primary role is to make others aware of the LMC's potential for accommodating varied teaching methods, diversified course content, varied student activities, and the range and depth of media available to meet the needs of students. LMC professionals should develop in-service roles that allow *them* to initiate and conduct in-service programs at one time, and at another time to participate in and work to improve in-service initiated by others.

LMC-Initiated In-Service

It is recognized that teachers generally lack basic knowledge about the use of media (including technology) in teaching and learning. Short term, structured, in-service workshops for teachers may have to encompass very basic information and practice in the following areas:

1. Orientation programs geared to the service potential of the LMC, district-level services, and the extended media system.

2. Overview of the LMC instructional program for students.

3. How to use various devices such as projectors, video equipment, and microcomputers.

4. How to evaluate and select media.

5. How to design and produce media.

6. How to use standard LMC tools such as the catalog and various indexes.

In-service of a more comprehensive or specialized nature may be structured for longer periods of time, since it requires deeper teacher involvement. Programs can be developed for individual departments or grade levels, with participation limited to those working in the area. Other programs can include the entire school staff in general activities designed to improve teaching and learning. The following types of programs cover general concepts of the LMC:

1. The preview, evaluation, and selection of media related to curriculum development and improvement.

2. Independent study potential of the LMC for various content areas.

3. Remediation potential of the LMC for students having difficulty in the content areas.

4. Developing resource and/or teaching units in various content areas using the LMC as a base of operations.

5. Developing individualized student learning packages in various content areas using the LMC as a base.

6. Initiating cooperative reading guidance programs in the school using the LMC as a base.

On occasion, in-service work initiated by LMC professionals should have a twofold purpose. For example, one purpose may be to teach teachers how to use television effectively in their work; another may be to enable the teacher to contribute a product to the LMC. This exchange of information for talent may be extended to other creative production work. The in-service objective is structured to produce two vital outcomes: greater teacher competency and needed teacher input into the LMC system.

School administration should be informed and should support any in-service program that promises to benefit the teaching-learning process in the school. Without administrative support and, more important, without the interest and support of the teaching staff, such in-service work is impossible. If the library media specialist is a member of a principal's council, or other school committees, steps can be initiated through that group to bring about desired in-service programming.

Some school districts pay in-service participants for their time, others provide credits toward future salary increments, and still others merely allow release time for in-service work. Various combinations of these approaches are found.

Pay, course credit, and release time from teaching are inducements to participate in in-service work. Interest, the acknowledged need for new skills and knowledge, and an excitement about new ideas are refreshingly different motivating forces. It would be desirable to have all or many of these forces at work in the school.

A vital consideration in the strategy to improve teacher competency is the method chosen for devising and carrying out the in-service program. The most beneficial results are obtained when members of the teaching staff are involved in structuring and carrying out the program.

Library Media Specialists as Participants

Few in-service programs can operate effectively without the skills of LMC personnel. For example, in any project designed to improve curriculum, teachers should interact with LMC personnel to:

- Review the availability of media related to the various projects.

- Preview and select new media to be included in the projects.

- Obtain assistance in planning, designing, and producing media to be included in the package.

- Structure student activities that require the extensive use of media beyond the textbook.

- Structure activities requiring independent and small-group use of the LMC.

- Determine what media skills students will need in order to function independently in the LMC and to integrate the teaching of needed skills into teacher-prepared programs.

Regional education centers in some states have been active in designing and offering continuing education opportunities for school personnel. It is likely that activity at this level will expand. In some states, the state department of education has initiated workshops and institutes to improve the competency of teachers and other school specialists. Activity at this level may be associated with legislation mandating continuing education as a condition for maintaining teacher certification.

In Connecticut, a summer institute program established by the state department of education offers an array of special programs. Those who offer special institutes, following a careful selection and approval process, are compensated for their efforts. Participants earn continuing education credit and are paid a stipend for attending. Library media specialists may design and offer programs or may become participants in a wide range of offerings.

DESIGN AND PRODUCTION OF MEDIA

Design and production is a rapidly expanding element of the comprehensive school LMC. It provides the resources and services needed to create new media or to modify existing forms to be used in teaching and learning. Although resources, services, and facilities will vary, depending on the pattern of services offered at the district or regional levels, at least a minimal level of capability is needed in each school—capability to be determined through the planning process.

Design is based on a knowledge of research, subject matter, media, and a systems approach to designing instructional systems. The function of the design process is to translate this knowledge and a knowledge of learners into specifications for instructional system components—"all of the resources which can be designed, utilized, and combined in a systematic manner with the intent of bringing about learning."[10] In the design phase, one analyzes an instructional situation to determine what idea or message must be conveyed, what medium would best convey the message, what device if any is required for the utilization of the medium, what technique or method is best suited to get the message to the learner, and in what setting or physical environment this is best achieved. In order to accomplish the objectives established, it may be necessary to combine several media, use one new medium, or modify an existing form in varied ways. The design generally ends with the writing of specifications for the component required to accomplish the task.

The design function usually involves the library media specialist working with the person who initiated the request. The results of the consultation may be the creation of a new medium or the modification of an existing form. A teacher usually initiates a request and states the instructional problem and objectives. The teacher may or may not check back to discuss the work in progress, but will receive the product when it is completed.

Production follows design. The production worker, technician, or aide takes the effort of the design phase and translates it into one or several different instructional system components as required. In production, there may be several levels of service. A minimal production capability level will fulfill the most common teacher and student needs: graphics, slides, audiotapes, and videotapes. More sophisticated levels would provide for such services as interactive video and microcomputer software production.

The production of disposable media is an essential school service usually reserved for teachers. This is a typing, word processing, and duplicating service. Although typically associated with a separate service unit in the school and with district level-printing services, if resources are available, the LMC can accommodate this activity.

Teachers

Teachers should be made aware of the design and production capabilities of the school and district through school or district in-service curriculum development projects, as well as other vehicles for communication. In-service may be oriented to a range of LMC and district services as well as "how-to" short courses.

Where space and resources permit, teachers should have the option of either designing and producing their own media or having the service provided. In the latter case, the availability of LMC staff becomes a significant factor.

Students

Under favorable conditions, students have access to media production facilities and resources as needed to complete projects related to their studies or personal needs. LMC personnel provide the same level of assistance available to teachers.

Design and production would be an appropriate component of the LMC instructional program, as would courses in media. Media courses offered by other departments of a school receive support services as needed from the LMC.

CURRICULUM DEVELOPMENT AND IMPROVEMENT

The curriculum of the nation's schools has been subjected to extensive criticism—from content to quality. Schools and districts have responded positively to the growing opportunity to improve existing programs and to create new programs.

The library media specialist, working with administrators and teachers, should be involved in the process in at least four areas: content, methodology, activities for students, and providing media to meet the needs of students and teachers. Beginning with the research phase of curriculum development, activities intensify on a day-to-day basis in the implementation phase.

The professional in library media has expertise not ordinarily found in other curriculum workers. As an information specialist, the research ability, bibliographic knowledge, and skill in manual and online information searching set the LMC professional apart. As a subject specialist, the professional can contribute in selected content areas. This background is supplemented by a knowledge of current literature in the field of education. It is also reasonable to assume that the library media specialist will have a broad view of existing programs as a result of day-to-day contacts with teachers and students.

Involvement in curriculum development and improvement, in large measure, provides the information needed for planning and the determination of needs: media, facilities, personnel, budget. Involvement also enables the library media specialist to exert influence in methods, activities, and media utilization.

Curriculum Development

The curriculum is all of the learning activities planned, organized, and carried out under the auspices of the school. It develops out of the philosophy of a particular social group for the educational experiences of its young. The overall process typically requires at least five steps:

1. Analyzing—diagnosis of need, review of existing curriculum, and study of current literature.

2. Planning—formulation of objectives and selection of content and experiences.

3. Programming—development of curriculum including organization of content and learning experiences.

4. Implementing—pilot test of curriculum, revision if necessary, and final implementation.

5. Evaluating—evaluation before piloting, after piloting, and periodic monitoring and evaluation after implementation.[11]

Selecting subject matter—what is known about the subject—is a problem, in part because of the information explosion. Following are some criteria for the selection of content:

1. To what extent is the specific subject matter required in a field of knowledge? What prerequisites are needed to study in this field?

2. To what extent has the subject matter been consistently selected as representative of the field?

3. To what extent can the subject matter be used in a practical way to achieve success?

4. To what extent will the subject matter be of interest to learners?

5. To what extent does the subject matter contribute to meeting the goals of society for its young?

The criteria may be applied to subject matter selection in one or more of the following ways: the best judgment of the individual curriculum worker, consensus of a group of experts, direct experimentation in the field, or an analysis of what people in a given field of work do, in order to determine the subject matter needed to perpetuate or improve activities in the field. Curriculum planners usually focus on objectives and content first; only later do they come to terms with media. The thinking is that they should not be tied to what is currently available in the way of resources. This line of thinking is reasonable, since the design and production capabilities of school districts and the ability of the commercial market to respond to educational needs can enable this process to succeed.

If the library media specialist has a background in the subject field, he or she should be a full participant in subject matter selection. Beyond content selection the library media specialist should be a principal contributor in three related areas: media, instructional methodology, and the programming of student activities.

Media, the printed and audiovisual resources to be employed in the teaching-learning process, fall readily into a principal area of expertise of the library media specialist. The task is to coordinate the search of the curriculum team for media that will satisfy subject matter requirements. Subject matter needs and criteria for selection are viewed in the light of knowledge about students who will be the recipients of and participants in the program. A review of media selection aids, an analysis of media currently available in the school, assistance in the direct preview and evaluation of media, an explanation of the LMC's financial potential to provide media, and guidance in designing and producing media are basic contributions to be made.

The library media specialist must be able to guide curriculum workers toward the exploration of methodologies that focus on the three *I*s: individualization, independent study, and inquiry. Whether the school provides homogeneous or heterogeneous grouping of students, whether there are formal groups or a "nongraded" program, whether teaching is by teams or by individual teachers, the three *I*s should be a primary thrust.

Individualized instruction refers to a program that is tailored to the individual, with recognition of his or her differences, interests, needs and mode of thinking and learning. This goal corresponds to a principal aim of education, which is to develop the unique personality of the individual within the framework of our democratic society.

Independent study is considered one of the most important elements in individualized instruction. In independent study, the student works in a free atmosphere on a project of his or her own choosing or on a project selected cooperatively with a teacher. Through this process, the student can explore and expand special interests, refine work-study habits and skills, and become a more self-directed learner. Teacher guidance, adequate facilities, and extensive media collections are essential factors in this process.

The third ingredient in the three *I*s approach is *inquiry*, which means seeking information or knowledge by questioning. Though associated primarily with the study of science and the scientific method in schools, inquiry should be considered an integral part of any program. There is no one specific way to carry on a program of inquiry; it may be approached either deductively or inductively. By whatever means inquiry is developed, procedures require a focusing of student attention on a meaningful problem, student freedom to move around gathering information, and available quantities of media. The three *I*s are interrelated aspects of an educational program designed for an LMC approach. The library media specialist can offer teachers the following options: media as an alternative to lectures and texts; LMC and other system facilities as an alternative to a strict classroom orientation; cooperative teaching endeavors using LMC personnel; and methods of structuring individual, small group, and whole class activities.

Programming student learning activities is a part of a total teaching strategy. It must be based on a knowledge of individual differences. In the implementation phase of the curriculum, teachers will recognize the implications of students' learning styles, which may be categorized as visual (reading), aural (listening), or physical (doing things). Any one person may use more than one style.

Curriculum Implementation

When the library media specialist has been involved in curriculum planning and works effectively in that capacity, implementation activities fall into place in the ongoing instructional program. Schools that develop instructional methodologies geared to the extensive use of media rather than a traditional textbook orientation rely heavily on the LMC. The library media specialist should meet with individual teachers or groups on a continuing basis to coordinate LMC services with instructional needs. The purposes of these meetings are to guarantee the availability of media when and where needed; select those media forms best suited to the capabilities of students; guarantee the availability of space and LMC personnel when and where needed; structure tentative activities for individual students, small groups, and entire classes which will provide for optimum use of and benefit from the LMC system; assess teacher needs for background information and teaching tools; and arrange for teacher and student review of utilization skills and techniques. Meetings of this type are best scheduled to coincide with the initiation of units of study or with areas of transition in a nongraded approach.

The schedule of the library media specialist should be flexible enough to permit attendance at meetings and to meet with teachers on an individual basis in the LMC or other locations. Continuity in meeting with individual teachers about their instructional needs and individual student requirements is vital to the success of the school. Capturing the individual teacher's attention and interest guarantees success in student use of the LMC. Interaction with teachers rates high on the list of priorities for LMC staff time.

Participation in activities outside the confines of the LMC is a natural extension of the LMC. Whether it is merely to view student projects elsewhere in the building, to attend department meetings, to observe effective instruction in the classroom, or to teach cooperatively with subject specialists on a long- or short-term basis, freedom to move about is essential. Other LMC staff should also be involved outside the LMC. A technician may be involved in taping an assembly program, setting up and operating equipment for special projects, and so on. Availability of LMC personnel for service throughout the building assures teachers that the LMC system can meet their needs and fosters interaction of teaching personnel with the LMC.

The design and production of media are integral to the implementation phase, though much of this work can be accomplished during curriculum development. Library media specialists should be available to help teachers and students produce media for individual and group use in teaching and learning. Much of the work during this phase consists of modifying existing media forms.

A basic task for the library media specialist is to continually evaluate the LMC system in order to determine whether it is meeting the needs of the instructional program. Standards and objectives guide this process.

SUMMARY

- Achievements represent the primary goals and intended output of the LMC system. Principal areas of focus are guidance and consulting services, instruction and in-service, design and production of media, and curriculum development and improvement.

- Guidance and consulting services provide a dual focus: guidance directed to students and consulting services to teachers. This is the most significant area of achievement.

- Instruction and in-service provide a formal program of instruction for students and in-service training for teachers.

- Design and production provide for the creation of new or modified media forms by students and teachers.

- Curriculum development and improvement focus on the library media specialist's role in curriculum activities.

ACTIVITIES

1. Determine how planning should be carried out to integrate intended LMC achievements into the school's program.

2. For a selected school, analyze the intended achievements. What priorities have been set? To what extent are specific goals achieved?

3. For a selected school, analyze the curriculum (one area such as social studies) to determine how LMC achievements relate.

4. Investigate one or more of the following topics: (1) district LMCs; (2) regional education centers; (3) individualization, independent study, inquiry; or (4) computer applications to LMC and school instructional programs.

NOTES

[1]Ralph Ellsworth, *The School Library* (New York: Center for Applied Research in Education, 1965), v.

[2]Department of Education, *Standards of Learning Objectives: Library/Information Use* (Richmond, Va.: Department of Education, 1986), 1. Reprinted by permission.

[3]Department of Public Instruction, *Media Program Recommendations: Guidelines for School Media Programs* (Raleigh, N.C.: Department of Public Instruction, 1986), I-4.

[4]Division of Education and State Library, *Information Skills for South Dakota Students* (Pierre, S.D.: South Dakota State Library, 1986), 1. Reprinted with permission.

[5]State Department of Education, *Instruction in Library Media Skills* (Hartford, Conn.: State Department of Education, 1984).

[6]National Assessment of Educational Progress, *A Framework for Assessing Computer Competence: Defining Objectives* (Princeton, N.J.: Educational Testing Service, 1986), 7.

[7]Ibid.

[8]State Department of Education, A *Guide to Computers in Education: Instruction* (Hartford, Conn.: State Department of Education, 1985), 4-5.

[9]Daniel Oran and Jay Shafritz, *The MBA's Dictionary* (Reston, Va.: Reston Publishing, 1983), 160.

[10]Kenneth Silber, "What Field Are We In, Anyhow?" *Audiovisual Instruction* 15 (May 1970): 22.

[11]State Department of Education, *A Guide to Curriculum Development: Purposes, Practices, and Procedures* (Hartford, Conn.: State Department of Education, 1981), 14.

BIBLIOGRAPHY

Callison, Daniel. "School Library Media Programs and Free Inquiry Learning." *School Library Journal* 32 (February 1986): 20-24.

Chisholm, Margaret. "The Librarian as Educator." *Catholic Library World* 57 (November/December 1985): 117-21.

Department of Education. *Standards of Learning Objectives: Library/Information Use*. Richmond, Va.: Department of Education, 1986.

Department of Public Instruction. *Media Program Recommendations: Guidelines for School Media Programs*. Raleigh, N.C.: Department of Public Instruction, 1986.

Division of Education and State Library. *Information Skills for South Dakota Students*. Pierre, S.D.: Division of Education and State Library, 1986.

Eisenberg, Michael. "Curriculum Mapping and Implementation of an Elementary School Library Media Skills Curriculum." *School Library Media Quarterly* 12 (Fall 1984): 411-18.

————. "Managing the Library and Information Skills Program: Developing Support Systems for Planning and Implementation." *School Library Media Activities Monthly* (March 1986): 27-33.

Ellsworth, Ralph. *The School Library*. New York: Center for Applied Research in Education, 1965.

Loertscher, David. "The Second Revolution: A Taxonomy for the 1980's." *Wilson Library Bulletin* 56 (February 1982): 417-21.

National Assessment of Educational Progress. *A Framework for Assessing Computer Competence: Defining Objectives*. Princeton, N.J.: Educational Testing Service, 1986.

Oran, Daniel, and Jay Shafritz. *The MBA's Dictionary*. Reston, Va.: Reston Publishing, 1983.

Pruitt, Ellen, and Karen Dowling. "Searching for Current Information Online ... How High School Library Media Centers in Montgomery County, Maryland, Are Solving an Informational Problem by Using DIALOG." *Online* 9 (March 1985): 47-60.

Schon, Isabel. "The Effects of a Special School Library Program on Elementary Students' Library Use and Attitudes." *School Library Media Quarterly* 12 (Spring 1984): 227-31.

_____. "A Special Motivational Intervention Program and Junior High School Students' Library Use and Attitudes." *Journal of Experimental Education* 53 (Winter 1985): 97-101.

Silber, Kenneth. "What Field Are We In, Anyhow?" *Audiovisual Instruction* 15 (May 1970): 21-24.

State Department of Education. *A Guide to Computers in Education: Instruction*. Hartford, Conn.: State Department of Education, 1985.

_____. *A Guide to Curriculum Development: Purposes, Practices, and Procedures*. Hartford, Conn.: State Department of Education, 1981.

_____. *Instruction in Library Media Skills*. Hartford, Conn.: State Department of Education, 1984.

5

PERSONNEL

OBJECTIVES

Identify and describe the types of personnel needed for effective service in the school LMC.

Write job descriptions for various positions in a selected school LMC.

Organize personnel for a selected school LMC.

Library media personnel are the principal assets of the LMC. They are responsible for providing the range of resources and services needed by teachers and students. In years past the school librarian's role encompassed the functions of reading specialist, curriculum generalist, subject specialist, guidance counselor, and administrator. Adding to this list the qualifications of the audiovisual specialist (curriculum generalist, subject specialist, instructional technology expert, and teacher) brought about a new professional position — library media specialist. To this background has been added in recent years the capabilities of an information scientist.

Although it has been possible to prepare an individual for this role, it usually is not possible for one person to perform all of the tasks envisioned for the LMC. Therefore, considerable effort is needed to define the LMC system and to design professional and support positions needed to have a positive impact on the educational program of the school.

SCHOOL-LEVEL CONSIDERATIONS

School Administrators

Leadership of the principal of the school and district level administrators determines the level of effectiveness of the school and LMC. As noted in chapter 2, however, only 64 percent of library media specialists in nationally recognized secondary schools believed that the school principal was an advocate for the LMC.

One expects the school administrator to know what the philosophical and educational implications of the LMC are for the school. Unfortunately, some administrators do not have an understanding of the roles of personnel to be employed, the ramifications of each position, the relationship between library media positions, and the potential relationship of library media staff to the instructional program and to students and teachers. There are a number of reasons for this lack of understanding.

Today's school administrator, much like those of the past, is a product of the classroom, and in that capacity may have had only a limited opportunity to rely on an LMC for resources and services. The graduate program which prepared the administrator for this new role probably gave only passing consideration, if any, to the LMC in the school. The administrator may have been involved in few LMC programs as a child and young adult. Also, the administrator may not have had an opportunity to really see anything of demonstrated value in LMCs.

Many educators have been highly supportive of LMC programs. However, there have also been some detractors. J. L. Trump, educational innovator and LMC critic, probably set the stage in the 1960s for much of the thinking of school administrators. In his view,

> Some independent study occurs in the library. Two kinds of students use the library. There are those with advanced or unusual projects who find specialized resources located there. For example, less frequently used and specially valuable printed, audio, and visual references are kept there for safeguarding. Other students come to the library because it is a quiet place. They frequently bring most of their study materials with them. Strict silence is the rule.[1]

Although substantial efforts to effectively integrate the LMC into the educational program were launched in the 1960s and 1970s through demonstration programs at national and state levels and special awards for school administrators who contributed significantly to the development of school LMCs, much remains to be done. Efforts are being made to provide assistance to principals through the publication of guides. For example, the Department of Education of South Carolina produced an administrator's guide to the LMC. The role of the principal was defined as follows:

THE ROLE OF THE PRINCIPAL

> The success of the media program depends largely on the principal's understanding and support. Improved programs will result when the principal supports the philosophy of a unified media center and encourages a spirit of cooperation between the media specialists and the faculty in promoting maximum use of the facility.

THE PRINCIPAL...

provides leadership in the development of an exemplary media center in the school.

provides a suitable budget and counsels with the media specialist for a wise expenditure of funds.

allows time for the media specialist *to plan* media activities with the teachers, and includes the media specialist on curriculum study committees.

appoints a faculty library committee to assist the media specialist in planning and evaluating the media program, and interprets the media center to the community in a positive way.[2]

Service Approaches

Two approaches embody opposing views of the LMC. One approach provided by national guidelines proposes a staffing pattern predicated on a high degree of interaction between library media specialists, students, and teachers in the educational process. This implies interaction in curriculum development, instruction and in-service, the design and production of media, and guidance and consulting services to students and teachers. This is the *leading service* approach, and commands the greatest interest and attention. The second approach is present in situations in which LMC staffing is inadequate, resulting in a severely handicapped program offering minimal services, not in any way compatible with the needs of users or the philosophy of the library media field.

One cannot project an optimum LMC program for a school of 1,000 students where staff will be limited to a single library media specialist and a part-time clerk. Unfortunately, this situation has been prevalent in many schools and has resulted in ineffective services to students and teachers. Another result has been frustration and eventual "burn-out" for the LMC professional. Planning is needed to relate personnel and other assets to the service approach for a school LMC. The service approach should be articulated and embedded in the comprehensive plan for the LMC and district.

PERSONNEL CONSIDERATIONS

Accountability for performance is possible only if there is a clear delineation of the duties of each position in the school LMC. When we know what a person is supposed to do, how it is to be done, and how well it should be done, an appraisal of performance can be made.

In many professions, there is reasonable doubt as to what tasks should be assigned to personnel of varying backgrounds and abilities. In the past, school libraries had only two categories of personnel: the professional and the clerical. The professional librarian had at least a four-year college education and the clerk had at least a high school diploma. There was usually a minimum of position exchange on the job. Although the professional frequently became involved in so-called clerical or mechanical functions, only infrequently did the clerical assistant perform professional tasks. The major reason for this condition was the vast amount of clerical and mechanical work involved in operating a library. The school audiovisual specialist, at one time, primarily performed tasks related to equipment distribution and maintenance.

Job Descriptions

Job descriptions are a means of describing job functions once they have been defined and may also serve a valuable purpose as the basis for recruitment and the employment of new personnel. Descriptions may be developed as a result of an analysis of tasks performed by an employee in carrying out a specific job. In the case of certified personnel, descriptions may have most of the elements prescribed by the certifying agency. Where properly associated with the planning and organizing, functions of management, jobs and job descriptions result from the analysis of organizational goals and objectives, decisions about the organizational structure needed to achieve goals and objectives, and the sorting out of key activities of personnel within the organization. Planning takes into account such concerns as certification, educational levels, and other factors which pertain to effective decision making.

Although the form of job descriptions will vary from district to district, and one should anticipate the need to conform to district policy where such a policy exists, the description will usually require at least the following: job title, distinguishing characteristics of the job, and a summary of major duties. The description may also indicate reporting lines and may include a statement of qualifications for the position. The format of the description may call for, as an example, the numbering of major duties, or it may be structured into a narrative form.

It is expected that job descriptions for district directors, supervisory personnel, and heads of school LMCs will contain specific, key activities for these positions. Each job description should also cite key activities which are held in common by this group. Each description should contain a statement which:

1. Focuses on the need to relate to the total system, to coordination with other units.

2. Relates to the need for the manager to do something new and creative on the job.

3. Deals with the need to work effectively with coworkers.

4. Provides for the assumption of responsibility for special projects as assigned.

5. Deals with the need to assume responsibility for professional growth and development.

Position Classification

The job description, in addition to defining the parameters of the job, also indicates its relative position in a larger scheme of position classification for the district. In the position classification scheme, one can visually scan the hierarchy of positions, from the job requiring minimal skills and educational background to the most complex job requiring the highest credentials. It is also possible to see other jobs rated in the same fashion according to level of responsibility, experience, and education. The position classification scheme is used for general personnel purposes, including the development of salary schedules.

The generalized position classification scheme in figure 5.1 illustrates the vertical and horizontal dimensions of a system. Once it has been agreed that the description fits the job, the position is ranked vertically by level of responsibility and difficulty, and horizontally with other types of jobs in the district that have similar general characteristics. Since the library media specialist is the first professional position in the LMC, the position is ranked relatively higher than clerical and technician levels in the vertical dimension. The library media specialist can be equated with other instructional personnel whose responsibility and educational attainment are essentially the same and whose positions are governed by state certification requirements, so these positions fall into the same classification and appear on the same horizontal level. Teachers of English, social studies, and science, for example, fall into this class. Noncertified personnel, having equal responsibility and educational attainment, may also appear in this class.

Where a multiple staffing pattern is employed in the LMC, and the head of the LMC is delegated the authority to supervise personnel, this position is usually classed with those of other department heads. Some school systems pay an additional stipend for a position at this level of responsibility based on the number of individuals in the department. Certification for department head status is not ordinarily a state requirement, though the school district may ask for higher qualifications for these positions, including more education and more years of experience.

Clerks or aides are usually classed with others in the clerical ranks who have similar qualifications. Employment in these categories is dependent upon education, experience, and various examinations. Some school districts class these positions under Civil Service.

	Position	**Corresponding Positions**
Class 7	District Director	District Math Coordinator
Class 4	Head of LMC	Department Heads Science Social Studies
Class 3	Library Media Specialists	Teachers
Class 2	Technicians	Technicians, Paraprofessionals
Class 1	Aides, Clerks	School Office Clerks

Fig. 5.1. Generalized position classification scheme.

LMC technicians are ranked with technicians at the district level and with various other jobs requiring similar education, experience, and responsibility. It is within the realm of possibility that the technician would be ranked horizontally with skilled, maintenance craftsmen (unless, that is, these craftsmen have a strong bargaining agent, in which case their salary rank may be superior to that of the library media specialist and teacher).

Position classification groups jobs in broad classes based on responsibility, experience, and educational qualifications. Job descriptions discriminate between the jobs performed by personnel in each class. There may be several job descriptions for library media specialists, technicians, and aides who are expected to perform different functions.

Selection of Personnel

The selection of new personnel should be guided by the needs of the school LMC and district as articulated in the planning process. In most school districts, selection would be part of the total personnel planning process and would involve, at least, the district director in activities associated with securing qualified library media personnel for the district. Where personnel are to be selected to work in school LMCs, the head of the LMC and school principal should have significant input into the selection process. For example, on-site interviews are particularly useful and provide the opportunity for school personnel to judge whether a candidate is suited to the work situation and vice versa.

The unified approach to library media services in the school LMC and district suggests that whenever possible, at every level—aide, technician, library media specialist—new personnel should be broadly prepared in three areas: library science, information science, and instructional technology.

Certification as a "media specialist" or "media generalist" does not necessarily provide that guarantee. For professional staff, one should also expect a specialty or concentration in one area of media as well as subject matter competence in at least one field such as science or social science. This is particularly important where staff is limited and flexibility is needed to respond to the needs of users. A high degree of specialization in one medium, to the exclusion of others, may be a detriment where balance is needed to offer a comprehensive program.

The replacement of personnel should be considered in the context of the needs of the LMC. Prior to the announcement of the need to fill a particular position, a review and decision are needed relative to the possibility of restructuring the organization, the possibility of not filling the position at all, the possibility of seeking a person whose qualifications are suited to new or expanded service requirements, and the possibility of employing someone at a different level in the personnel classification scheme of the district. When an appropriate decision has been made, the selection process may be initiated.

Procedures for selecting and employing personnel will vary from district to district. One would expect the district personnel office to be in contact with college and university placement offices as well as specialized schools and selected placement agencies. Other sources for personnel would be a state employment office, or in some cases, a state department of education. Advertising positions in newspapers and professional journals is a common practice. Prospective candidates would file a formal application, supply college placement papers if appropriate, and file transcripts and letters of recommendation. State certification would be one requirement for most professional positions. For some positions, particularly clerical, examinations are usually required. Personal interviews of prospective employees should be conducted by one or more members of the district staff.

STAFFING THE LMC

The 1975 AASL/AECT guidelines have provided a generalized view of the number and types of people recommended to operate a comprehensive LMC program. The numbers and types of staff people cited in these guidelines are based essentially on the consensus of the two national groups involved in formulating standards. The basic relationships among staff size, media collections, size of facility, and financing are again predicated primarily on consensus. According to the guidelines, personnel needed to staff a modern, unified LMC program include:

> *Head of School Media Program:* A media specialist with managerial competencies who is designated as responsible for the media program at the individual school level. Qualifications vary with such factors as the size of the school, size of media staff, and type of program.

Media Professional: Any media person, certified or not, who qualifies by training and position to make professional judgments and to delineate and maintain media programs or program components. Media professionals may include media specialists, television or film producers, instructional developers, radio station managers, and technical processing (cataloging) specialists, whose duties and responsibilities are professional in nature.

Media Specialist: A person with appropriate certification and broad professional preparation, both in education and media, with competencies to carry out a media program. The media specialist is the basic media professional in the school program.

Media Technician: A member of the media staff with technical skills in such specialized areas as graphics, production and display, information and materials processing, photographic production, operation and maintenance of audiovisual equipment, operation and maintenance of television equipment, and installation of systems components.

Media Aide: A member of the media staff who performs clerical and secretarial tasks and assists as needed in the acquisition, maintenance, inventory, production, distribution, and utilization of materials and equipment.

Director of District Media Program: A media professional with appropriate certification and advanced managerial, administrative, and supervisory competencies who qualifies for an administrative or supervisory position.[3]

Assuming adequate financial support to develop an optimum program in the school, the specific staffing pattern would be influenced by both the national guidelines and local requirements. For example, the 1975 AASL/AECT guidelines recommended that a school with an enrollment of 1,000 students have a designated program head, two to three professionals, three to five technicians, and three to five aides.

It is probably correct to assume that the ratios proposed in the guidelines for LMC personnel are suitable for a specific school LMC. This LMC would also have other assets, in the proportions recommended in the guidelines. All would be the result of planning for the LMC and school. The recommendations of three states are provided in figures 5.2-5.4 for comparison.

The following minimum staffing pattern is recommended for schools. Please note that each phase should occur at three-year intervals.

Building Level	Phase 1	Phase 2	Phase 3
100 or Fewer			
Specialist	½	1	1
Associate	½	½	1
Support	½	½	½
201-500			
Specialist	1	1	1
Associate	½	1	1
Support	½	½	1
501-1000			
Specialist	1	1	1
Associate	1	1½	1½
Support	1	1	1½
Over 1000			
Specialist	1	1	2
Associate	2	2	2
Support	1	2	2

Fig. 5.2. Nevada—Staffing pattern. From *Media Standards for Nevada Schools* (Carson City, Nev.: Department of Education, 1987), 3. Reprinted with permission of the Nevada Department of Education.

Category	Phase I	Phase II	Phase III
Professional Staff **K-8**	Minimum Qualifications: Teacher's Certificate plus 18 semester hours of library and media coursework.	Teacher's Certificate plus 18 semester hours of library and media coursework.	Teacher's Certificate plus 32 semester hours of library and media coursework.
	Size of Staff: 1 full-time for each 500 students.	1 full-time for each 500 students.	1 full-time for each 250 or major fraction thereof.
9-12	Minimum Qualifications: Teacher's certificate plus 18 semester hours of library and media coursework.	Teacher's certificate plus 18 semester hours of library and media coursework.	Teacher's certificate plus 32 semester hours of library and media coursework.
	Size of Staff: 1 full-time for each 600 students.	1 full-time for each 600 students.	1 full-time for each 250 or major fraction thereof.
	Provision should be made for balance in staff competencies for library media and computer services. A graduate degree in library media is highly desirable.		
Support Staff **K-12**	1 half-time clerical aide for each library media professional.	1 full-time aide (clerical and/ or technical) for each library media professional.	1 full-time clerical aide and 1 full-time technical aide for each library media professional.

Fig. 5.3. Illinois—*Recommended Standards for Educational Library Media Programs* (Springfield, Ill.: State Board of Education, 1986), 6. Reprinted by permission.

Standard	Educational Resource	Considerations
3301-35-03(B)(2)(b)	Each library shall be staffed by a certificated librarian or by an aide or volunteer supervised by a certificated librarian ...	A staffing ratio of librarians to buildings or students is not specified. One certificated librarian for each district is required. The additional assignment of certificated staff and aides to buildings is at local discretion provided services are available for at least the length of the minimum school day. Staffing at the building and district levels should be determined following the definition of the level of services necessary to meet expectations.

Standard	Educational Resource	Considerations
		Library aides and volunteers must be supervised by a librarian who holds appropriate certification. For example, a librarian supervising both elementary and secondary programs must have a K-12 certificate in educational media or library science.

Fig. 5.4. Ohio—Minimum standards. From *Quality Library Services K-12* (Columbus, Ohio: Department of Education, 1986), 15. Reprinted with permission of the Ohio State Board of Education.

Library Media Specialists

The Manpower Project, initiated by the American Association of School Librarians and funded by the Knapp Foundation, provided significant information for the 1960s and beyond.[4] The project was designed to determine the kinds of personnel needed to operate school library media centers. The goals of the project focused on recruitment, analysis, and education. Phase I of the project dealt with a task analysis conducted in 694 elementary and secondary schools judged to have quality LMCs. The *Behavioral Requirements Analysis Checklist*, a Manpower Project publication, provided a compilation of competency-based job functions and task statements for library media personnel.[5]

More recently, activities or competencies of library media specialists have been defined by state certification requirements, school districts, professional associations, and research. For example, the library media specialist must be appropriately certified by a state department of education. Within each state, certification is usually issued on completion of a program of education at a college or university approved by the state department of education.

Certification

In Connecticut, the certificate for the library media specialist position in the schools (K-12), called "media specialist," has both provisional and standard categories. Provisional certification requires completion of twenty-four graduate credits in media as part of a planned degree program at a master's or sixth-year level. In addition to this requirement, candidates must also have earned a minimum of eighteen credits in education and psychology as an undergraduate or graduate student, completed a field practicum of six credits, and received recommendation from a college or university approved by the state department of education. The standard certificate further requires completion of an additional six credit hours (total of thirty credit hours) in the degree program and three years of successful experience.

Competencies required for certification are:

1. Design, implement, and evaluate media programs. (Media programs are here defined as all the instructional and other services furnished to students and teachers by a media center and its staff.)

2. Evaluate, select, acquire, organize, produce, and retrieve media. (Media is here defined as printed and audiovisual forms of communications and their accompanying technology.)

3. Teach students, staff, and faculty to utilize media and its accompanying technology by applying valid instructional methods and techniques.

4. Assist students in the interpretation of print and nonprint materials.

5. Apply principles of administration and supervision for effective leadership and operation of the media center program.

6. Formulate the educational specifications and contribute to the design of school media facilities.[6]

Essentially the same conditions apply to certification for district-level positions. In order to obtain such certification in Connecticut (a general certificate for school administrators, called "intermediate administrator"), a candidate must enroll in an institution which offers a sixth-year level program in administration and supervision approved by the state department of education. For provisional certification, the candidate must earn fifteen credit hours in specific coursework dealing with administration and supervision, receive the recommendation of the institution, and hold a standard teaching certificate (including media specialist certification).

Reciprocal agreements between various states may enable an individual to obtain certification in another state. Otherwise, a review of credentials will be made to determine eligibility. Since the term *library media specialist* is used in a generic sense, one can expect that its definition will differ from state to state, as will educational requirements.

Research

The *New Directions* study (cited also in chapter 1), provided evidence of the competencies needed by school library media specialists (and other professionals in the library-information field).[7] The competencies—knowledge, skills, and attitudes—in specific areas were also categorized under entry-level, mid-level, and senior-level. Information from this study can be used by academic institutions preparing library media specialists and by schools, districts, professional associations, and others to create model job descriptions and other materials.

Using *New Directions* as a guide to the role of the library media specialist would require merging the following competency lists:

- Competencies generic across all work settings and all functions (apply to all professions).

- Competencies generic across all library work settings and library functions.

- Competencies generic across all functions in school libraries (LMC).

- Depending on the nature of the position in the LMC, specific competency lists, such as management and reference.

Entry-level competencies, generic across all functions within the school LMC setting, are:

Knowledge

Knowledge of alternative approaches to the organization of information.

Knowledge of alternative approaches to retrieval of information.

Knowledge of the users of the services and products, their characteristics and information habits.

Knowledge of the mission, goals, and objectives of the organization served.

Knowledge of the structure of the organization and the role of the library (or information center) within the organization.

Knowledge of the various projects and key personnel within the organization.

Knowledge of the policies and procedures relevant to the library (or information center).

Knowledge of the various resources available within the library (e.g., personnel, equipment, etc.).

Knowledge of the users' information needs and requirements.

Knowledge of the collection, and of related collections.

Skills

Establish rapport with users and colleagues.

Make decisions and recommendations based on available information.

Work independently and in groups.

Isolate and define problems and develop the necessary criteria and action for their solution.

Attitudes

Like people in general.

Like children.

Like to help people.

Be sensitive to others' needs.

Like to work with others/as a team.

Like to work on one's own.

Be supportive of coworkers.

Be determined/tenacious.

Be flexible/versatile.

Be objective.

Be open-minded.

Have patience.

Be resourceful.

Have a sense of ethics.

Be willing to take initiative.

Pay attention to detail.

Be service oriented.

Be willing to promote the library and its services.

Have a desire to grow professionally.

Have a desire to remain current in specific and general subject fields.

State Guides

The Mississippi guide to managing school LMCs is a competency-based handbook for certified library media specialists, administrators, and evaluators. In five chapters (titles representing intended achievements or goals), twenty-five competencies are cited. For each competency, a list of descriptive actions are cited. The five achievements and competencies are shown in figure 5.5.

I — The library specialist and the principal establish the library media program as an integral part of the total instructional program.

Competency 1 — The library media specialist works with the administration and teachers.

Competency 2 — The library media specialist works with the administration in the development of a budget.

Competency 3 — The library media specialist shall be involved in instructional planning with teachers.

Competency 4 — The library media specialist serves as a resource person in curriculum development and implementation.

Competency 5 — The library media specialist assists teachers in the production of materials.

II — The library media specialist provides guidance and assistance to students in the use of the library media center and its resources in order to meet instructional objectives and individual enrichment.

Competency 6 — The library media specialist provides sequential instruction to students.

Competency 7 — The library media specialist assists students in locating materials and answering reference questions.

Competency 8 — The library media specialist encourages reading, provides reading guidance, and maintains an awareness of students' reading habits and interests.

III — The library media specialist establishes an inviting atmosphere conducive to individual and group inquiry, research, study, and leisure activities.

Competency 9 — The library media specialist assumes responsibility for student behavior.

Competency 10 — The library media specialist plans the arrangement of the library media center's space and furniture.

Competency 11 — The library media specialist plans, prepares, and arranges bulletin boards, displays, and exhibits.

IV — The library media specialist organizes a media program that assures optimum use of resources and facilities by both students and teachers.

Competency 12 — The library media specialist provides the needed equipment and media materials for teachers to accomplish instructional objectives.

Competency 13 — The library media specialist establishes and maintains a balanced, comprehensive collection of media (print and nonprint) and equipment.

Competency 14 — The library media specialist assumes the responsibility for classifying, cataloging, and organizing materials for easy access.

(Fig. 5.5 continues on page 120.)

Fig. 5.5. — *Continued*

Competency 15 — The library media specialist provides control of all materials and equipment by conducting a yearly inventory of all media and equipment and discarding inappropriate and obsolete items.

Competency 16 — The library media specialist maintains equipment and assumes responsibility for its repair.

Competency 17 — The library media specialist establishes circulation procedures for ease of accessibility by students and teachers.

Competency 18 — The library media specialist maintains accurate records and statistics on utilization of materials, services, and facilities.

Competency 19 — The library media specialist schedules and encourages the use of the library media center and its resources to provide for optimum use.

V — The library media specialist exercises leadership in the development of the library media program.

Competency 20 — The library media specialist exhibits effective public relations.

Competency 21 — The library media specialist seeks opportunities for professional growth.

Competency 22 — The library media specialist communicates regularly with the principal and/or coordinator.

Competency 23 — The library media specialist develops and maintains an effective working relationship with school staff.

Competency 24 — The library media specialist distributes written communication to keep teachers informed of services and materials.

Competency 25 — The library media specialist conducts inservice activities for teachers on the utilization of media within the instructional program.

Fig. 5.5. Achievements and competencies for managing school LMCs. From *Mississippi School Library Media Programs: A Guide for Management* (Jackson, Miss.: State Department of Education, 1985). Reprinted by permission.

The job description for media coordinator in North Carolina, includes six major functions to be performed by the library media specialist (see figure 5.6).

REPORTS TO: Principal

SUPERVISES: Coordinates and directs the activities of library/media aide(s), student assistants, and/or volunteers.

PURPOSE: To provide the leadership and resources for implementation of a school library/media program that serves as an integral part of the instructional process.

DUTIES AND RESPONSIBILITIES:

1. MAJOR FUNCTION: *Manages Instruction*

   Adhering to the *Teacher Performance Appraisal Instrument* criteria, the media coordinator instructs students and faculty in using and/or producing media to integrate into the curriculum and facilitate the teaching/learning process.

2. MAJOR FUNCTION: *Manages Public Relations*

   The media coordinator initiates interaction with students, staff, administration, and the general public for purposes of integrating, promoting, and expanding the media program.

3. MAJOR FUNCTION: *Plans for the Media Program*

   The media coordinator designs and implements short- and long-range plans which allow a balance among integrated skills instruction, literature appreciation, planning with teachers, and collection management and development.

4. MAJOR FUNCTION: *Manages Resources*

   The media coordinator establishes and carries out procedures for effective and efficient selection, acquisition, cataloging, processing, accessing, and maintaining materials and equipment.

(Fig. 5.6 continues on page 122.)

Fig. 5.6.—*Continued*

5. MAJOR FUNCTION: *Manages the Facility*

The media coordinator organizes the facility and resources in such a way that they reflect the philosophy and goals of the school and its media program.

6. MAJOR FUNCTION: *Carries Out Professional Responsibilities*

The media coordinator provides opportunities for personal and professional growth for him/herself as well as for the school's staff and students. S/he also carries out assigned non-instructional duties; adheres to established laws, policies, rules and regulations; and submits accurate reports promptly.

June, 1987

Fig. 5.6. Job description, media coordinator. From *Media Program Recommendations: Guidelines for School Media Programs* (Raleigh, N.C.: Department of Public Instruction, 1986), II-4. Reprinted with permission of the North Carolina Department of Public Instruction.

Profile—The Library Media Specialist

A study of personality and communications behaviors by Barbara Herrin provided a profile of successful school library media specialists. Although it is difficult to generalize from a group of five model female library media specialists to the entire population of successful professionals, the researchers concluded that the successful library media specialist is one who:

Has a positive self-concept.

May be shy/reserved but projects warmth.

Is bright, stable, enthusiastic, experimenting/exploring, trusting.

Is able to be self-sufficient.

Is confident of worth as an individual.

Enjoys people, work, variety/diversity.

Views change as a positive challenge.

Values communication.

Communicates effectively as an individual.

Is caring and especially attentive to others.

Is able and willing to clarify communication.

Is relatively self-disclosing.

Is uncomfortable with conflict.

Is confident of ability to deal with difficult situations in professional manner.

Is neither critical nor domineering.

Has no great need for achievement, power, or economic advantage.

Views self as leader in curriculum development.

Is willing to take the risks of being a leader.[8]

Support Staff

In an effective LMC, the library media specialist is assisted by a staff of technicians and aides. Students and volunteers may also be viewed as essential personnel since they frequently perform some of the tasks associated with the jobs of technicians and aides.

Technician

A job description for a library media technician is provided in figure 5.7.

Technicians have competencies in one or more fields, e.g., graphics production and display, information and materials processing, photographic production, operation and maintenance of instructional equipment, television production, and installation of system components. Large schools requiring multiple support personnel for their media centers may employ technicians, even though system-level staffing includes technicians, as well.

(Fig. 5.7 continues on page 124.)

Fig. 5.7.—*Continued*

Duties and Responsibilities:

A. MAJOR FUNCTION: *Equipment Management*

Provide instruction in the operation and use of instructional equipment.

Repair and maintain equipment.

Maintain cumulative records listing repairs and the condition of equipment.

Supervise the use of specialized equipment, such as television, videotaping equipment, photographic lab, computer lab, etc.

Assist in the installation of system components, such as computer networking, closed-circuit television systems, and film chains.

B. MAJOR FUNCTION: *Production*

Produce graphics and display materials, such as transparencies, posters, charts, graphs, displays, exhibits, and materials for television programs.

Involve and help students and teachers with production techniques when making their own tapes, slides, transparencies, charts, etc.

Perform photographic production work, such as still photography, motion photography for films, videotape recording of television broadcasts, televising local and in-school events, and developing black-and-white film.

C. MAJOR FUNCTION: *Miscellaneous Tasks*

Assist in the technical processing of information and materials by performing such tasks as bibliographic searching and processing of materials.

Fig. 5.7. Recommended job description for media technician. From *Media Program Recommendations: Guidelines for School Media Programs* (Raleigh, N.C.: Department of Public Instruction, 1986), II-7. Reprinted with permission of the North Carolina Department of Public Instruction.

Aide

A job description for a library media aide is given in figure 5.8.

Aides with secretarial and clerical competencies perform tasks related to the ordering, receipt, maintenance, inventory, production, circulation, and use of materials and equipment. The media aide should become familiar with library automation, since computers are used to simplify routine media center tasks. Media aides working directly with users must be able to respond effectively to their needs. They carry out all tasks under the direction of the professional members of the media staff, reporting, as appropriate, to designated professionals or technicians.

Duties and Responsibilities:

A. MAJOR FUNCTION: *Order and Process Materials*

Prepare order cards.

Type purchase orders.

Unpack new materials and check invoice.

Collate new materials.

Complete information on catalog cards and/or type new sets when necessary.

Prepare materials for circulation.

File shelflist and catalog cards above the rod.

B. MAJOR FUNCTION: *Circulate Materials*

Assist students at desk.

Keep circulation records as required.

Prepare and distribute overdue notices.

Shelve materials.

Deliver materials and equipment.

(Fig. 5.8 continues on page 126.)

Fig. 5.8.—*Continued*

C. MAJOR FUNCTION: *Maintain Collection*

Read shelves.

Help take inventory.

Repair materials and equipment.

Prepare books for bindery.

Prepare materials for information file.

Check in periodicals/prepare for circulation.

D. MAJOR FUNCTION: *Work with Students and Teachers*

Help students and teachers find materials.

Give assistance in production of materials/use of equipment.

Supervise student pass system.

Read stories to small groups (not to be confused with media coordinator's role in literature appreciation).

Supervise and assist with reinforcement activities.

E. MAJOR FUNCTION: *Miscellaneous Tasks*

Type bibliographies, reports, correspondence, worksheets, etc.

Check supply inventory and reorder when needed.

Process incoming mail (file catalogs, open letters, etc.).

Plan and/or help with bulletin boards and displays.

Help make games, activities, recordings, transparencies, learning centers, etc., for media coordinator.

Help with housekeeping chores (plant watering, dusting, etc.).

Fig. 5.8. Recommended job description for media aide. From *Media Program Recommendations: Guidelines for School Media Programs* (Raleigh, N.C.: Department of Public Instruction, 1986), II-6. Reprinted with permission of the North Carolina Department of Public Instruction.

Student Assistants and Volunteers

Student assistant and volunteer programs should be carefully planned and coordinated with the total LMC operation. Policies and procedures should be developed, and appropriate supervisory practices initiated to ensure a proper delineation of roles and to facilitate the flow of activities.

There can be a significant benefit to students who are members of a club that enables them to learn more about the operation of an LMC. They can make a contribution to the school by assisting in the selection of media. They can also benefit from participation in literary discussion activities, film-oriented programs, and media production activities. The special function volunteer—a creative storyteller, artist, or teacher—can significantly enhance an LMC program.

Reality Staffing

In the real world of LMCs, optimum staffing patterns rarely exist. There are some alternative staffing patterns which can be explored for such situations.

At the secondary school level, the assignment of one or more teachers to the LMC on a part-time basis could provide a significant educational benefit. This becomes an opportunity to involve them in media selection, reference, and reading guidance in areas related to their own subjects, thereby expanding the LMC service base for students and teachers.

Another alternative for both elementary and secondary schools would require the examination of the functions of specialists, such as reading consultants and resource teachers, who work with a few students at a time. These professionals may be prime candidates for service emanating from the LMC. If the LMC is viewed by school administrators as the principal service center for all media, the school can capitalize on both LMC resources and the skills of these professionals in a broader context.

The decision to use professional and other personnel in this manner should be followed by a carefully developed in-service program designed to integrate the particular skills of these employees into the total LMC program. If the plan is deemed another "cafeteria assignment," or a punitive action on the part of administration, the conflict engendered can do considerable harm to the LMC and to interpersonal relations in the school.

Deployment of Personnel

Where effective, comprehensive planning has been employed, the organizational structure and staff deployment for the LMC will have been resolved. Under any circumstance, planning is needed to effect optimum programming levels using the talents of available personnel.

If national guidelines are used as a gauge, a school of 1,000 students would have an LMC staff consisting of a designated head of the LMC, two or three professionals, three to five technicians, and three to five aides. All other elements cited in the guidelines — media, facilities, and program — would also be in balance. Given this ideal situation, information would still be needed to make effective decisions on the deployment of staff, including the availability of resources and services from a district center, the availability of resources and services from commercial vendors, the availability of resources and services from a district LMC system or systems external to the district, program elements and level of service desired for the school, the curriculum and instructional methods employed by teachers in the school, and perhaps most important, detailed information about the student body.

In a situation where staff is inherited, that is, not selected specifically for the intended program, effective deployment may be constrained by the lack of qualifications of existing staff. Training and development, of an intensive nature, may cure the problem. However, transfer to another situation may help, as would separation.

Career Ladder

The career ladder offers an individual the opportunity to enter the field at various levels and to advance to a higher level (in terms of duties, salary, and status) when adequately prepared and when a vacancy occurs. The employee also has the option of remaining at the initial employment level. In addition to vertical mobility, the opportunity also exists for movement horizontally within the system.

The option is always open for the individual who has gained skill and experience through education and continuous employment within the school district to leave and secure employment in business and industry. Employment may be in either library- or nonlibrary-related positions, at a level commensurate with the training, education, and experience attained in the initial employment structure.

Where a career ladder has been formalized in a school district, employee growth and development are an integral part of the scheme. Provision would be made for extended release time to attend in-service programs directed to the type of training and experience needed by the individual on the job. Formal course work leading to college degrees would be an integral part of the plan for upward mobility.

Education is necessary to make the career scheme work. Articulated programs of library media education, associate degrees through doctoral programs, exist to accommodate the needs of such personnel. On- and off-campus courses and specialized in-service offerings are also possibilities.

The technician level of the ladder may be equated with either associate or bachelor's degree work, depending on the nature of the job. The library media specialist and head of the LMC positions would typically require a master's level program as well as certification issued by a state department of education. For similar positions in a district library media center, the same pattern would be followed.

Figure 5.9 illustrates the ramifications of the career ladder showing vertical progression from the aide position to the head of the LMC. Options to move horizontally are also shown. If district supervisory positions and district director were included in the scheme, the educational requirement would be shifted upward to the sixth-year level and additional certification would be required to cover district-level responsibilities.

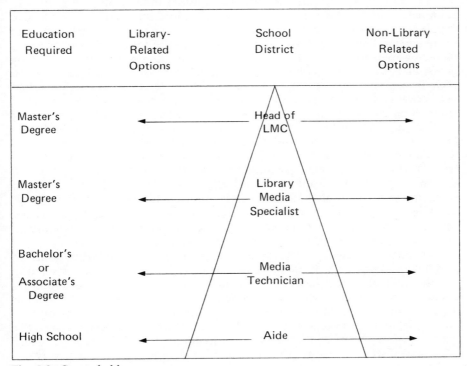

Fig. 5.9. Career ladder.

Supervision

The individual designated as head of the LMC must represent management to employees, interpret policies and procedures, and carry out the objectives of the organization. This person also represents employees to management, bringing out the views and needs of personnel.

The work of the head of the LMC involves both technical and inter-personal skills, since the role requires leading, directing, and controlling the work of others. The person who assumes a supervisory role should expect to shift emphasis from personal performance to the performance and productivity of employees. At the heart of the job is the need to motivate and train employees in order to achieve a high level of performance and to achieve the goals and objectives of the LMC. It is assumed that the head of the LMC has also been delegated the authority to require certain standards of work and conduct from employees and to appraise their performance.

In the process of working with and through individuals and groups to achieve the goals and objectives of the organization, the head of the LMC can expect to experience, either directly or indirectly, interpersonal conflicts and misunderstandings. Interpersonal problems can arise for a variety of reasons, including personality conflicts, prejudice and discrimination, conflicting goals, and ineffective communication. An effort to understand people from their own points of view can enable the supervisor to anticipate individual needs, wants, and problems, and to deal with them in a constructive manner. Counseling can be used as a vehicle for improving performance, resolving conflict, and establishing a work environment conducive to both high standards of performance and employee self-actualization.

Employee training and development are essential to maintain existing levels of performance. They are imperative if goals and objectives are oriented to new or expanded efforts in the delivery of resources and services. Also, since employees are evaluated on the basis of their effectiveness and efficiency, the obligation exists to provide every means available to prepare them to cope with job requirements. If the employee fails, or performs in a haphazard fashion, responsibility rests with the supervisor.

No single means exists to identify training and development needs of personnel. Indications of these needs come from many sources, including established goals and objectives, the literature of the field, and from employees themselves. Usually, entry-level clerical and technical staff receive training prior to assuming full responsibility for the job. This training may be on-the-job, or, if the number of trainees warrants the effort, in a group setting in the school LMC or at the district level. At other levels, including the head of the LMC and district director, personnel usually assume their new roles as described by someone in the organization, or as perceived by themselves. There is the assumption that since the person was effective in a previous position, he or she will be equally effective in the new assignment. Although this approach may be adequate in some cases, the need exists for personnel development at all levels of the organization.

The head of the LMC and other supervisory personnel have direct responsibility for the identification of training and development needs. A part of the identification process is the observation and critique of performance, taking steps to provide corrective action which may include the demonstration of appropriate techniques and skills. In some instances, needs can be satisfied in-house, or at a district level where personnel may have the expertise needed to conduct a formal in-service program. However, development may also be extended to matching the personal needs of individuals with specialized courses or programs external to the LMC and district.

Appraisal is the systematic evaluation of an employee's job performance and potential for development. Personnel appraisal, training, and development are interrelated functions of the head of the LMC and other supervisory personnel. If carried out properly, the appraising process can facilitate mutual understanding between the supervisor and the individual being appraised.

Appraisal methods used within school districts are many and varied. Any process used by supervisors, at any level, should be approved through appropriate administrative channels in the school district. A traditional and common appraisal method is the use of rating scales. In this familiar process, the supervisor uses a printed form that contains a number of employee qualities and characteristics to be evaluated, such as quality of work, quantity of work, job knowledge, initiative, dependability, and so on. The traits are then evaluated on a continuous (continuum) or discontinuous scale (boxes or numbers). Rating scales have been and continue to be used because they are easy to construct, easy to use, and easy to understand. They also have serious drawbacks, since they provide only the illusion of precision and, like most other instruments, are subject to such common problems as personal bias, leniency or strictness, and the tendency of supervisors to either "play it safe" by neither condemning nor praising, or to evaluate an entire set of characteristics in the same way as a particular trait (e.g., "accepts responsibility") for which an accurate assessment can be made. Where an MBO system is used with professional staff, appraisal may be oriented to the achievement of task-oriented, performance objectives. Consideration must also be given to such concerns as relating performance to the total system, working effectively with coworkers, and growth and development. (See appendix D for an appraisal instrument.)

Mutual understanding and appraisal on a continuing basis appear to be two elements necessary for appraisal to accomplish the fundamental goal of providing better quality service.

SUMMARY

- Library media personnel are the principal assets of the LMC. Library media specialists, technicians, and aides are needed to create optimum conditions for teaching and learning.

- Job descriptions differentiate roles to be performed by LMC personnel.

- The head of the LMC represents management of the school and district to LMC employees and the views of employees to management.

- The career ladder permits entrance into the field with minimal education and experience. Through a combination of education and in-service, the individual may move up the ladder to become a library media specialist.

- The principal must be an advocate of the LMC if it is to maximize its contribution to the success of the school.

ACTIVITIES

1. Compare job descriptions for school LMC personnel to those for personnel in academic and public libraries.

2. Compare staff deployment patterns in school LMCs to those in academic and public libraries.

3. For a selected school district, compare the functions of the district director and head of the school LMC.

4. Investigate one or more of the following topics: (1) certification of LMC personnel, (2) education of LMC personnel, or (3) supervision.

NOTES

[1]J. Lloyd Trump, "Independent Study Centers: Their Relation to the Central Library," *Bulletin of the National Association of Secondary School Principals* 50 (January 1966): 45-51.

[2]*Administrator's Guide to the Media Center* (Columbia, S.C.: Department of Education, 1984), 2.

[3]American Association of School Librarians and Association for Educational Communications and Technology, *Media Programs: District and School* (Chicago and Washington, D.C.: American Library Association and Association for Educational Communications and Technology, 1975), 109-10.

[4]American Association of School Librarians, *School Library Manpower Project Phase I—Final Report* (Chicago: American Library Association, 1970).

[5]American Association of School Librarians, *Behavioral Requirements Analysis Checklist* (Chicago: American Library Association, 1973).

[6]*Connecticut Teacher Certification Regulations* (Hartford, Conn.: State Department of Education, 1980).

[7]José-Marie Griffiths and Donald W. King, *New Directions in Library and Information Science Education* (White Plains, N.Y.: Knowledge Industry, 1986), 208-10.

[8]Barbara Herrin, and others, "Personality and Communications Behaviors of Model School Library Media Specialists," *Drexel Library Quarterly* 21 (Spring 1985): 86-87.

BIBLIOGRAPHY

Administrator's Guide to the Media Center. Columbia, S.C.: Department of Education, 1984.

American Association of School Librarians. *Behavioral Requirements Analysis Checklist*. Chicago: American Library Association, 1973.

_____. *School Library Manpower Project Phase I—Final Report*. Chicago: American Library Association, 1970.

American Association of School Librarians and Association for Educational Communications and Technology. *Media Programs: District and School*. Chicago and Washington, D.C.: American Library Association and Association for Educational Communication and Technology, 1975.

Barron, Daniel, ed. "The School Library Media Professional in the Negotiations Process." *School Library Media Quarterly* 11 (Summer 1983): 265-316.

Cain, Carolyn. "Media Specialists and the Quest for Lifelong Learning." *School Library Journal* 29 (October 1982): 109-13.

Connecticut Teacher Certification Regulations. Hartford, Conn.: State Department of Education, 1980.

Ely, Donald. "The Role of the School Media Specialist: Some Directions and Choices." *Journal of Research and Development in Education* 16 (Fall 1982): 33-36.

Griffiths, José-Marie, and Donald King. *New Directions in Library and Information Science Education*. White Plains, N.Y.: Knowledge Industry, 1986.

Herrin, Barbara, and others. "Personality and Communications Behaviors of Model School Library Media Specialists." *Drexel Library Quarterly* 21 (Spring 1985): 69-90.

Hug, William. "Perceptions of Mergers among Library/Media Technology Professionals." *Journal of Research and Development in Education* 16 (Fall 1982): 1-5.

Kenny, Sue, and James Kenny. "Personality Patterns of Public School Librarians and Teachers." *Journal of Experimental Education* 50 (Spring 1982): 152-53.

Media Program Recommendations: Guidelines for School Media Programs. Raleigh, N.C.: Department of Public Instruction, 1986.

Media Standards for Nevada Schools. Carson City, Nev.: Department of Education, 1986.

Penland, Patrick. "Certification of School Media Specialists." *Journal of Research and Development in Education* 16 (Fall 1982): 9-12.

Pichette, William. "Evaluating the School Librarian." *Bulletin of the National Association of Secondary School Principals* 68 (April 1984): 124-30.

Quality Library Services K-12. Columbus, Ohio: Department of Education, 1986.

Recommended Standards for Educational Library Media Programs. Springfield, Ill.: State Board of Education, 1986.

Trump, J. Lloyd. "Independent Study Centers: Their Relation to the Central Library." *Bulletin of the National Association of Secondary School Principals* 50 (January 1966): 45-51.

Vincelette, Joyce, and Fred Pfister. "Improving Performance Appraisal in Libraries." *Library and Information Science Research* 6 (April-June 1984): 191-203.

6

FACILITIES AND FURNITURE

OBJECTIVES

Describe major alternatives in the design of facilities for the school LMC.

Write educational specifications for LMC facilities in a selected school.

FACTORS IN PLANNING

There are many factors to consider in the planning and construction of a new school or the remodeling of an older school or LMC, involving general community sentiment and typical management practices in the district. Also, educational planners and architects must plan in terms of the future. Flexibility of design is imperative, so that educational innovations may be incorporated into the structure at a later time. The ultimate conversion of schools to other uses is another practical concern for the 1980s and beyond. Planning and construction reflect a compromise between ideals and ideas, and it is in this context that the LMC is designed.

Rationale for Space

An attempt to plan the LMC so as to create effective patterns of use by the media staff, teaching staff, and students requires considerable effort. Many questions must be answered before the architect can move ahead with the work, and these questions can be answered only if the library media specialist is involved in total school planning and in writing educational specifications as they relate to the total school concept. It is advisable not to have a fixed, single concept about the form of the LMC before involvement with other school personnel and their ideas. Rigid thinking and the rejection of other ideas will limit the library media specialist's involvement and opportunity for leadership.

Besides a knowledge of educational philosophy, of the external and internal organization of the school, and of the relationship of the LMC to other areas of the school, other factors are important in organizing the spaces needed to operate a program effectively. Some questions to be answered are:

- What number and type of staff will be available to operate this program?

- What hours will the facility be open for use?

- What spaces are required?

- How will spaces be used?

- What media will be included in the collection?

- How will media be organized for use?

- What specialized equipment will be required?

- What areas are to be shared by students and teachers?

- What areas are reserved for the exclusive use of teachers and/or students?

- How should spaces relate to each other?

- How should each space be programmed for use?

The 1975 AASL/AECT guidelines, which appear to have their greatest impact on the design of facilities in new schools, state what "should be" in schools. The same quantitative standards are applied to schools at any level, elementary through secondary. The one qualifying factor, often overlooked in the quest for guidance in planning, is that the guidelines are directed to the LMC *as it should be* in the context of the school *as it should be*. Guidelines make an assumption about educational programming—that the internal organization of the school has been structured to incorporate the "ultimate" in teaching and learning conditions.

The school district may have a special planning team of its own to do preliminary work concerning size of building, general configuration, and cost estimates. This might also be the task of educational or architectural consultants, who work with school people to get the job done. In most school districts, teachers and other professionals participate in the development of educational specifications for a new school. The term *educational specifications* is synonymous with *building program*, a term used in other fields.

Role of the Head of the LMC

Although it is unlikely that the head of the LMC can know all there is to know about facilities planning, one must at least be aware of an appropriate role in the process. Familiarity with the fields of education and library media service is essential if this role is to be performed with distinction. Responsibilities should include the coordination of all media and communications systems throughout the school, including multimedia instructional installations, auditoriums, public address systems, microcomputer labs, and so on. Focusing specifically on the writing of specifications for the LMC, the planner looks first to the objectives, policy, and program that make up the school's philosophy. Where there is a district director, he or she would assume a leadership role in the planning process, coordinating efforts at all levels. Input from the head of the LMC and other staff would be part of the coordinating process.

Educational specifications for the LMC, then, are compatible with the total school program. Specific areas to be considered follow:

1. Introductory matter.

   a. A statement of the philosophy and objectives of the LMC as it relates to education in the school.

   b. A statement defining the LMC's orientation to the entire educational plant, whether it is one building or several.

   c. A statement providing general directions relating to all areas. One might mention here requirements such as carpeting, ventilation, the need to provide flexibility of space, and conduit or raceway for future electrical or electronic equipment.

2. Definition of each space required. At this point, national, state, and local standards or guidelines will be of value. The guidance provided by regional accrediting groups will also be helpful, as will authoritative literature. For *each* space, the following information is needed:

   a. Name of the space.

   b. Size of the space.

   c. Type and number of occupants of space.

   d. A description of the function of the space. This will include:

      • Relationship to other spaces in the LMC.

      • Activities anticipated for the space.

- Any special considerations such as the environment or atmosphere intended.

- Problems (such as security, and the need for special locks).

3. Built-in equipment. This is a separate list of what is required for each space, such as clocks, cabinets, shelving, and sinks. These items are usually part of construction costs and are handled by the building contractor.

4. Furnishings and equipment. The selection and purchase of furnishings and equipment may be included in an architect's contract for an additional sum, or may be a responsibility assumed by the educational staff of the district. No matter how the problem is handled, the library media specialist should prepare a separate list of movable furniture, such as desks, carrels, and audiovisual equipment.

5. Personnel requirements. A separate list of staff requirements will be prepared as part of the total package of information prepared for the new school.

The Architect

The architect who is selected to plan a school, or to remodel existing facilities, usually discusses the concept "form follows function." In other words, the intent is to design plans for the physical structure based on function, as described by educators.

The architect either will have had experience in school building design or will have educational consultants available for assistance. Frequently, the educational concepts incorporated into the new school actually come from the architect, because his or her experience in the field provides a broad picture of a building's potential. This can be a benefit to unimaginative educators, or it can be a serious detriment, depending on the architect. Educational facilities planners must be aware of existing and projected innovations in education and must be ready to listen to new ideas and to manipulate them to fit the situation.

The architect assists in the development of the building project in three essential stages: decision, design, and delivery. In the decision stage, he or she may participate in feasibility studies, financial analysis, programming, and research required as preliminary work. The design stage calls for planning and developing all of the project details and the preparation of construction documents. The delivery stage calls for the administration of the construction contract and may call for management of the actual construction project and services related to furnishing the building. The architect provides basic services in the schematic design, design development, construction documents, bidding or negotiation, and construction phases.

Schematic Design Phase

Through conferences with various school personnel, the architect studies and analyzes the educators' requirements. He or she then prepares schematic design studies; these are drawings and other documents that illustrate initial efforts to translate the educational requirements. The architect also provides as much information as possible about construction and materials. After the educators have reviewed this phase and approved the work, and the architect has submitted a statement of probable construction costs, this phase is considered complete.

Design Development Phase

This phase provides for the refinement of schematic design studies. The architect prepares more detailed drawings and provides data about the appearance of the structure, electrical and mechanical systems to be used, the types of materials to be used, and a more refined statement of construction costs. Again, review and approval by educators are required before the architect moves on to the next phase.

Construction Documents Phase

In this phase the architect prepares working drawings and specifications based on the design documents that have been approved. The work to be done is described in technical language: the materials and equipment; type of workmanship required; structural, mechanical and electrical work; site work; and special equipment requirements. This is also the phase in which the architect assists in the preparation of bidding information, proposal and contract forms, and so on. At this point, any additional adjustments to probable construction costs will also be made.

Bidding or Negotiation Phase

The architect provides the educators with advice and assistance in obtaining bids or negotiated proposals and in awarding the construction contracts.

Construction Phase

The architect administers the construction contract through a number of activities:

Preparing needed supplementary drawings.

Reviewing the construction schedule, materials, samples, and so on.

Making periodic visits to the site to review progress and see that work is proceeding according to the contract.

Issuing certificates of payment for the contractor.

Preparing change orders in work approved by the educator.

Determining the date of project completion, providing the educator with the written guarantees prepared by the contractor, and issuing a final certificate of payment to contractors.

Alternatives in Facilities Organization

The typical, traditional, and most common organizational pattern for physical facilities has been the single, centralized library media facility. In the past, the school library suffered from three basic faults: (1) it has had perimeter shelving to house collections, with seating in the center of the room, which creates distractions for users; (2) the circulation desk has often been located on one side of the reading room, which leads to considerable noise and confusion in the LMC, and (3) students have had to walk through seating arrangements or completely around seating to reach media.

What are the major alternative organizational patterns for library media facilities? First, consider that there is a great deal of physical difference between a self-contained library media facility and one that is part of an academic building. The self-contained facility usually offers the educational planner and the architect broader opportunities for design. The facility that is developed within the physical structure of the school starts with many design problems simply because it must fit, like a jigsaw puzzle piece, into the total school. There are a number of alternative patterns of organization in use today; these are discussed below.

School as an LMC Concept

The optimum organization of a library or LMC has long been conceived of as a totally integrated exchange: the LMC as a school—the school as an LMC. Although this concept is never fully translated operationally in terms of using media for learning, physically the translation has been made. The learning center or multi-instructional area concept in elementary school design has been responsible for a pattern that includes open space instead of traditional classrooms, team teaching and flexible grouping for instruction, and total integration of media into the teaching-learning space. Figure 6.1 is a generalized representation of this pattern. An elementary school with an open interior design provides space for three major areas: primary grades, media resources, and intermediate grades. Although the figure shows a rectangular shape, squares, circles, octagons, and other forms are also used. The concept is intended to provide total flexibility of space, personnel, and media.

```
┌─────────────────────────────────┐
│                                 │
│         Primary Grades          │
│                                 │
│         Media Resources         │
│                                 │
│       Intermediate Grades       │
│                                 │
└─────────────────────────────────┘
```

Fig. 6.1. School as an LMC concept.

A Centralized LMC System

Usually, centralization of an LMC program means physically combining the system elements that are most compatible and interrelated from a service point of view, either in one area of a school building or in one part of a campus. A pure or absolute translation of the LMC system concept on a centralized basis would physically relate specialized laboratories, multimedia instructional facilities, and the LMC in one defined geographic area. The instructional direction of the school would be based on a high orientation to this centralized learning core. Other spaces, commonly referred to as teaching stations, would be distributed geographically and would provide for other forms of teacher-student interaction.

A less absolute but more common interpretation of centralization merely dictates the physical unification of traditional library/audiovisual elements in the facility called an LMC. The organizational pattern arranges basic services functionally, providing space for reference services, and distributing other media by form (books, periodicals, etc.). Ordinarily, planners of facilities are cautioned to limit seating in general use areas to no more than 100 in one space. This means simply that if a facility is to seat 150 users, it should be organized into at least two distinct supervisory areas. Actually, evidence and experience provide us with a better gauge of the number of students to be accommodated in a single area. A maximum of 50 students is recommended; 20 to 30 would be even more desirable. Figure 6.2 provides a generalized view of a typical centralized LMC.

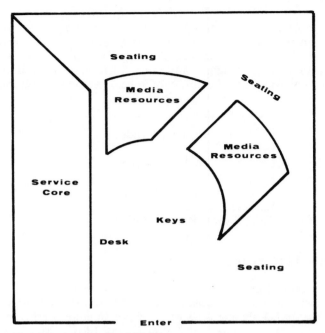

Fig. 6.2. A centralized LMC.

Centralized Divisional or Resource Center Schemes

Divisional and resource center schemes are principal variations in large centralized school LMC facilities. They provide ways to handle large numbers of students and also to concentrate space, media, and personnel on a single subject or related group of subjects studied in the school. Using one of these approaches provides some flexibility in the types of media housed in a specialized collection.

The division collection has been used with varying degrees of success in colleges and public libraries. Collections may be limited to books or may encompass other printed and audiovisual forms as well. Decisions about using this approach may be made arbitrarily by the LMC staff, with due recognition of the interrelationship of media housed together and student-faculty needs, or it may be the result of a compromise with administration and teaching staff in establishing priorities. The more common approach is to group two or more subject disciplines, such as math and science, languages, and social sciences, into divisions. The allocation of space to the various divisions is usually arbitrary, and divisions are separated by double-faced shelving or other types of readily movable dividers rather than by permanent walls. Space allocations for the divisions will ultimately be governed by an evaluation of space requirements based on the quantity and types of media housed in a division, in addition to actual use by students and teachers; sometimes a reorganization of the divisional structure will be necessary.

The "resource center" approach differs slightly from the divisional approach. It refers to carving seating space out of a standard arrangement of shelving for media. For example, a resource center in science would mean providing seating for twenty-five to thirty students among the 500-600 range of the Dewey classification; an English resource center, among the 800s, and so on. This is a simple, effective technique for patterning seating in a large facility. Figure 6.3 depicts these two alternatives in a generalized scheme.

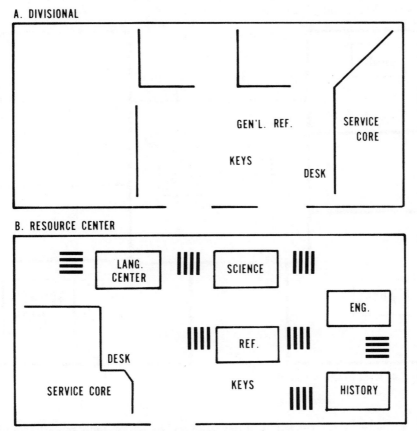

Fig. 6.3. Centralized divisional and resource center schemes.

A Decentralized LMC System

A decentralized LMC (see figure 6.4) would have a modest central facility or service core, with satellites (which are also called centers, departmental resource centers, or learning centers). The satellites may house general collections selected to serve the needs of a particular grade level or they may be subject-oriented, in much the same manner as the divisional or resource center plans considered above. The pattern has received its greatest promotion at the secondary level, under the strong influence of the professional educator rather than LMC personnel. In fact, decentralized centers may not even be a part of a service system coordinated with the LMC.

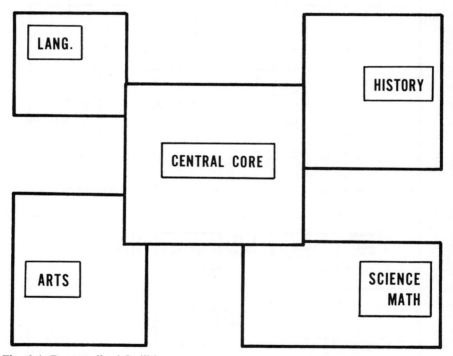

Fig. 6.4. Decentralized facilities.

Usually, decentralized facilities are seen in senior high school facilities and, to a lesser degree, in intermediate or middle schools, which may house any grade combination from four to eight. The philosophy behind the pattern, however, arose from the idea of a classroom collection of printed and audiovisual media at the teachers' fingertips. This fingertip principle is difficult to overturn; only rarely does the alternative concept of sharing resources succeed in replacing it. At the secondary level, where many teachers do not have a permanent room as a base, the departmental office has provided the requisite fingertip control. It is a logical progression from the classroom, to the departmental office, to the departmental resource center. If teachers of the same subject are physically concentrated in specific areas (often located a fair distance from an existing LMC), an understandable interest in a center to serve the department is generated. This interest is even stronger if the LMC system operating in the school is inadequate; conditions become ripe for change.

Whether to provide centralized or decentralized facilities for student and teacher utilization of media and services is an important consideration. For decentralized facilities, the existing patterns of organization and control are:

1. A resource center fully supported and operated by a specific department in the school. Total responsibility is in the hands of the department chair.

2. A resource center supported and operated jointly by a given department and LMC. Each has clearly defined responsibilities for programming.

3. A resource center supported and operated by the LMC as a system component.

The principal advantages of decentralized facilities seem to be that access to media and equipment may be faster from teaching areas and study centers, location and size may be conducive to study and research activity, and it is sometimes easier to add auxiliary facilities than to expand a centralized facility. Disadvantages of decentralized facilities seem to be extensive duplication of media and equipment, the need for additional personnel, and larger budgets for resources and personnel.

LOCATION OF THE LMC

The centralized facility is most common and is recommended unless unusual circumstances prohibit this pattern. Centralization, in this context, is simply the organization of the LMC facility in one defined area. The centralized facility may occupy one or more floors of a building, but the parts of the facility will be physically connected. This does not limit the system.

The LMC facility should be located in an area of the school or campus directly related to instructional areas. The private, residential school should choose a site orientation on campus that relates to both academic facilities and student residences, thus splitting the travel distance for users. A major issue in the location of the LMC in any school will be the time and distance one must travel to use the facilities. For some, this factor overshadows any other consideration, so it is highly desirable to make the LMC as accessible as possible. If the centralized facility is to be an integral part of the school, it is recommended that the facility be near major academic areas; also, it should be located on the main floor relating to the main entrance to the school. Attempting to do both of these things may be contradictory. If the LMC is to be used after school hours, then provision must be made for direct access to the media facility while the remainder of the school is closed to the public. Direct access does not necessarily mean first floor. The main problem with trying to get a "first floor front" location is that many other school departments seek the same space. The school business office, health suite, guidance suite, auditorium, and gymnasium all might choose the same location. Since the principal concern is access to the LMC after school hours, an architect can meet the requirement in several ways. For example, if the LMC is located on a second floor of an academic building, a direct-access staircase and elevator to accommodate the physically handicapped can lead to the facility or a lobby at the main level can route users of the building to various locations, including the LMC.

It is usually recommended that the LMC not be located in proximity to playgrounds, a gymnasium, music areas, shops, or other areas that might generate a great deal of noise. This obviously limits possible locations. However, location is important.

Provision should be made during the planning stages for expansion of the facility. Various options are possible during this time, such as expanding within the school building by adding spaces initially programmed for other purposes. In order to allow for potential expansion, the facility should not be bounded by corridors which, because of fire or other regulations, could not be used for expansion. Other problem areas could be stairwells, heating plants, or other permanent obstacles. Whether the philosophy of the school will permit expansion of the facility at a later time is immaterial at the planning stage; providing the conditions for further expansion is important.

Relating Space to Program

One way to study the various spaces needed in an LMC is to categorize them. Decide which spaces are provided essentially for support functions and which are necessary to primary functions. If the intent and purpose of each of the functional spaces is known, a simple classification scheme can provide for two basic areas based on support and primary use. Figure 6.5 illustrates an adaptation to the space program recommended in the 1975 AASL/AECT guidelines.[1] In cases in which square footage was cited as a range of figures (e.g., workroom — 300-400 square feet) the largest figure has been used here. Note that support space amounts to 41 percent of the grand total.

Although the library media specialist is not expected to develop plans, it is helpful to test out visually the relationships required in planning. It can be helpful to cut out squares, ellipses, or other shapes, to label them, and to move them around on a board, simply to test out relationships based on the functional requirements of the LMC system. Using the basic support and primary spaces provided, one can begin to test out the relationships between individual spaces.

Support Space	Sq. Ft.	Primary Space	Sq. Ft.
Entrance, circulation and distribution	800	General function space: reading and browsing, individual viewing and listening, individual study and learning, storytelling, information services (15% @ 40 sq. ft. per student)	6,000
Administration: 4 @ 150 sq. ft.	600		
Work space	400		
Maintenance and repair	200		
Stacks	400	Conference rooms (3 @ 150 sq. ft. each)	450
Magazines and Newspapers	400	Small group viewing and listening	150
Equipment distribution and storage	400	Group projects and instruction in research	1,200
Television			
Studio 40' x 40'	1,600	Media production laboratory	800
Storage	800		
Office with workspace	150	Darkroom	200
Radio 20' x 25'	500	Center for professional materials for faculty	600
Storage and control center for remote access (est.)	1,000	Computerized learning laboratory	1,000
Total Support Space	7,250	Total Primary Space	10,400

Grand Total: 17,650 square feet

Fig. 6.5. Space allotments, school of 1,000 students.

Figure 6.6 shows one way of relating the types of spaces required for the LMC. The LMC is first broken down into its smallest functional components, then restructured to form a composite picture. In this illustration the smallest functional space is called a unit. Two or more related units are then merged to form a cluster of related functional units. Two or more clusters are merged to form either the support or the primary space. This pattern does not imply that it is possible to then separate physically the two types of spaces defined (for example, one cannot assign all of the primary space to one floor and all support space to another floor). Support spaces are what the term implies. They support the primary space program where the principal activities of users take place.

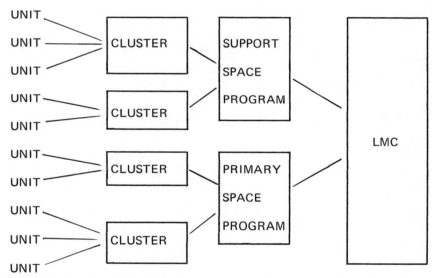

Fig. 6.6. Relationship of spaces.

Flexibility

Flexible is defined as "characterized by ready capability for modification or change, by plasticity, pliancy, variability, and often by consequent adaptability to a new situation."[2] It is a term that has been used in educational circles in reaction against the former rigidity of space, curriculum, and personnel. It is a key concept in educational facilities planning. The term is used and overused. As Ronald Gross stated, "There is some truth to this criticism: flexibility is a high abstraction and only gets its meaning when broken down into specific requirements to fit particular cases."[3] He cited architect William Caudill, who abandoned the term in favor of words with a high degree of specificity: *expansible space*, which can allow for ordered growth; *convertible space*, which can be economically adapted to program changes; *versatile space*, which serves many functions; and *malleable space*, which can be changed at once and at will.

Although these terms are applicable to the entire school, they are particularly appropriate to a discussion of space requirements for a library media center. Terms may be used in various combinations. For example, when considering the need for a facility that can be enlarged as teaching-learning concepts change and as media collections threaten to take over all available floor space, the concept of expansible space focuses the attention of planners more directly on the need to build a facility that by its very nature will grow in size and change in form. One may think of expansible space in two ways; the first is simply a "pushing out walls" idea of getting additional room when needed, the second is expansible and convertible space in tandem. This second approach recognizes that change and innovation can be applied to a facet of a media operation that requires additional space, while another related aspect of the media program is reduced. In creating a new equilibrium, one expands where needed by taking advantage of the concept of convertible space, which implies that because of the use of nonload-bearing walls, it is economically feasible to expand one area and reduce the size of its adjacent area.

School LMCs have developed what Caudill has referred to as versatile space. Most general use space is versatile and can serve many functions simultaneously. In a single area, one might see students and teachers reading, viewing, listening, writing, and discussing. Also, use might be made of paper, pencil, and book, while information retrieval via microcomputer and computer-assisted instruction might be "happening" at the same time, in essentially the same space. To a considerable degree this is possible, and it is a practical solution to the space utilization problem in schools. If space is at a premium, the pattern of assigning specific functions to individual spaces can leave one area unused for extended periods of time, while other areas are overcrowded.

The concept of malleable space—that is, space that can be changed at once and at will—while compatible to a degree with the concept of versatility, implies the ability to convert to a totally different pattern of use. For example, adjacent conference rooms that seat six to eight people can become one seminar room seating sixteen if a folding partition is moved. The same space, if conditions are properly prepared, can also become a facility for group viewing of television.

Perhaps the term *flexibility* will continue to be used successfully in programming educational facilities. Supplying enough descriptive information to make *flexible* meaningful to the reader does not limit the term.

CENTRALIZED FACILITIES

The centralized facility is treated in detail here because it remains the most common way to organize the LMC system. The decentralized and open space plans are treated as extensions of, or deviations from, the centralized approach. As noted, there are two types of space—primary and support.

Primary Space

The total space provided for primary program functions consists of a group of discrete units that can be combined and programmed as functional clusters of related services spaces. Figure 6.7 illustrates a patterning or relationship of the various primary system components, showing six clusters that contain related functional units.

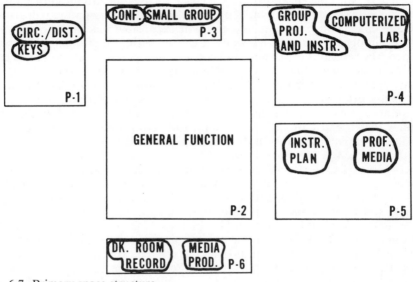

Fig. 6.7. Primary space structure.

Cluster 1 contains a service unit (circulation) and a keys unit; these provide a transition to the important business to be conducted by students and teachers in the LMC. The two units provide basic information about the location and use of media and about all LMC services.

The service unit may serve as a general security checkpoint. Its major functions include circulating and distributing all media to be used anywhere in the school or community, booking audiovisual equipment for use at various teaching stations (this equipment to be stored elsewhere), distributing portable equipment to be used by students and teachers in the LMC, and handling the reserve media collection.

The keys unit provides two types of informational sources. The catalog provides information about what is in this LMC collection (alternatives include printed book catalogs, microform catalogs, and computerized catalogs featuring video display). The second part of the keys unit consists of bibliographies that are used as guides to information that exists in the media universe. Obviously, the larger the LMC, the more comprehensive this collection will be. The cluster should be situated so that users who do not have business to conduct at the keys unit can pass by it easily.

Cluster 2 is referred to as a general function area. It should be large enough to accommodate a minimum of 15 percent of the student population at one time. If the school has a high orientation toward the extensive use of media, independent study, and flexibility of scheduling, then it would not be unrealistic to expect the general function area to accommodate as much as 75 percent of the student population. Many unit possibilities exist, and they have been experimented with in school, public, and academic libraries.

Factors that govern specific unit development in individual schools include media storage requirements, LMC personnel, and student and teacher needs. The general function area is probably the most critical in the entire LMC operation.

Cluster 3 contains two types of spaces: conference rooms and a small group space for viewing and listening. Unit functions imply a degree of group interaction among students, between students and teachers, among teachers, and among LMC personnel and these groups. In addition to the free flow of ideas, this concept anticipates the free movement of bodies in a variety of activities. This is an extremely important cluster, one that is rarely provided for adequately. Each conference room should allow for multipurpose activities, including group discussion, project development, listening, and viewing. Users should not have to move through the general function areas of the LMC to get to this cluster, though it should be situated conveniently in relation to the general function areas. Conference rooms should be grouped in units of two, with movable partitions so that the space can also be used for seminar groups, group viewing, and so on. Another desirable grouping would be four conference rooms that could be used independently, as a large group space, or as any intermediate combination. It is not always possible to arrange for exactly the combination wanted, sometimes due to community fire regulations. In these cases, *flexibility* means using options within the conference rooms. Soundproof rooms, clearly defined by fixed floor-to-ceiling walls, are required. It should be possible to remove these walls with a minimum of cost and disruption of program if required.

Cluster 4 includes two learning centers, each of which is equivalent in size to a standard classroom in a modern elementary school. Though in practice the units—one for group projects and instruction in research, and one for a computerized learning laboratory—represent different use requirements, they are compatible. If we can assume that the space for group projects is one in which classes of students meet to "kick off" individual and group learning projects under the direction of library media specialists and teachers, it is reasonable to assume also that students will be channeled to other learning spaces, such as the computerized laboratory, general function areas, and so on. This unit may actually take two forms: the first, as an area in which students may receive formal instruction and also relate to each other and to media organized here temporarily; the second, as an area providing for formal multimedia presentations relating to LMC utilization and/or the specific learning needs of the students. Adopting this latter function for the space would depend, in large part, on the number and size of multimedia lecture spaces provided throughout the school.

The computerized laboratory envisioned could provide audio-video programming or house an array of microcomputers. The optimum situation would find teachers creating programs for the system and integrating these programs with independent study aspects of learning. If the LMC is integrated with academic areas of the school, it would be desirable to provide direct access to this cluster from a corridor. In any event, access should be provided so that class groups need not use the general function area as a corridor.

Cluster 5 is composed of two units: professional materials for faculty and an instructional planning unit. Functions can be mixed or clearly distinguished. The professional media unit would relate to professional collections housed in a system LMC. If no district-level collection exists, the school collection will be larger and more generalized. In any case, media relating to teaching, including periodicals and curriculum guides, would be housed here. It would be a place where teachers could relax, catch up on professional work, or meet with teachers from other areas.

On the other hand, an instructional planning unit would be designed to accommodate teaching teams and would be organized around the types of furniture and equipment needed to plan instruction on a day-to-day basis. Long-term planning would also be accomplished here through the preview and evaluation of media related to instruction. This unit could also provide facilities for the design of new media forms.

The last primary space considered here (Cluster 6) should be planned to accommodate both creative and routine activities related to designing and producing new media and to modifying existing media for use in a learning situation. This cluster would include a general production unit and a more specialized unit with a darkroom and recording facilities. A few qualifying comments are needed about the best use of this cluster, since media production is assuming new proportions in school LMC programming. The extent of services offered by the district must be considered. Ordinarily, graphics work is one of the first services provided by a district center. If service beyond that offered at the district level is needed, or if this service is not provided at the district level, then a full program of services should be offered at the school level, including typing and duplicating services. Another consideration is the need for darkroom facilities. Generally, film development is handled through a commercial photographic company, even in LMCs, for school districts with as many as 50,000 students. If the school photography club needs darkroom facilities, the LMC may be the place for it. If photography is a part of a school graphic arts program or some other program, then sharing facilities might be more practical than duplicating them.

In some schools, students as well as faculty need access to media production facilities. The question is whether students and teachers can use common production facilities or whether separate work areas are needed. If teachers wish to discuss professional business in this environment, they may prefer not to have students in the area. An instructional planning unit for faculty could alleviate problems of this type. Teacher use of the media production unit would then be limited to actual production time, while consultation with LMC personnel would be carried on in the instructional planning unit. An alternative plan might also provide separate planning spaces in the production unit, with joint use of production equipment. Schools that foster an informal relationship between teachers and students will feel no pressure in this case.

Support Space

The various types of space needed to support primary functions of the LMC program can readily be grouped into clusters of related service units. Figure 6.8 details the types of support space needed in the LMC and the possible relationships of service clusters.

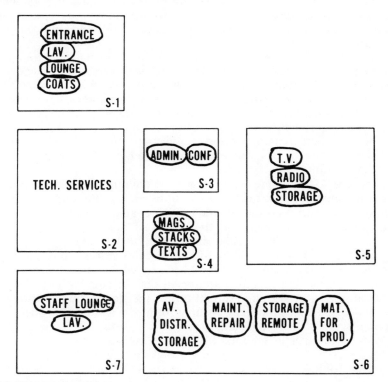

Fig. 6.8. Support space structure.

Cluster 1 should contain an entrance lobby and may also contain lavatories, coatrooms, and a student lounge. A centralized LMC that is physically separated from other teaching-learning areas in the school should provide a main entrance that relates externally to high density traffic areas of the school or campus, so long as the complications of potential noise and activity do not preclude such a location. This entrance should be the primary point of ingress and egress, providing a transition point that gives students time to acclimate themselves to a new set of conditions. Exhibits and displays can be provided, at this point, in wall-mounted or free-standing cases; through tackboards of various sizes and shapes, including floor-to-ceiling tackboard for one or more areas; or by means of various free-standing panel display units. In campus-type schools, public lavatories should be available.

Although coatrooms have been phased out of library media facilities at all levels, the fact remains that students who intend to spend several hours working in and moving about an LMC would appreciate having a place to store coats and books. An area of student lockers could be provided, each of which would have a shelf for books and hooks for coats. Locks could be obtained at a service desk, so that security would not be the responsibility of the LMC staff. (Twenty such units would occupy only twenty linear feet of space, two feet deep.)

Cluster 1 also provides for the comfort of users by having a lounge unit. The size and actual function of this space must be determined through an evaluation of need. The lounge usually provides casual seating, low tables, lamps, and so on. The furniture groupings serve to structure discussion areas within the unit. This would also be considered a minimal security area. Sometimes the unit serves a dual function; the space is used for a noncirculating collection of media or as a noncirculating reserve collection. In such cases, security is provided either directly or by forcing access through a checkpoint adjacent to the circulation unit.

If the LMC is integrated in an academic building, then lavatories, coatrooms, and lounge areas may well be omitted, assuming that reasonable proximity to comfort units outside the LMC is available. The security factor is an individual school problem, so the design of the cluster should provide options for rigid or flexible formal supervision of this area.

Cluster 2 incorporates the basic technical services units required to acquire media and equipment for the LMC, to provide necessary processing services, and to move media and equipment out for circulation and distribution. Organization of the units should reflect the flow of media through the cluster. Since this is a prime receiving area for media and equipment, it should have direct access to a corridor and to an elevator, if the LMC does not have a first-floor location. The school LMC that occupies a building of its own provides direct access to the outdoors through this cluster.

Cluster 3 houses administrative space for staff and, in larger facilities, conference and secretarial space. There is some difference of opinion about quarters for administrative functions. The national guidelines recommended some 600 square feet of administrative space for an LMC in a school of 1,000. Some argue, however, that 150 square feet per professional is an excessive amount, and some point out that not every professional needs office space. The rationale for assigning administrative space is to provide a fixed location for the professional who spends part of the day selecting media; meeting with sales representatives, members of the teaching staff, and students; and working on other administrative tasks related to the center. Considering that some LMCs have an extended-hours program and are open perhaps six days a week and until 9:00 or 10:00 each evening, this space becomes vital. An alternative to providing an administrative unit that houses four professionals is to distribute the administrative space throughout the primary structure, such as an office at the keys unit and/or circulation unit, or offices relating to specific professional work stations in the general function cluster. If the distribution does not, in fact, reduce the total usable space for general function programming, this pattern is most desirable. Where maximum flexibility is required in the general function cluster, office space can be provided by using movable metal units, with or without doors. The principal disadvantage here is that the sound level cannot be adequately controlled.

An administrative conference room provides meeting space for the LMC staff, allows for the continuing review and discussion vital to selection, and provides a suitable meeting space for faculty and student LMC committees. Another option is to provide private administrative space for the head of the LMC (150 square feet would be generous), a conference room of the same size, and secretarial space. Other space could then be distributed throughout the LMC. We can assume that as school LMC facilities and staff size increase, one secretary will be required to handle the administrator's correspondence and other paperwork.

Cluster 4 units are grouped together because of their basic storage nature. The units are magazine storage, stacks, and textbooks. Media stored here are ordinarily those to which only limited access is required.

Magazine storage can be handled in a variety of ways in the LMC. The current trend is away from binding periodicals and toward providing backfiles on microforms. The equivalent of one year's file of periodicals should be available in the LMC general function cluster for immediate access. Even if backfiles are to be maintained on microforms, it is desirable to store three to five years' worth of periodicals in the magazine storage unit for class projects.

The stacks are primarily a dead storage unit for little-used media that are considered to be of value to the collection. Multiple copies of resource media and kits of media may also be stored here. Direct access to media is fundamental to the modern school LMC; hence, these stacks imply limited use and access.

A textbook storage unit is included in the cluster as an alternative. If the LMC is to be the principal location for the storage and distribution of all media to be used in the school, then textbook management also should become a function of the LMC. This function may require additional staff, depending on the number of textbooks used in the school. Limited access to this unit is anticipated; it is desirable, however, to provide access to a service corridor for delivery of texts to teaching stations without passing through the primary structure.

Cluster 5, which houses television and radio units, is supportive in nature because the units are production space, their output being received both in the LMC and throughout the school. They are treated as optional spaces because the extent to which these facilities are needed in each school will be governed in part by the services that the district media center offers. Because of the nature of the equipment involved, direct access to a corridor is essential and double doors are required. Storage and office space are a part of the cluster.

Cluster 6 units are grouped functionally because they all involve audio-visual equipment service. The "materials for production" unit provides storage space for the media production unit. Direct access to the primary structure is required.

Maintenance and repair services in the individual school can be gauged only in relation to the services offered at the district level. If the district LMC provides comprehensive maintenance and repair services, then only the essential minimal and basic repairs need to be handled in the school. In the absence of services at a district level, facilities for simple maintenance and repair must be provided at the individual school level and contracts must be made with commercial firms for major repairs and servicing as required.

The space designated for a remote access control unit may house a mini-computer having terminals located in the computerized laboratory for student use and throughout the school. If the planning approach has been comprehensive, the minicomputer may also serve various LMC needs as well as school and district administrative requirements. If the computerized laboratory is intended to house only microcomputers, remote access space may be converted for other uses.

The audiovisual equipment distribution and storage unit in this cluster relates directly to teaching stations. Direct access to a corridor must be provided to move equipment expeditiously to needed locations. Equipment for use in the LMC, however, would be stored in the circulation/distribution unit.

Cluster 7 represents a staff convenience center. If the LMC is independent of other academic buildings and is also open for extended hours, this is an essential cluster. It would also be desirable for those schools in which the LMC is a separate facility in a campus-style arrangement. Any LMC facility that operates on an extended-hours basis needs such a cluster because after-hours access to other school facilities is generally curtailed. The fact that the staff in a large school may number twelve to twenty members gives added weight to the need for convenience facilities.

Figure 6.9 suggests one pattern for relating primary and support space.

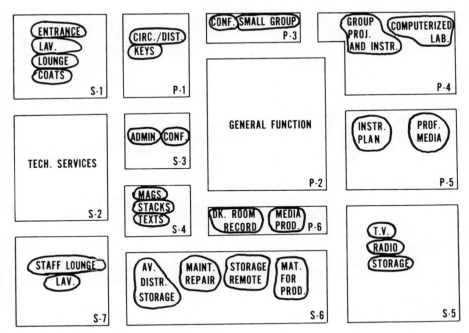

Fig. 6.9. Relating primary and support space.

Traffic Patterns

Not enough attention has been paid to the movement of individuals and groups through an LMC of any size. The basic problem to be solved is how to get users where they want to go, in the shortest possible time, with the least inconvenience to themselves and other users. Ralph Ellsworth developed a generalized traffic pattern whose concept is adaptable to any centralized LMC.[4] Traffic moves from the entrance-circulation to the keys area (or bypass), through the media collection, to various user spaces (see figure 6.10).

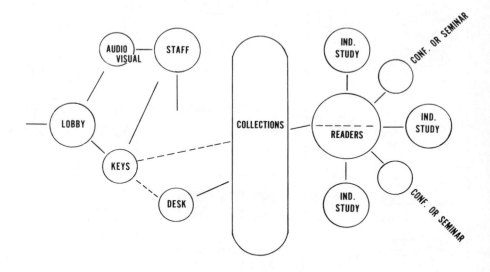

Fig. 6.10. Traffic patterns.

Internal Physical Environment

The "environment for learning" that the LMC creates says a great deal about the program philosophy of the school and can be a determining factor in encouraging students and teachers to spend their time profitably in a learning situation.

The general conditions discussed below apply to all or most spaces of the LMC.

Temperature Control

It should be possible to control conditions thermostatically throughout the LMC regardless of external weather conditions. The LMC needs an integrated heating-cooling system capable of a dual function throughout the year—a total climate-control system capable of automatically adjusting and controlling the temperature and flow of air.

Architects are among the chief proponents of air conditioning LMCs and school facilities in general, for reasons that go beyond pure considerations of comfort. Air conditioning allows the architect wide latitude in interior planning; he or she can literally "put the pieces together" without concern for windows that must perform a ventilating function. For example, in the case of an LMC that is integrated with an academic building, the entire LMC can be placed in an internal location, with no need to provide windows to ventilate the various components in the facility. In the light of experience with typical air conditioning systems in schools, however, it would be highly desirable to have an environmentally conditioned facility that also provides some manual method of controlling the flow of air, such as windows that open.

A consideration of windows leads logically to a consideration of the architect's use of glass in building schools. The use of glass in schools that are provided with climate control is generally limited to external considerations of aesthetics, general cost factors of building materials, and perhaps "bringing the outside into the building" aesthetically to capitalize on a particularly spectacular view. One should also consider that direct sunlight through glass makes it difficult to control the internal climate and creates other problems because of glare and reflected light. Climate control and vandalism were major factors in the trend away from exterior walls of glass to building schools without windows.

Artificial Lighting

No specific prescription for lighting in the various areas of the LMC will be made here, though some observations can be made. A recommendation to avoid illumination levels which would tend to bleach out images on computer display terminals, television screens, microfiche projectors, and other rear screen projection is reasonable.

Through the use of artificial lighting, the LMC can create conditions that accommodate the potential needs of users. Both incandescent and fluorescent lighting can be used to provide varying environmental patterns and visually more interesting ceilings. At least in the general function cluster, lighting should be zoned and controlled by dimmer switches that control the intensity of lighting in the various areas. Besides meeting specific lighting needs in various areas, this method can also provide interesting environmental conditions.

Ceilings

Although it is not often considered worthy of an aesthetic treatment, the ceiling of the LMC does offer many possibilities. In the self-contained, campus-type facility, the architect can design various types of ceilings. The loft plan, which provides large open spaces uninterrupted by load-bearing walls, lends itself very well to extraordinary modifications of traditional flat ceilings. Although the multiple-level academic building generally precludes much in the way of relief from the ordinary, particularly if the LMC has other building levels above it, even here both interesting and practical variations in ceiling height can be planned for various areas. For example, the entrance and catalog keys clusters can have lowered ceilings and lighting that differs significantly from that in the general function cluster. Ceilings in conference and other areas can also be modified to provide a varied pattern.

Acoustical Treatment

The best acoustical treatment for an LMC facility comes from a combination of factors, including ceiling treatment, flooring, the heating-ventilating system used, and the size and general configuration of areas. It also helps to arrange book stacks, equipment, and furniture so that the number of students in any area is limited to between twenty-five and fifty.

Flooring

Carpeting is recommended as a suitable floor covering for the LMC. Although it is initially more expensive than tile, carpeting is much acclaimed as a surface that is both easier to maintain and longer wearing.

Architects and others frequently recommend varying the height of floors. Split-levels, depressions that form storytelling areas, or raised lounge areas visibly defined by three or four stairs are commonly employed. However, there are several reasons to avoid this variation in floor level: (1) some physically disabled children cannot readily negotiate flights of stairs or even one or two stairs — this is a consideration not to be taken lightly; and (2) changes in the organization of the facility are difficult to make if a permanent physical barrier has been incorporated. A balcony, whether it is for stack storage or for other student utilization purposes, presents the same problem. Although a ramp or an elevator might solve these problems, such solutions are often not considered during the planning stage.

Wall Treatment

The walls—now that they are no longer used primarily for book stacks— can provide special acoustical or visual effects. New and used brick, slump brick, tile blocks with various patterns formed by epoxy paints, paneling, laminated plastic papers, and paints in a variety of colors can be employed satisfactorily.

Internal environment planning should coordinate all factors: acoustics, climate control, flooring, ceilings, walls, and lighting. The interior decorator is frequently cited as a required member of the school design team. The LMC is a prime area for the creative talents of a gifted decorator.

Security

The amount and variety of valuable equipment as well as printed and other media have made LMCs the target of theft. The installation of an electronic control system at the service (circulation) area should be a prime consideration in the design of new facilities. Thereafter, unless attention has been given to this possibility during the planning stage, significant remodeling may be required to accommodate a system.

Since the theft of equipment is usually associated with "after hours" activity, provision should be made to control this problem. Guards, guard dogs, and lights have been tried by schools. Electronic monitoring systems can detect and report to a control center any intrusion into the LMC or school building.

LMC FURNITURE

Seating

The pattern established for student and teacher use of the LMC is based on an estimate of learning needs and is programmed in the educational specifications for the new school. Various estimates are available for the allocation of user space. In the 1960s, Ellsworth recommended that 60 percent of user space be reserved for study carrels, 15 percent for group study (conference) rooms, 8 percent for flat-top tables, and 17 percent for lounge furniture. The national guidelines recommended that 30 to 40 percent of seating be reserved for study carrels. The decision on how much space to allocate for types of seating will be made in the context of planning based on intended LMC program output.

Carrels

Study carrels are of two varieties, dry and wet. The dry carrel provides a visually private workspace for the individual, while the wet carrel adds at least an electrical outlet for use of audiovisual equipment. If carrels are to be purchased, they should be "wet." Many types are available commercially, others may be fabricated for use. For example, it is possible to modify existing, four-position tables for study carrel use. In any event, the following advice is worth heeding: unless the carrels are finished with a plastic laminate, the problems arising from student graffiti will be very trying.

Carrels should provide visual privacy. Although most commercially available carrels close the user in on three sides, it is desirable to leave one side open so that the individual does not feel closed in.

Workstations

Unless microcomputer activity is confined to the computer lab, the workstation may be substituted for carrels (workstations rather than flat tables may also be used in a lab). The workstation (see figure 6.11) will typically accommodate a microcomputer, with modem for remote access; a video display; a printer; and a work surface for writing. To conserve space, a shelf is used to stack components. The selection of workstations which provide for adjustable table and shelf height, plus the addition of a chair which is also adjustable in height, will usually satisfy ergonomic considerations. Electrical service for micro use and telephone lines (for remote access of databases) are a major concern. Noise may also become a significant factor.

Fig. 6.11. Workstation.

Carrels and workstations arranged in single or double rows along walls or partitions, facing in the same direction, can be used to advantage. At least four feet should be allowed from the front of one carrel to the front of the following one to provide for access to seating. They may be grouped in clusters (see figure 6.12).

It is not unusual to find in an LMC a casual corner for recreational reading, with lounge chairs and tables. Individual seating and two-seater lounge furniture with suitable tables and lamps can be used effectively. Lounge furniture that provides space for three persons is not recommended.

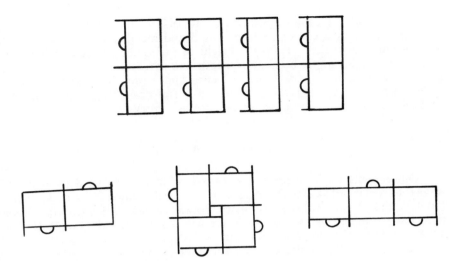

Fig. 6.12. Carrels/workstations.

Tables selected for the LMC should seat no more than four students. These tables may be round or rectangular in shape. If several tables are to be used, there should be a mixture of types. Elementary school level height of tables will vary from twenty-five to twenty-eight inches, junior high level from twenty-seven to thirty inches, and senior high level from twenty-nine to thirty inches. Tables may be all wood or a combination of metal and wood, or plastic. Table tops should be laminated plastic.

A highly recommended alternative to standard library tables, for conference rooms and other group activity spaces, is the trapezoid table. As shown in figure 6.13, trapezoid tables can be arranged in many ways.

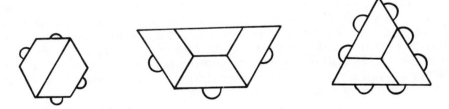

Fig. 6.13. Trapezoid tables.

Many kinds of chairs are available for use in the LMC—solid wood, molded plastic, or a combination of wood and metal, and with or without arms. Chair height depends on the height of the tables selected. Elementary level chair height ranges between fourteen and seventeen inches, junior high level between sixteen and eighteen inches and senior high level, eighteen inches. Chairs which may be adjusted to various heights are desirable for specialized uses such as microcomputer use at a workstation.

Other Furniture

Other items of furniture requiring attention are the card catalog and service (circulation) desk. The height of the card catalog does make a difference, since the general size of patrons is always a factor. Elementary schools must have a catalog that its patrons can reach. At the secondary level, there is a temptation to provide card catalog units with a counter height work surface above; this limits the catalog to a maximum height of about forty-two inches, and the user must constantly bend over to reach the drawers. Where technology has, or will, replace the card catalog (e.g., video terminals) attention must be given to furniture and space requirements in order to accommodate several users.

Many libraries have service (circulation) desks that are unnecessarily large. The circulation desk should be compact, made up of modular units that are joined together. At the elementary school level, desk height is suggested, while at the secondary level, the unit should be counter height.

In most school LMCs, the service (circulation) area is also used to store reserve media, so storage shelving is required. This is also a logical place to store portable equipment that is to be used in the LMC.

Storing Media

The concept of the LMC as a unified system implies an integrated collection of printed and audiovisual media. On the one hand are those who interpret this to mean merely providing access to printed and audiovisual media under one roof. The opposite interpretation of integrated collections attempts to place all media dealing with the same subject together on the shelves. In this plan, books, 8mm films, filmstrips, realia, and videocassettes are assigned to the same shelf location.

Neither of these approaches is completely satisfactory. Operationally, there is a great deal of evidence that effective service to users can be provided when the collections are divided on the basis of media format. This has been one of the principal, traditional methods—separate shelving for periodicals, books, microforms, and records. The second approach—shelving all media together—is philosophically in tune with the concept of the unity of knowledge. Practically speaking, it is also possible to shelve selected media forms together in one order (books, 8mm films, reel-to-reel tapes). For collections that are extremely modest in size and that are not expected to grow and expand, this may be desirable. Two factors are decidedly against this approach: first, shelving a substantial collection of media takes much more space than does separate shelving of audiovisual resources, for which compact storage is available; and second, media forms are incompatible in size and shape. Until it is somehow practical to store together all media, including study prints, art prints, transparencies, audio and video cassettes, and records, a partial attempt accomplishes very little.

The open-stack (direct-access) arrangement is the current pattern for the storage of books and other media in the school LMC. This means that users can go directly to the shelves or storage units for items needed. Usually, seating and work space are provided in direct proximity to stored media.

Books

Practices developed over a long period of time have created the book storage pattern in use today. Even though one cannot see authors' names, book titles, or colorful book jackets, and though there is the problem of books falling over, the existing pattern for shelving books has rarely been considered worth challenging. Only the physical storage of paperbacks has broken the pattern.

Shelving used in the LMC may be wood or metal. Wood has been the standard for open-stack collections, metal for closed stacks. In the past, wood was considered quality shelving, while metal was considered an inexpensive installation. Today, however, metal shelving has taken its place in open-stack collections on a par with wood because of the many styles available, the use of woodgrain end panels, and the variety of colors available.

All shelving purchased should be three feet on center and fully adjustable. It is suggested that consideration be given to purchasing from reputable companies that will continue to produce the specific type of shelving purchased for years to come. It is recommended that top and bottom shelves not be used initially, and that shelves be only two-thirds full. Shelving that is constructed with backs keeps books from slipping away. However, in situations where ranges of shelving are used it is preferable not to use backs, because they tend to visually close the space. Adjustable back stops can be used.

The height and depth of book shelving vary with the grade level of the school. It is suggested that shelving height for elementary schools be six feet. Though this is a foot higher than ordinarily recommended, the additional height is suggested here for two reasons: (1) the top shelf space can be used for display purposes, as long as the book collection remains modest in size; and (2) as the collection expands, this becomes the first line of defense. The first area for expansion becomes the top and bottom of shelving units. The recommended height for junior and senior high schools is seven feet.

Depth of shelving varies for different collections. For general nonfiction and fiction collections, the recommended depth of shelving is eight to ten inches. We suggest a nine-inch depth as a standard. For an oversized collection, ten to twelve inches is recommended. Reference book shelving should be twelve inches deep. Although shelving will be adjustable so that space between shelves can vary, recommended space between shelves is ten to twelve inches. In the elementary school, shelving for picture books should be forty-two to fifty inches high, and twelve inches deep. The space between shelves should be fourteen to sixteen inches. A special feature, and one very much needed, is the addition of upright partitions spaced every seven to eight inches in order to prevent these books from spilling over.

The pattern of shelving all books along perimeter walls is no longer accepted. Recommendations today call for free-standing, double-faced stacks in ranges. The suggested maximum length of a range is fifteen feet, although occasionally a length of eighteen feet can be tolerated. The walking space permitted between shelving is thirty-two to thirty-six inches. In a school situation, no less than thirty-six inches of space between ranges is suggested. If it is anticipated that there will be continued heavy traffic for specific types of books, such as reference or picture books, five to six feet between ranges would be needed. The needs of the physically handicapped are a continuing concern.

Counter height shelving (no less than forty-two inches high) is often used to create patterns of use in the LMC. Limited use of shelving of this height is suggested, because it is a nuisance for the user to stoop to read the shelves and to lift books placed at that level. A practical and beneficial trend is the practice of adding a unit of forty-two-inch-high shelving to the end of each range (see figure 6.14); the user can stand here and can comfortably review books selected before moving on to the seating area.

Fig. 6.14. Counter height shelving.

Estimates of book capacity for full three-foot units are: general fiction and nonfiction, thirty volumes; reference books, eighteen volumes; and picture books, sixty volumes. A common guide or estimate for general collections is 125 volumes per seven-foot-high section of six shelves.

Other media usually stored on shelves are record collections and periodicals. Periodicals are stored with covers showing, while record storage is similar to that of hardbound books. The rationale for these different approaches is obscure. The original assumption was that periodicals had colorful covers, record albums did not. For periodicals, there are two options. The first is standard periodical shelving, which is twelve inches deep and provides a sixteen-inch slant shelf. This arrangement can also provide storage capacity for several back issues beneath the shelf, which can be raised. Second is the free-standing periodical rack. Options are also available for records: (1) standard record shelving available at a depth of sixteen inches, or (2) the record bin. One must weight the relative advantages of each, such as the coordination of record and periodical shelving with book shelving (see figure 6.15).

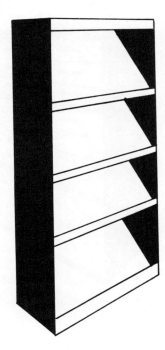

Fig. 6.15. Record and periodical storage.

Pamphlets and Transparencies

Vertical files can be used for both pamphlet materials and transparencies. Generally, legal-size metal files are used. These are available in a variety of colors and may be three or four drawers in height. They are arranged in banks, either free-standing or against a wall. Other types of storage are available for transparencies, but are not generally recommended.

Filmstrips and Films

These materials may be stored in many ways. The compactness of free-standing stacking units is recommended. Slotted units are preferred, so that cans may be moved in either direction to accommodate additional filmstrips. Filmstrips, audio cassettes, 8mm films, microfilm, and microfiche should be stored in free-standing stacking units as shown in figure 6.16. The units, which are available in metal and in a variety of colors, can be expanded.

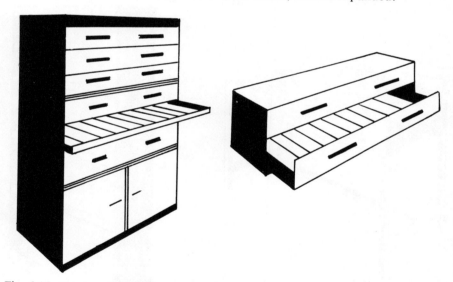

Fig. 6.16. Storage of filmstrips, audiotapes, 8mm films, and microforms.

If 16mm films are to be stored in the individual school LMC, either closed cabinet storage or open shelving may be used. Videotapes may be stored on standard shelving. Shelving of the twelve- to sixteen-inch deep variety should be available to store sound filmstrips and kits; slides (which may be stored in units as they would be used); models; dioramas; and miscellaneous, odd-sized media.

Manufacturers have endeavored to provide a way to store all media forms related to the same subject together in the LMC. Two approaches are being used. The first provides for shelving inserts to be used for various media forms. This method still separates media forms but allows them to be physically stored on shelves in the same general location. The second approach provides varied packaging alternatives for media forms, boxing them in a book format so that they can be shelved in a Dewey Decimal class. Adjustable shelving is supposed to provide for the accommodation of various sized packages to house media.

SUMMARY

- The library media specialist plays an important role in the planning of schools in general and of LMCs in particular. The development of educational specifications, also called a building program, provides the architect with a narrative outline of the educational program of the school and LMC that is then translated into a functionally and aesthetically designed building.

- Alternative concepts for LMC planning include a media system that is totally integrated with instructional spaces; a physically centralized facility which may be patterned in traditional fashion, with arrangement by media forms; a divisional or resource center approach, which groups all media related to the same subject; and a physically decentralized system, which endeavors to place satellites, or centers, in proximity to potential high-use areas within a single building or a group of buildings.

- The entire space requirement of the LMC may be viewed as encompassing two fairly distinct types of space: primary space, which includes functional areas for students, teachers, media, and services; and support space, used to provide the "backup" services that make the LMC function effectively and efficiently.

- The internal environment created for the LMC says a great deal about the philosophy of the school. The relationships of such factors as ceilings, flooring, walls, climate control, and acoustics should be considered.

- Furniture selected for the LMC should suit program requirements, with due consideration given to the utilization of technology and the needs of users.

ACTIVITIES

1. For a selected school, critique the design of the LMC.

2. Describe the roles of educators, architects, and others who would be involved in the design of LMC facilities.

3. Compare LMC facilities and furniture in a selected school to those in selected academic and public libraries.

4. Investigate state and local building codes and state department of education regulations or guidelines for the design of LMCs.

5. Investigate one or more of the following topics: (1) security systems, (2) lighting, (3) interior decorating, (4) environmental conditioning, or (5) ergonomics.

NOTES

[1]American Association of School Librarians and Association for Educational Communications and Technology, *Media Programs: District and School* (Chicago and Washington, D.C.: American Library Association and Association for Educational Communications and Technology, 1975), 95-103.

[2]*Webster's Third New International Dictionary* (Springfield, Mass.: G. & C. Merriam Co., 1986), 869.

[3]Ronald Gross and Judith Murphy, *Educational Change and Architectural Consequences* (New York: Educational Facilities Laboratories, 1968), 15.

[4]Ralph Ellsworth and Hobart Wagner, *The School Library: Facilities for Independent Study in Secondary Schools* (New York: Educational Facilities Laboratories, 1963), 52.

BIBLIOGRAPHY

American Association of School Librarians and Association for Educational Media and Technology. *Media Programs: District and School.* Chicago and Washington, D.C.: American Library Association and Association for Educational Communications and Technology, 1975.

Cohen, Aaron, and Elaine Cohen. *Automation Planning and Space Management: A Blueprint for Libraries.* New York: R. R. Bowker, 1981.

_____. *Designing and Space Planning for Libraries.* New York: R. R. Bowker, 1979.

_____. "Remodeling the Library." *School Library Journal* 24 (February 1978): 30-33.

Gross, Ronald, and Judith Murphy. *Educational Change and Architectural Consequences.* New York: Educational Facilities Laboratories, 1968.

Hannigan, Jane, and Glen Estes. *Media Center Facilities Design.* Chicago: American Library Association, 1979.

Knight, Nancy. "Library Security Systems Come of Age." *American Libraries* 9 (April 1978): 229-32.

Lushington, Nolan, and Willis Mills. *Libraries Designed for Users: A Planning Handbook.* Hamden, Conn.: Shoe String Press, 1979.

7

MEDIA AND EQUIPMENT

OBJECTIVES

Identify and describe the types of media and equipment suitable for use in the school.

Design an evaluation/selection process for a selected school LMC.

Design a technical services operation for a school district LMC.

The term *media* is used to encompass all forms (printed and audiovisual) and channels for the communication of information. In its broadest meaning, *media* also includes equipment.

Various terms have been used to describe mixed collections of informational and recreational resources which convey varied messages to users. Some of the terms used are:

1. *Print and nonprint materials.* The reverse of this could be audiovisual and nonaudiovisual, though some insist that the term audiovisual is sufficiently broad to include printed sources.

2. *Materials.* Used independently or with other terms for resources stored and distributed by libraries.

3. *Resources.* Used synonymously with *materials.*

4. *Carriers.* Used by Ellsworth to encompass all forms.[1]

5. *Media.* In *Webster's*, used as the plural of medium, meaning "through or by which something is accomplished, conveyed, or carried on."[2]

6. *Media.* In national guidelines "are all the forms and channels used in the transmittal process."[3]

MEDIA AND EQUIPMENT

The library media specialist coordinates the selection, acquisition, and organization of media at the school level. A parallel activity is the selection and acquisition of equipment. Representative quantities of media and equipment recommended by Ohio and Illinois are provided in figures 7.1 and 7.2.

LMC media resources will be of two types: primary and secondary. Primary source media consist of the record of events in original form, whereas secondary sources represent media developed from the primary sources. Examples of primary sources are original manuscripts or documents, taped interviews, on-the-scene filmed or videorecorded experiences, and specimens. Secondary sources are represented by a secondhand reporting of the original. Secondary sources form the major portion of school LMC collections.

Printed media are generally well known and are sometimes treated as a single medium because of the mode of presentation. The book, however, although it is a printed medium, appears in both hardbound and paperbound formats, which in the eyes of the user are quite dissimilar. Types of books that have unique qualities or purposes include bibliographies, reference sources, general fiction and nonfiction of the trade book variety, and textbooks (which do have a place in LMC collections). A book may contain many of the elements usually classified as audiovisual: opaque pictures of many types, transparent overlays, graphs, diagrams, charts, cartoons, comics, maps, and programmed material. Books may be used in a cross-media approach with records, tapes, and other media in an instructional system.

Magazines and newspapers record information considered not stable enough to be formally incorporated in book form. As carriers of new information, they can play a vital role in the LMC collection. Used in conjunction with the basic indexes available, they are a principal vehicle for use in student investigative experiences. Pamphlets, government documents, and ephemera provide a way to expand the range of experience through the printed word.

The use of audiovisual media in the LMC presents a variety of problems. Equipment for the LMC should differ from models designed for classroom use. An effort should be made to provide the user with the most effective use of the medium under difficult physical conditions (such as lighting), while at the same time providing minimal distraction to others. Some equipment is appropriately designed for the LMC. Most is not. However, portable equipment purchased for general use in the school can be modified for use in the LMC.

(Text continues on page 179.)

	Phase I	Phase II	Phase III
Books	Elem. – 2,500 to 6,000 volumes or 12 per pupil. Sec. – 8,000 to 10,000 volumes or 18 per pupil.	Elem. – 4,000 to 8,000 volumes or 15 per pupil. Sec. – 10,000 to 15,000 or 20 per pupil.	Elem. – 8,000 to 10,000 volumes representing 8,000 titles or 22 books per pupil. Sec. – 15,000 to 20,000 volumes or 25 per pupil.
Magazines	Elem. – 15-24 titles. Sec. (JHS or MS) – 75-85 titles. Sec. (HS) – 100-125 titles.	Elem. – 25-39 titles. Sec. (JHS or MS) – 85-100 titles. Sec. (HS) – 125-150 titles.	Elem. – 40-50 titles. Sec. (JHS or MS) – 100-120 titles. Sec. (HS) – 150-175 titles.
Audio Recordings (disc and tape)	600 or 2 per pupil.	800 or 4 per pupil.	1,000 or 4 per pupil.
Sound Filmstrips, Filmstrips, Slides, Sound Slides, and Transparencies	500 or 1 per pupil.	750-1,000 or 2 per pupil.	1,000-1,500 or 3 per pupil.
Microcomputer Software, Instructional Films, Video Programs, and Microforms	The collection should be of sufficient quantity to meet curricular needs. Districts may share among school collections, district collections, or with some other centralized service. Multimedia kits and collections should reflect staff and student needs respecting learning/teaching styles.		
Projectors, Slide (2 x 2)	1 per 5 teaching stations plus 2 per media center.	1 per 4 teaching stations plus 3 per media center.	1 per 3 teaching stations plus 4 per media center.
Viewers, Filmstrip (silent and sound)	1 per teaching station plus 5 per media center.	2 per teaching station plus 10 per media center.	2 per teaching station plus 15 per media center.
Viewers, Slide (2 x 2)	1 per 5 teaching stations plus 1 per media center.	1 per 3 teaching stations plus 1 per media center.	2 per teaching station plus 1 per media center.

Projectors, Filmstrip (at least one with sound)	1 per 5 teaching stations plus 1 per media center.	1 per 4 teaching stations plus 2 per media center.	1 per 2 teaching stations plus 4 per media center.
Projectors, Opaque	1 per media center.	2 per media center.	4 per media center.
Projectors, Overhead (10 x 10)	1 per 2 teaching stations plus 2 per media center.	1 per teaching station plus 2 per media center.	1 per teaching station plus 2 per media center.
16mm Projectors	Elem.–1 per 10 teaching stations plus 1 per media center. Sec.–Same, except plus 2 per media center.	Elem.–1 per 6 teaching stations plus 1 per media center. Sec.–Same, except plus 2 per media center.	Elem.–1 per 4 teaching stations plus 1 per media center. Sec.–Same, except plus 2 per media center.
Projectors, 8mm (reel to reel, loop cartridge, magazine, etc.)	1 per 4 teaching stations plus 2 per media center.	1 per 3 teaching stations plus 3 per media center.	1 per 2 teaching stations plus 5 per media center.
Record Players (w/ ear phones)	Elem.–1 per teaching station. Sec.–1 per 15 teaching stations plus 2 per media center.	Elem.–1 per teaching station. Sec.–1 per 10 teaching stations plus 5 per media center.	Elem.–1 per teaching station. Sec.–1 per 5 teaching stations plus 10 per media center.
Tape Players and/or Recorders	Elem.–1 per teaching station. Sec.–1 per 15 teaching stations plus 2 per media center.	Elem.–1 per teaching station. Sec.–1 per 10 teaching stations plus 5 per media center.	Elem.–1 per teaching station. Sec.–1 per 5 teaching stations plus 10 per media center.
Video Recorders with Monitors	Elem.–1 per floor. Sec.–1 per 15 teaching stations.	Elem.–2 per floor. Sec.–1 per 10 teaching stations.	Elem.–1 per 2 teaching stations or 2 per floor. Sec.–1 per 2 teaching stations.
Microcomputers	1 per grade level plus 1 per media center.	1 per teaching station plus 1 per grade level plus 2 per media center.	2 per teaching station plus 1 per grade level plus 3 per media center.

Fig. 7.1. Ohio standards for media and equipment. From *Quality Library Services K-12* (Columbus, Ohio: Department of Education, 1986). Reprinted with permission of the Ohio State Board of Education.

	Phase I	Phase II	Phase III
Books K-12	Basic collection selected from standard book reviewing and selection aids.		
	3,000 titles or 10 volumes per pupil, whichever is greater.	5,000 titles or 15 volumes per pupil, whichever is greater.	6,000 to 10,000 titles representing 10,000 volumes, or 20 volumes per pupil, whichever is greater.
Periodicals			
K-6	6-8 titles.	9-12 titles.	13-40 titles.
7-8	12-15 titles.	16-25 titles.	26-50 titles.
9-12	25-40 titles.	41-60 titles.	61-125 titles.
K-12	Necessary magazine indices and duplication of titles as required for research and instruction.		
Recorded and Graphic Materials.	Filmstrips, film (8mm, super 8mm, and 16mm), audio recordings—tape and disc, videotape—tape and disc recordings, slides, transparencies.		
K-8	3,000 titles.	5,000 titles.	7,000 titles.
9-12	Access to sufficient duplicate items to insure satisfaction of 90% of initial requests.		
Sound Filmstrip Projector			
K-12	1 per 12 teaching stations plus 1 per library media center.	1 per 8 teaching stations plus 2 per library media center.	1 per 4 teaching stations plus 2 per library media center.
9-12	2 per library media center.	1 per 10 teaching stations plus 3 per library media center.	1 per 5 teaching stations plus 3 per library media center.
Overhead Projector			
K-12	1 per 5 teaching stations plus 2 per library media center.	1 per 3 teaching stations plus 2 per library media center.	1 per teaching station plus 2 per library media center.
Opaque Projector			
K-12	1 per floor level.	1 per floor level plus 2 per library media center.	1 per floor level plus 3 per library media center.

Equipment			
Filmstrip Viewer with Sound Capability K-12	2 per library media center.	4 per library media center.	6 per library media center plus additional units as needed.
2 x 2 Slide Viewer/Projector with Sound Capability K-12	1 per library media center.	2 per library media center.	4 per library media center plus additional units as needed and slide sorter light table.
16mm Sound Projector K-12	1 per 12 teaching stations plus 1 per library media center. 1 per floor in multistory buildings.	1 per 8 teaching stations plus 2 per library media center.	1 per 4 teaching stations plus 3 per library media center.
8mm or Super 8 Projector K-8	1 per library media center.	2 per library media center.	1 per 10 teaching stations plus 2 per library media center.
9-12	2 per library media center.	1 per 10 teaching stations plus 2 per library media center.	1 per 8 teaching stations plus 2 per library media center.
Variable Speed Record Player K-6	1 per 5 teaching stations plus 1 per library media center.	1 per 3 teaching stations plus 2 per library media center.	1 per 2 teaching stations plus 3 per library media center.
7-12	1 per 12 teaching stations plus 2 per library media center.	1 per 8 teaching stations plus 2 per library media center.	1 per 4 teaching stations plus 2 per library media center.
All Schools	1 set of earphones per player.	1 set of earphones per player.	1 set of earphones per player plus portable listening stations as needed.

(Fig. 7.2 continues on page 178.)

Fig. 7.2. — Continued

	Phase I	Phase II	Phase III
Audio Tape Recorder/Player			
K-6	1 per 5 teaching stations plus 3 per library media center.	1 per 3 teaching stations plus 3 per library media center.	1 per 2 teaching stations plus 3 per library media center.
7-12	1 per 10 teaching stations plus 3 per library media center.	1 per 8 teaching stations plus 3 per library media center.	1 per 4 teaching stations plus 3 per library media center.
All Schools	1 reel-to-reel per school plus appropriate accessories.		
Mobile VTR System (with Deck, Monitor)			
K-12	1 per library media center.	2 per library media center plus additional receivers for off-air teaching station use.	3 per library media center plus additional units as needed.
	Take into consideration program availability based on scheduling, off-air recording, playback equipment, and prerecorded materials.		
VTR Camera			
K-12		1 per building.	1 per building.
Cable Television	Minimum – 1 cable drop per building as available plus appropriate hardware.		
Computer Terminal and/or Microcomputers	Sufficient quantity to meet the needs of the curriculum. Minimum – 1 per building and 1 per library media center.		

Fig. 7.2. Illinois standards for media and equipment. From *Recommended Standards for Educational Library Media Programs* (Springfield, Ill.: State Board of Education, 1986). Reprinted by permission.

Types of Media and Equipment

Still Pictures

Two types of still pictures are available for use in the schools: opaque and transparent. Opaque media such as art prints, study prints, posters, and book illustrations can be used in the original form or modified by means of an opaque projection device. The term *transparent media* refers to a group of visual media whose image is viewed when light is passed through them. Included here are filmstrips; the photographic slide (usually a 2-by-2-inch mounted piece of film); the microscope slide, which has the potential for use with a microscope or as a projected medium; microfilm (reel-to-reel) and microfiche, which are photographs in miniature form; and transparencies.

Devices for the projection of still media include filmstrip projectors, slide projectors, and overhead and opaque projectors. With the exception of the opaque projector, which requires almost total darkness, these devices can be used in an LMC where the light can be somewhat controlled. Filmstrip, slide, and overhead projectors can be used in seminar or conference rooms using either a screen or a light-colored wall as a projection surface. If the overhead lighting in the general-function area of the LMC can be controlled, then these devices can also be projected on a wall-mounted screen or suitable wall space in that area. Transparencies may also be viewed by using a light box similar to a slide sorter or by simply placing a sheet of plain white paper behind the transparency as a background.

Use of standard filmstrip and slide projectors can be modified in several ways. They can be used in a study carrel, with the image projected through a rear screen device (which may be built-in or portable), or by direct projection against the rear or side of a carrel. If there are no carrels, the projectors can simply be used on a flat table surface and shown on either a portable desk top screen or a rear screen unit. Devices whose principal viewing method is rear screen projection are recommended for LMC use. These models offer considerable flexibility; they can be used by individuals and small groups in a variety of locations in the LMC. Figure 7.3 illustrates front and rear screen equipment for the projection of still media.

Fig. 7.3. Devices for the projection of still media.

Microfilm and microfiche also fit the still picture category. They are the microforms that have been used most often in the LMC for the storage of newspapers and periodicals. Simple readers enable the viewer to read and take notes, while the reader-printer also prints "hard copy," which may be taken away for further study (see figure 7.4).

Fig. 7.4. Microfilm/microfiche equipment.

Motion Pictures

Sound film in an 8mm or 16mm format provides many benefits in the teaching-learning situation. Sound and light control are factors that require attention in the LMC. Conference or seminar rooms, where available, can be adapted for use if a wall-mounted screen or light-colored wall can be used as a projection surface. Portable rear screen units and headphones provide additional ways of modifying projector use. Rear screen units, whose sound is controlled by the use of headsets, are recommended for the LMC. Figure 7.5 illustrates front and rear screen equipment for motion projection.

Fig. 7.5. Motion picture projection equipment.

Audio

Audio media include records, tapes, and compact disks. Record players and tape recorders are used throughout the school, and they may be used successfully with headphones in an LMC. Two types of tape recorders are available—reel-to-reel and cassette. Although most schools have moved to the cassette format as a matter of convenience, reel-to-reel continues to be popular for production activities. The newest format, compact disks and their players, are becoming more common and are to be preferred over other recordings because of their quality of sound and more permanent nature of the disks.

A cross-media approach, combining visual and auditory material, is common in schools today. Equipment is available for either standard projection or rear screen use with headphones to control sound. Figure 7.6 illustrates audio and cross-media equipment.

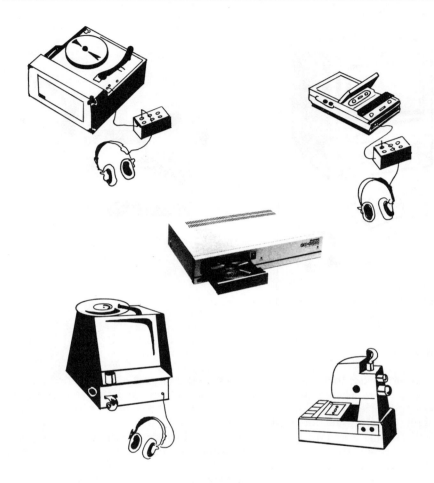

Fig. 7.6. Audio and cross-media equipment.

Television

This medium fits both motion picture and cross-media categories. It is the ultimate synthesizer of multiple uses of media. Television is used in a passive learning mode through the use of videocassettes as well as remote access public/cable/instructional television. In an active mode, it is used as a primary production medium associated with classroom and school activities. It is also used in an interactive mode in what is termed *long distance learning*. Figure 7.7 illustrates television equipment.

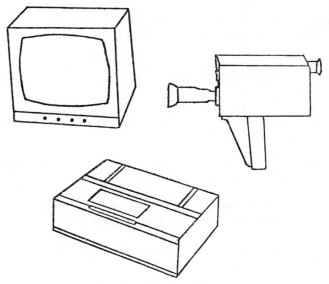

Fig. 7.7. Camera, recorder, and monitor.

Microcomputers

The microcomputer is a fairly recent but highly significant technology in the nation's schools. In a few short years it has been elevated in stature to join the 3 Rs as a staple of the curriculum. Figure 7.8 is a picture of a microcomputer.

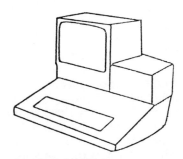

Fig. 7.8. Microcomputer.

In the LMC, management can be facilitated through the use of appropriate word processing and spreadsheet software. The microcomputer is also applied to the intended achievements of the LMC:

- *Guidance and Consulting* — Information retrieval online from remote databases. New CD-ROM technology is now returning the database to an on-site location.

- *Instruction and In-Service* — Directed instruction and in-service related to microcomputer applications.

- *Design and Production* — The production of software programs or modification of existing programs.

- *Curriculum Development* — Applications to various subject areas as well as assistance in computer science instruction.

Other forms typically associated with, or described as, audiovisual in nature are discussed below.

Field Experience

Educators have always desired to expose the learner to all of the universe through lifelike experiences, but the obstacles to this goal are obvious. The field trip is an attempt to provide firsthand experience of one aspect of life. From the kindergarten trip to the post office and fire station, through visits to museums, aquariums, and observatories, to the summer trip to Europe and the planned year of study abroad, the school has tried to capture the essence of the world for the learner. While no recommendation is made here that the LMC staff begin conducting world tours, a file of potential field experiences can be maintained.

Graphics

Used in the context of the school media program, graphics refer to a variety of visual forms including graphs, diagrams, charts, posters, cartoons, and comics. Occasionally graphics are described as nonpictorial, in an attempt to differentiate between the still picture and graphics. They can be used in numerous ways, either in the original or as projected media. Maps and globes are technically also graphics, though they are usually treated separately. Globes are spherical models of the earth, and three principal types are generally found in schools: political, physical political, and slated-outline globes. Maps are flat representations of the earth's surface, and again, three principal types are found in the school: physical, political, and special purpose.

Instructional Kits

A kit may include any number of related media geared to a particular subject. Kits, which in some school districts may be boxed for distribution, may incorporate filmstrips, records, audio- and videotapes, 16mm films, three-dimensional media, books, pamphlets, and teacher guides. Instructional kits are available commercially or may be developed in the schools.

Realia

The medium of animate or inanimate real things covers a wide field. *Realia* usually refers to objects and specimens that can be gathered through extensive field experiences. An object is a real thing, as is the specimen. They differ in that the specimen is representative of a class of like objects. Gerbils, baby chicks, and "resource people" who make themselves available to the school may also be classed as realia.

Three-Dimensional Media

In the absence of the real thing or experience, the LMC can provide three-dimensional representations of the real: models, mockups, and dioramas. Models provide a visual and manipulative experience for students. A model of a space capsule, an ear, or a human torso (capable of being disassembled and reassembled) can provide the student with the opportunity for a realistic appraisal of things as they are. Mockups are usually operating, full-scale models developed for specific training purposes or analysis; a school does not necessarily need a full-scale mockup. Dioramas are miniaturized scenes in-depth that incorporate a group of modeled objects and figures.

Media Production

Media most frequently cited for local production include graphics, transparencies, slides, and tapes (audio and video). Equipment available for production is of two types: portable, which can be taken into the field (including still and motion cameras, audio and video); and fixed position equipment (dry mount press, copystands, duplicating machines).

BUILDING MEDIA COLLECTIONS

Media Collections in the New School

Collection building for a new school should begin a year in advance of a school opening. A minimal initial collection of at least one-third of the total potential collection should be available. Although it is fairly common practice to purchase preselected, "opening day" collections, no generalized collection can fully suit the needs of a specific school. Each school develops a personality of its own based on the community, types of students, faculty, educational methodology, and so on. Therefore, the packaged collection should be combined with other carefully screen selections.

The media collection should begin with as comprehensive a reference collection as is possible with the funds available. Collection building begins with such traditional media as dictionaries, encyclopedias, almanacs, and other general purpose reference tools. The one possible exception to this guideline would be in the building of collections for K-4 elementary schools, where reference sources suited to the needs of these children are less plentiful. The fact remains, however, that an LMC designed to serve both students and teachers should concentrate on reference sources first.

If funds are adequate, the selection of reference tools should be coupled with the purchase of media needed by teachers in instructional situations. These are parallel directions. Maps, globes, transparencies, and other media are vital to teachers if they are to do even a minimal job of teaching.

Beyond these two basic areas, selection should proceed to develop collection strength in scope and depth. A focus on the curriculum should lead naturally to a concentration of effort, subject by subject, to bring together media best suited to teaching and learning. In most subject areas, both print and audiovisual media for individual student use are available on two or more levels of difficulty. This means that the initial purchase of reading matter about any subject should include not merely one title, but perhaps three titles, written at three levels of reading difficulty. This approach provides for the needs of students at three different levels of reading ability. It also allows for a natural progression in students' understanding, because they can begin reading books that provide information with a minimal challenge in terms of vocabulary and comprehension, then move to more difficult work as the need arises. Coupled with this approach is a specific need for more multiple-copy purchasing than has generally been the case in school LMCs. Items of proven value should be purchased in multiple copies. This approach is preferable to simply expanding the scope of the collection by purchasing single copies of media that may or may not be used. A rule of thumb used for reserve collections in college libraries is one copy for fifteen students. It would not be unreasonable for the LMC to provide one copy of a particularly valuable or popular item for every ten to fifteen students needing such information.

Collection building beyond the initial stages calls for a continuing assessment of student and teacher needs in relation to curriculum, existing collections, and market availability. It is therefore desirable to focus on a given subject and search for those media that make a definite contribution to the area. Each medium has a unique set of attributes that determine its appropriateness to the task at hand. A degree of both qualitative and quantitative control can be added to the analysis and evaluation of collections through the use of standard retrospective selection tools.

School Closings

In some areas of the country, school and LMC closings, rather than openings, have become the prevailing pattern due to a decreasing student population. Rather than developing educational specifications for new schools and acquiring media, equipment, and furniture, this situation has resulted in the development of plans to redistribute resources in a manner that is both equitable and geared to improving the effectiveness of existing school LMCs.

Most schools can readily use additional resources. However, school and LMC closings can present difficult problems. The size of the school district and its organizational structure, a knowledge of enrollment projections for schools remaining open, and plans for future retrenchment are factors that will influence decision making.

Decisions relative to the distribution of resources should be made at the district level, with appropriate input from school LMC personnel. Inventory control of all school resources at this level can facilitate the process, since information on the status of each school LMC—media, equipment, furniture—will be readily available.

Although media, equipment, and furniture may be treated as separate elements, their relationship must be considered in any distribution plan. Also, a plan should consider the needs of school LMCs, in relation to program, as well as the need to update equipment and furniture in existing schools. Options exercised in the distribution process include assigning the bulk of all resources to the "poorest" LMCs, assigning an equal share to all LMCs, and assigning resources based on LMC proposals indicating need and potential utilization. Although the last approach has merit, the tendency is toward "sharing the wealth" and avoiding conflict.

Balance in the Collection

The LMC collection may be considered "balanced" if it is sufficiently broad to meet the basic informational and recreational needs of students and teachers, and sufficiently specific in content and media forms to meet the direct instructional needs of the school with due consideration for the age-grade-ability levels of students.

Resource Sharing

The concept of resource sharing is both very old and very new. It is viewed as a means of reducing or containing expenditures for media, as a means of locating and accessing information needed by users, and as a means of cooperatively expanding and accessing the resources of a region through various collection development and technological network schemes.

As a major goal of the profession in the 1980s, resource sharing focuses on a user's right of access to media, wherever they may be located. The goal is moderated by a recognition of the right of certain types of organizations not to make their holdings generally available to the public because of the nature of their collections.

Resource sharing is not new to school LMCs; the process of exchanging needed materials has been going on for years. In some areas, district LMCs were established to facilitate exchange and to create shared resources such as professional collections, film libraries, and other special collections for distribution to schools as needed. The questions remaining for the 1980s is, "To what extent will school LMCs and districts become involved in single or multi-type cooperatives and utilize technological networks to extend their capabilities?"

SELECTION

The key to developing media collections is the ability to translate knowledge about school needs into action through an evaluation, selection, acquisitions, and organizational process. The library media specialist should be aware of:

1. The curriculum of the school and district.

2. Innovative practices in various subject fields (content and methods).

3. The marketplace.

4. Technology available and suitable for use with audiovisual media.

5. The abilities and interests of students.

6. The needs of teachers.

7. Technical services practices including centralized and commercial processing and network potential.

8. Media selection policy, procedures, and criteria for selection.

9. Fiscal policies and budget allocations.

Media Policy

Written policies and procedures should be developed by representatives of the LMC staff, teaching staff, administrators, school board members, student representatives, and community representatives. It should become an official board of education policy. The purpose of the written policy is to state what the school and district will do in this field. A typical policy statement will:

1. Be compatible with the philosophy of education for the school and district.

2. Recognize nationally stated objectives for media selection, such as the *School Library Bill of Rights for School Library Media Center Programs* (see appendix F).

3. Recognize published guidelines dealing with copyright law (see appendix G).

4. Recognize specific community and student needs.

5. Recognize the right of individuals and groups, both within and outside of the school organization, to question and challenge media policies, procedures, and specific items selected for inclusion in the collections of the schools. Usually this right is recognized and specific procedures for filtering questions and challenges are established.

6. Include both the philosophy and the criteria used for the selection of media.

The media policy provides a blueprint for action in the schools. It provides LMC personnel with needed information on the why, how, and for whom of selecting. For others involved in the selection process, it provides a clearer understanding of the relationship of parties as well as definitive guidelines for involvement.

Who Selects and Why

Selection is a multifaceted operation that should involve many people at many different levels.

LMC Professionals

Responsibility for selection and the leadership role in selection must be assumed by the library media specialist, who is uniquely qualified by training and experience and by involvement in the school curriculum to coordinate this activity. The process involves relating a knowledge of school needs to a knowledge of existing media collections and the availability of media on the market.

A primary responsibility of the LMC professional is to create a balance in expenditures for various subjects in various media forms. Related to this responsibility might be that of deciding to add a new medium to the collection. Such judgments must include consideration of financing, space, equipment, and projected scope and depth of collections.

Teachers

Teachers should be included in the media selection process. They are generally knowledgeable about the content of their fields, they should know their students' capabilities, and they are primarily responsible for programming student activities in the school. Also, teachers will tend to use, and assign students to use, media with which they are familiar. It is reasonable, then, that they should share a degree of responsibility for selection.

Students

Students can be involved in the selection process in a variety of ways. Since one function of the LMC program is to provide for the personal needs of students, there should be considerable student participation both through individual recommendation and through a group structure. If time permits and media are available for preview purposes, actual try-outs in a teaching-learning situation can be most helpful in making selections.

Parent and Community Groups

Broad moves have been made in major cities to decentralize school districts in order to make boards of education more responsive to community needs. Community school advisory councils have sprung up, which have wide interests and powers. Nationwide, parents and communities have reacted to educational programs dealing with sex education, drug abuse, and other social concerns. It would appear that a meaningful dialog should be created with parents and the community relative to the most precious commodity of the community—its children.

Other Specialists

It is desirable to include in the selection process such specialists as school administrators, district coordinators, and supervisors. University and college personnel and private citizens whose experience may go somewhat beyond the ordinary may be consulted as needed. Their best contributions might be made in the context of curriculum development as consultants or reactors. Whether to include parent and community groups and other specialists should be spelled out in policy.

Organizing for Selection

The library media specialist can facilitate the evaluation-selection process by structuring committee activities. Selectors should be provided information about policy and procedures, reviewing sources, criteria for evaluation, and the availability of funds. At least one in-service meeting should be devoted to clarifying roles and procedures. On a continuing basis, committees should be given an overview of various fields or areas of interest through bibliographies and other means.

Using a secondary school as an example and given an LMC professional staff of four, each professional should be assigned to work with specific instructional departments in regard to selection and other purposes, such as curriculum implementation. A reasonable structure would include selection committees of teachers based on departmental lines, with representation from the LMC staff. This would provide for both horizontal (grade level) and vertical (within the subject) considerations. The LMC staff would have two functions: working with established teacher and student committees in evaluation, and working to gather reviewing sources and media for consideration by the selection committees. The final review of selections made by committees may be done by the LMC staff as a committee, or a formal coordinating committee may perform that function. The coordinating committee, through the LMC, would be responsible for advising the selection committees of purchases to be made.

The basic structural difference in an elementary school is that there would be an option to have grade level or subject area committees. Most elementary schools are still organized along traditional grade level lines. Many also have grade level chairs or coordinators. In this case, it would be advantageous to organize along grade level lines and leave vertical articulation in the subject areas to a coordinating committee. If a nongraded program has been established for the school, it would be advisable to organize along subject area lines in a manner similar to the secondary school model.

District-Level Coordination

In school systems that have a district LMC, one component of the district program may be a department devoted to the preview, evaluation, and selection of media. A highly structured program would have carefully detailed policies and procedures for selection and a firm organizational plan for committee work, culminating in the selection of a comprehensive list of media suitable for purchase in the schools. Figure 7.9 details the functions of a coordinating committee, media staff, and selection committees.

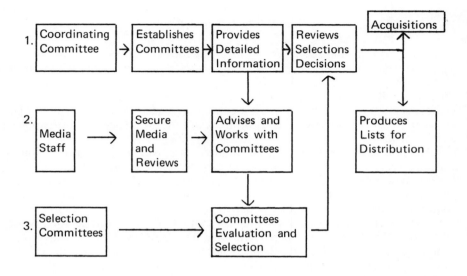

Fig. 7.9. Evaluation and selection process.

Direct Evaluation

In most schools or districts, selectors rely heavily on reviewing tools (where available) in making their decisions. However, direct, critical evaluation is desirable because many of the media produced are not adequately reviewed, not reviewed at all, or reviewed late. Equipment should be subject to direct evaluation.

Criteria for Selection

Criteria established for the direct evaluation of media should be compatible with and part of the media selection policy of the district. Prior to the initiation of direct evaluation, both the policy statement and criteria should be reviewed. If the ground rules are clearly understood, evaluation and selection can proceed in an orderly fashion with a minimum loss of time.

Although one can expect to find variations in criteria when moving from one medium to another, essentially the same broad criteria can be applied to all media. Any medium that is put to the test must be subject to scrutiny based on the following criteria:

1. *Authenticity:* Is the medium accurate and up-to-date? What are the qualifications of the author or producer?

2. *Appropriateness:* Is the medium appropriate to the subject matter? Are the vocabulary, content, concepts, and theme suited to the intended audience?

3. *Content:* Does the medium have an organized, well-balanced presentation? Does it relate to the needs of students? Does it provide outlines, charts, graphs, etc., that will be helpful to the user?

4. *Interest:* Will the message contained in this medium hold the attention of the user? Is it stimulating? Imaginative?

5. *Technical Quality:* Is the quality of production adequate — format, audio and visual qualities, ease of handling, and use of color?

A variety of evaluation forms are in use today; some are extremely comprehensive and others require only that the evaluator indicate purchase or no purchase. Somewhere between these two, a relatively simple, multipurpose form can provide the reviewer with enough information to make a valid judgment. (Figure 7.10 is a generalized data-gathering tool.) Forms should be accompanied by a direction sheet that includes an explanation of the criteria to be used in the evaluation process. A media profile is suggested rather than a grading score (excellent, average, poor) because a charting scheme has a higher visual effect on the reviewer. Comments are placed on the back of the form. Although written comments are extremely valuable to the reviewer, they have a way of crowding out other information.

```
┌─────────────────────────────────────────────────────────────────────┐
│  Type of Media _____  Subject Area(s) _____   │
│                                                                       │
│  Author or Producer _____  Grade Range: K-3, 4-6, 7-9, 10-12 │
│                                                                       │
│  Title  _____  Purchase: Yes__ No__ Hold __ │
│  = = = = = = = = = = = = = = = = = = = = = = = = = = = = = =          │
│                                                                       │
│  Media Profile—Grade on a scale of 1 to 5. One is poor, five is excellent. │
│                                                                       │
│      Authenticity          1   2   3   4   5                          │
│      Appropriateness       1   2   3   4   5                          │
│      Content               1   2   3   4   5                          │
│      Technical Quality     1   2   3   4,  5                          │
│      Interest              1   2   3   4   5                          │
│                                                                       │
│  = = = = = = = = = = = = = = = = = = = = = = = = = = = = = = = =      │
│                                                                       │
│  Comments—Please add on back of form.                                 │
│                                                                       │
│  Evaluator _____  School _____  Date _____          │
└─────────────────────────────────────────────────────────────────────┘
```

Fig. 7.10. Media evaluation form.

Both staff and students should participate in the selection of equipment. Those who are to use the equipment should have an opportunity to evaluate it in the teaching-learning situation. It also makes sense to include them in the establishment of policy and procedures for selecting equipment, the development of criteria to be used for various purposes in the school, and the evaluation process.

In the small school, the media selection committee may adequately serve this purpose. If specialized devices are to be evaluated, it may be desirable to bring in expert assistance. As with any selection process, the basic question is, "What purpose is this device to serve?"

If the district director coordinates a total program, there should be a district equipment selection committee composed of teachers in the field, administrators, and library media specialists. However, the availability of a district committee in no way diminishes the necessity for individual school action. In order to achieve the best results for a school, the school LMC staff must be actively involved in the system, with an interlocking relationship between school and district. The individual school media and equipment committee should be the representatives to a districtwide committee.

General criteria can be applied to the equipment used in the schools and the LMC system. Any consideration of equipment should begin with the question of purpose. Beyond purpose, the following criteria apply:

1. Is the device portable?

    Compact
    Lightweight

2. Is the device sturdy and reasonably attractive in design?

    Constructed of durable material
    Free of imperfections

3. Is it easy to operate?

    Controls accessible and clearly marked
    Few control mechanisms

4. Does the device meet performance standards?

    Does what the manufacturer claims
    Does what it is supposed to do well
    Meets school use requirements

5. Is the device easy to maintain and repair?

    Minor repairs simple, quickly effected
    Parts requiring cleaning easily accessible
    Parts can be replaced

6. Are the manufacturer and distributor reliable?

   Will the manufacturer continue this equipment line?
   Parts available when needed
   Types of services available on manufacturer and distributor
   agreements

7. What are the costs for comparable equipment?

8. Is there a model available from the manufacturer which is designed
   for individual use?

9. What modifications of the typical portable device can be made?

Equipment should be subjected to rigorous evaluation. It is always help-ful to consult published evaluations of equipment, such as those found in the American Library Association's *Library Technology Reports.*[4] It is also desirable to consult with other LMC personnel about the equipment they use, so as to gain their opinions about satisfactory and unsatisfactory performance records. Many do keep maintenance and repair records, which can be valuable.

Evaluation should include a demonstration of competitive equipment under identical conditions. If possible, there should be extensive try-out periods under varying conditions by LMC personnel, teachers, and students. These same individuals should be requested to use the directions provided with equipment to check on clarity and ease of operation. A technician, or someone who performs that function, should also go through the motions ordinarily employed in the in-school or district repair and maintenance of equipment.

A school or district will ordinarily try to standardize equipment—pur-chase the same make and model of a device from a particular manufacturer. This avoids some of the problems of training teachers and students to use different types of equipment. Maintenance and repair costs may also be signif-icantly reduced.

TECHNICAL SERVICES

It is usual for the user of a school LMC to want immediate access to any item in the collection, to items to be purchased, as well as to items to be obtained through interlibrary loan. Although this is impractical, every effort should be made to satisfy a need as expeditiously as possible.

Technical services housed within the school LMC will include such typical functions as acquisitions, preparation and organization, circulation/distri-bution, and the maintenance of media and equipment. Assuming as a primary goal the interaction of users with the LMC, wherever possible, responsibility for many technical services functions should be shifted to another unit of the system, such as a district LMC, a cooperative, commercial vendors, or some appropriate combination of these. The operation should be refined so that only in-house circulation/distribution continues to be a principal concern of technical services in the school LMC.

Acquisitions

The goal in acquisitions is to obtain what is needed, in as brief a period of time as possible, and in ready-to-use form. If possible, along with evaluation/selection activities, acquisitions should be handled at a district level.

To function effectively, the library media specialist should be familiar with the district fiscal year, the purchasing period allowed under existing regulations, standard requisition and purchase order forms and procedures, and bidding and contract regulations. Orders for new media and equipment should be placed as expeditiously as possible, with 60 to 75 percent of funds expended initially and the remainder held for special order needs. If the process of selecting media is an orderly, on-going activity that is an outgrowth of comprehensive planning, the LMC will have an already evaluated and approved "consider for purchase" file of equipment and media available at all times.

Preparation and Organization

Preparation and organization follow acquisitions; these are those processes associated with the physical preparation of media and the cataloging and classification activities. Because these activities can require a significant amount of time, this effort should be coordinated at a district level and, to the extent possible, handled by either a district or regional processing center or through commercial vendors. Since cost-effectiveness is an important concern, careful analysis and planning would be required before initiating district-level technical services.

Circulation/Distribution

All media forms and equipment eventually end up as part of the organized resources of the LMC, being processed to the point of storage. The circulation/distribution procedure begins when media must be retrieved for use (see figure 7.11).

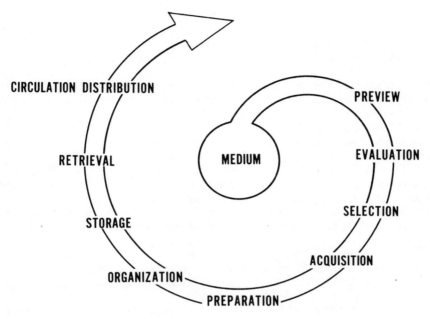

Fig. 7.11. Media cycle.

The term *circulation/distribution* describes two functions coordinated at a single LMC workstation. In the past, where separate library and audiovisual services were provided in a school, these functions were separate and distinct. In a school library, circulation generally implied active participation by a patron:

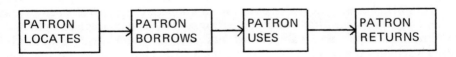

On the other hand, distribution, as an audiovisual concept, implied an active service function by staff:

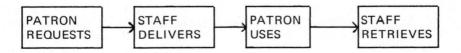

Circulation/distribution procedures should be kept as simple as possible. All media and portable equipment should be loaned, on at least an overnight basis, unless extraordinary conditions exist.

Although manual charge-out systems continue to be the primary vehicle for circulation, some school LMCs use mechanical or automated systems. Automation has now progressed to the point where commercially available systems, such as CLSI, can be utilized by a school district or regional, multi-type cooperative for circulation control. These systems include both patron and bibliographic data. These systems also have the potential to interface with a customized network (via a service network) such as OCLC, cable television, and home computers.

There are probably as many methods of handling equipment distribution in a school as there are school districts. In any case, no one system will be suitable for all because of the many variables found from school to school, such as physical layout of the building and the amount of equipment available. Flexible and efficient procedures are needed for an effective pattern of distribution.

The delivery of equipment to teaching stations should be reduced to a minimum. If the supply of equipment is adequate and security is regulated, equipment should be deployed to fixed locations throughout the school. Many newer schools have provided for decentralized storage of equipment. Patterns range from departmental storage at the secondary level, to first- , second- , and third-floor storage space in multilevel buildings, to cluster storage, where an equipment storage closet is expected to serve four to six classrooms. A pattern of assigning equipment to various grade levels in elementary schools, where rooms are close to each other, has also been used. Any of these patterns will reduce distribution from a central storage area. If equipment storage is decentralized, a reserve equipment pool must be maintained for emergency breakdowns or for conflicts in use.

Although decentralization of equipment offers definite relief for the LMC in terms of delivery, and places equipment close to the people who will use it, it is not without problems. Inventory, maintenance, and repair may plague the LMC staff. Unless teachers are willing to cooperate, the usual operational check of equipment after use becomes impossible. The concept of optimum utilization of equipment is abandoned, since assigning equipment permanently to a teaching station only guarantees that the assignment has been made, and that the potential for use by an individual teacher is probably greater than if the device were not located there. Certain devices may not be used at all; others may receive minimal use. There is also the problem of possession: once equipment is assigned, should a department be asked to relinquish a device?

If equipment delivery and operator services are reduced to a minimum, in-service training is needed to show teachers how to operate standard equipment. As an alternative, teachers could designate a student, or students, from each class to learn the fundamentals of projection and general equipment operation. This alternative is highly recommended for three reasons: the teacher's time is spent preparing students for learning experiences rather than readying equipment; student operators are a part of the group and feel an obligation to do a good job; and the LMC staff is relieved of the pressure to get student operators to various teaching stations, where they remain for educationally unproductive periods of time (ranging from fifteen to fifty minutes). Since the training of very young children is not possible, teachers in the primary grades should learn to operate the equipment. At this level, however, if paraprofessionals are available as teacher aides, they are the logical people to train. Projectionists or equipment specialists should be provided for fixed location operations, such as auditoriums, multimedia lecture halls, and automated learning laboratories.

The reservation and scheduling of equipment should be handled at the service desk. Teachers should also be able to request equipment reservations by telephone. In most schools, a day's notice is usually adequate for reservation, depending on the availability of equipment.

Maintenance of Media and Equipment

The effectiveness of the LMC program may be seriously impaired if media and equipment are not kept in good condition. The LMC system that has dog-eared books, dirty and scratched records, and projectors with blown-out lamps is doomed to failure. Beyond the maintenance performed in the individual school, there is usually a need for in-depth support at the district level or through contractual or other service plans with commercial firms.

Maintaining printed media is similar to maintaining audiovisual media at the individual school level. For printed media, cleaning and mending are regularly carried out with dispatch, using various supplies readily available from commercial library supply houses. Beyond the mending of torn pages and frayed bindings, printed media are regularly sent out to commercial firms for rebinding. The techniques of book mending and repair may usually be taught to a group of interested people on request, by a sales representative of these same commercial supply houses. Printed media are ordinarily given a casual inspection at the service desk or during an annual inventory.

Some of the maintenance tasks required for audiovisual media can be equated with those performed for printed media. For the most part, these tasks revolve around cleaning processes for the various audiovisual forms and the splicing of damaged 8mm and 16mm films or tapes. Supplies to accomplish these tasks are available from commercial library supply houses as well as from distributors of audiovisual equipment and supplies. Beyond this simple maintenance, it becomes a matter of replacement of the medium or, in the case of films, the replacement of footage. Inspection of most audiovisual forms is tedious and time-consuming. In most LMCs, no effort is made to inspect audiovisual forms, except those that can be scanned quickly or automatically machine inspected. It is more common to rely on either written or oral reports from users on the condition of media used. This procedure is acceptable as long as every effort is made to have reports filed, to remove worn or defective items from circulation, to provide the maintenance required, to replace the item, or to remove the item completely from the active rolls.

Equipment should receive an operational maintenance check after each use. This can be omitted if each user fills out a simple check form indicating the condition of the equipment before dispatching it to another user. A maintenance and repair file should be kept as part of the inventory file, and inspection and cleaning should be carried out and duly noted at regularly scheduled intervals. The file should also contain a record of lamp changes, minor adjustments, repairs, and annual service checks. Using a computer database is an ideal way to keep equipment and repair records.

To the extent possible, the repair of equipment should be handled by a district LMC or a commercial firm. The degree of sophistication of equipment (such as the presence of television studios and multimedia, large-group instructional areas) generally determines whether qualified equipment technicians will be employed in the school or district. Technicians perform maintenance, equipment repairs, and annual servicing. In some cases, technicians may also perform media production services.

Inventory/Weeding

Policy guidelines should apply to inventory, weeding, and the disposition of media and equipment. The inventory and weeding are essential, continuing activities which have a direct relationship to collection development, the maintenance of media and equipment, and resource sharing. The process provides an accurate accounting of resources on hand at a particular time. It can also provide for the systematic evaluation of the collection, the weeding of media no longer of value, the development of reorder lists, and the sorting of media to be repaired. Since the total inventory will, in large LMCs, take an extraordinary amount of time and will detract from direct services to users, alternatives include inventorying selected sections of collections during slow periods, as well as inventorying only parts of the collection each year.

Weeding the collection to remove outdated, unused, and worn media is a continuing task. A rule of thumb for weeding books has been approximately 5 percent annually. Estimates for the replacement of audiovisual media range from 10 to 15 percent based on normal wear, accidental damage, and curriculum revisions. In situations in which teacher specialists participate periodically in surveying collections, weeding may be considered an integral part of that task.

SUMMARY

- The term *media* is used to encompass all forms (printed and audiovisual) and channels for the communication of information. In its broadest meaning, media also includes equipment.

- In the selection of media and equipment for the school and district, selection committees should be guided by the formal selection policies of the school district.

- Criteria for the selection of media include authenticity, appropriateness, content, interest, and technical quality. Criteria for equipment include portability, attractiveness of design, ease of operation, performance standards, ease of maintenance and repair, reliability of manufacturer and distributor, and cost.

- Where possible, technical services activities should be coordinated and completed by a district center or commercial firm. This applies particularly to acquisitions, preparation and organization, and maintenance and repair.

ACTIVITIES

1. Describe the background information needed prior to the selection of media and equipment.

2. For a selected school district, review the basis for media, equipment, and technical services offered by the district LMC.

3. Compare service options and costs for centralized technical services versus commercially available services.

4. Investigate one or more of the following topics: (1) media selection policies, (2) television utilization in the schools, or (3) microcomputer utilization in the schools.

NOTES

[1]Ralph Ellsworth and Hobart Wagner, *The School Library: Facilities for Independent Study in Secondary Schools* (New York: Educational Facilities Laboratories, 1963), 39.

[2]*Webster's Third New International Dictionary* (Springfield, Mass.: G. & C. Merriam Co., 1986), 1403.

[3]American Association of School Librarians and Association for Educational Communications and Technology, *Media Programs: District and School* (Chicago and Washington, D.C.: American Library Association and Association for Educational Communications and Technology, 1975), 110.

[4]*Library Technology Reports* (Chicago: American Library Association, 1965, bimonthly).

BIBLIOGRAPHY

American Association of School Librarians and Association for Educational Communications and Technology. *Media Programs: District and School.* Chicago and Washington, D.C.: American Library Association and Association for Educational Communications and Technology, 1975.

Anderson, Eric. "The Amazing Library Computer." *Electronic Learning* 2 (March 1983): 68-71.

Armstrong, Margaret, and Betty Costa. "Computer Cat at Mountain View Elementary School." *Library Hi Tech* 1 (Winter 1983): 47-52.

Berglund, Patricia. "School Library Technology." *Wilson Library Bulletin* 60 (November 1985): 36-37.

Bernhard, Keith. "Computer Applications in the Library Media Center: An Introduction to Electronic Spreadsheets." *School Library Media Quarterly* 12 (Spring 1984): 222-26.

Clyde, Laurel, and D. Joan Joyce. "Selecting Computer Software for School Libraries." *School Library Media Quarterly* 13 (Spring 1985): 129-37.

"Computer Technology and Libraries." *School Library Journal* 31 (November 1984): 35-73. (*School Library Journal* special section)

Crowe, Virginia. "Choosing Technologies for School Library Media Centers: Hardware Selection." *Drexel Library Quarterly* 20 (Winter 1984): 51-63.

Ellsworth, Ralph, and Hobart Wagner. *The School Library: Facilities for Independent Study in Secondary Schools.* New York: Educational Facilities Laboratories, 1963.

Graham, Judy. "My Micro Chased the Blues Away." *School Library Journal* 29 (February 1983): 23-26.

Holter, Charlotte. "Selecting Books for Young Adults ... a Considerable Responsibility." *Catholic Library World* 57 (January/February 1986): 170-71.

Lathrop, Ann. "Microcomputer Courseware: Selection and Evaluation." *Top of the News* 39 (Spring 1983): 265-74.

Loertscher, David. "In-House Production of Computer Software." *Drexel Library Quarterly* 20 (Winter 1984): 16-26.

Magrill, Rose Mary. "Evaluation by Type of Library." *Library Trends* 33 (Winter 1985): 267-95.

Mancall, Jacqueline. "Teaching Online Searching: A Review of Recent Research and Some Recommendations for School Library Media Specialists." *School Library Media Quarterly* 13 (Summer 1985): 215-20.

Naumer, Janet. "Microcomputer Software Packages—Choose with Caution." *School Library Journal* 29 (March 1983): 116-19.

Niemeyer, Karen. "Software or Software? Getting Tough with Microcomputer Courseware Evaluation." *Catholic Library World* 57 (January/ February 1986): 178-80, 189-90.

Quality Library Services K-12. Columbus, Ohio: Department of Education, 1986.

Recommended Standards for Educational Library Media Programs. Springfield, Ill.: State Board of Education, 1986.

Smith, Lotsee, and Keith Swigger. "Microcomputers in School Library Media Centers." *Drexel Library Quarterly* 20 (Winter 1984): 7-15.

Tenopir, Carol. "Online Searching in Schools." *Library Journal* 3 (1 February 1986): 60-61.

Truett, Carol. "The Search for Quality Micro Programs: Software and Review Sources." *School Library Journal* 30 (January 1984): 35-37.

Walker, H. Thomas. "Library Resource Sharing in Maryland: A Case History in Successful Networking." *Catholic Library World* 55 (December 1983): 216-20.

Woolls, Blanche. "Selecting Microcomputer Software for the Library." *Top of the News* 39 (Summer 1983): 321-27.

8

THE BUDGET

OBJECTIVES

Describe alternative budgeting systems used in schools and school districts.

Develop a budget proposal for an LMC in a selected school or for a selected, district library media system.

Financial support of the LMC is critical. Any school or district has a limited amount of money to spend for existing programs and for the initiation of new programs. In many communities, the average school budget increase allowed by fiscal authorities can be predicted, year by year. In other communities, financial constraints will preclude growth and may, in fact, severely constrict all components of the organization.

BUDGET PREPARATION

The budget is a fundamental control mechanism of management. It should relate directly to comprehensive planning for library media services. In any district, the process for developing a budget will follow specifications required by the parent organization.

Background Information Needed

In order to develop a budget that is meaningful and related to LMC plans and programming, a continuing program of analysis and evaluation should include at least the following:

- *Inventories of media and equipment.* One must be completely knowledgeable about the quantity and quality of existing resources.

- *State of collections.* One should know, in terms of both standards and program needs, the relative strength of collections.

- *Costs of media and equipment.* This information is essential for planning expansion of collections and for projecting needed increases in funding.

- *Past performance.* One should have information (for a five-year period, if possible) about funds available to the LMC program, plus an analysis of how funds were spent. This provides an opportunity to visualize both a pattern of support for the LMC and the effectiveness of expenditures in relation to program needs.

- *Effectiveness of the LMC* in meeting its objectives. Essential to the entire budgetary operation is full knowledge of the degree to which objectives have been established for the LMC program and the degree to which these have been met.

- *Knowledge of state, national, and regional guidelines*; and of at least the average media expenditures for the state.

- *Knowledge of school and district priorities* and the relationship of the LMC to these priorities. One must know if curriculum development has created a priority for expanded science facilities, resources, and methodology. This information becomes essential to effective budgeting because of an assumed relationship between improved instruction and a need for LMC resources and services.

One who has held a position for some time may have all of the needed facts. For a person new to the system, information can usually be obtained from various school district personnel: principals and their assistants, for information about their priorities and budgetary planning; guidance and/or reading personnel, about student capabilities; curriculum directors, about curriculum development; federal and state funding sources; district financial officers, for budgetary procedures, an historical look at LMC expenditures for past years, and specialized funding for various district programs and projects; and state departments of education personnel, for statistics about average expenditures and program comparisons. The program planning method developed by Liesener, discussed briefly in chapter 3, provides a useful approach to the collection of this information.

National guidelines recommend that the annual per pupil expenditure for media and equipment in the school district should be at least 10 percent of the national per pupil operational cost, based on average daily attendance.[1] The per pupil operational cost includes the cost of administration, instruction, attendance services, health services, pupil transportation services, operation of plant, maintenance of plant, and fixed charges. It is estimated that this sum would support the total LMC system for a school district, including individual school programs, a district program, and various contractual arrangements made with other service agencies. The figure represents an estimate based on an assumption that a comprehensive LMC system actually operates in a district, and that education is guided by a focus on individualization, inquiry, and independent study.

The budget recommendations of two states are provided in figure 8.1 for comparison to the national guidelines.

Ohio

Standard 3301-35-03(B)(2)(d):

ANNUAL SCHOOL YEAR DISTRICT EXPENDITURES FOR LIBRARY MATERIALS AND EQUIPMENT SHALL AMOUNT TO AT LEAST ONE-HALF OF ONE PERCENT OF THE TOTAL GENERAL FUND EXPENDITURES FOR REGULAR INSTRUCTION FOR THE PREVIOUS SCHOOL YEAR AS ENTERED ON "FORM 625 OHIO COMMON CORE DATA."

Procedure and Interpretation

1. Compute the sum of columns A, D, G, and J from line 5.05 of the previous school year Form 625 Ohio Common Core Data.

2. Multiply the sum obtained in Step 1 by .005 (one-half of one percent).

3. The figure obtained in Step 2 is the current annual amount school districts are required to expend for library materials and equipment.

4. Expenditures of district funds to meet this figure may be from any source with the exception of certain federal funds which may not be used to supplant programs required by state standards.

5. The definition of what constitutes library materials and equipment is pursuant to local definition.

6. Proof of expenditures for library materials and equipment falls upon the district.

Illinois

	Phase I	**Phase II**	**Phase III**
District Library Media Expenditures K-12	A total from all sources equal to 1% of the State average per pupil instructional costs.	A total from all sources equal to 3% of the State average per pupil instructional costs.	A total from all sources equal to 6% of the State average per pupil instructional costs.

Fig. 8.1. Minimum standards—expenditures for Ohio and Illinois. From *Quality Library Services K-12* (Columbus, Ohio: Department of Education, 1986), 61; *Recommended Standards for Educational Library Media Programs* (Springfield, Ill.: State Board of Education, 1986), 6. Reprinted by permission.

The district usually has a clearly defined budget planning period. In most districts, this is a final aspect of the planning which has gone on during the year. In some districts, a great many people will be involved in budget planning, including LMC personnel at the school level. This is desirable and reflects a philosophy which recognizes the need for a broad perspective of financial need related to educational programming. Other districts continue to restrict budget planning to a central core of administrative personnel. In the former situation, involvement in budget building becomes an integral part of the library media specialist's job. In the latter case he or she may have to intrude on the traditional process.

A federal government handbook designed to be a vehicle or guide for program cost accounting or for accounting in a program, planning, budgeting, and evaluating system provides the means for relating a specific expenditure to all *dimensions*, thereby providing for complete accountability.[2] Figure 8.2 includes excerpts from the handbook.

The three most important dimensions for financial record keeping are fund, object, and function. Other dimensions recommended for use are operational unit, program, source of funds, and fiscal year.

The library media specialist who has learned to function as a leader in the school has the support of administration, teachers, and students. Support within the school is gained by effective participation in a principal's advisory council, by involving teachers and students in committee work related to the LMC, and by coordinating an effective LMC system throughout the school. Support outside the school is gained by creating an awareness through news media, through favorable reports by children to parents, and by continuing contact with the community as it relates to the school. Support at the school district level is gained through effective action and participation of LMC personnel in curriculum development and related professional activities. The

A FUND
1 General Fund
2 Special Revenue Fund

B OBJECTS
100 Salaries
  110 Regular Salaries
300 Purchased Services
  360 Printing and Binding
400 Supplies and Materials
  410 Supplies
  420 Textbooks
  430 Library Books
  440 Periodicals
  490 Other Supplies and Materials
500 Capital Outlay
  540 Equipment
  550 Vehicles
  560 Library Books

C FUNCTION
1000 Instruction
  1100 Regular Programs
    1110 Elementary Programs
    1120 Middle-/Junior High Programs
    1130 High School Programs
2000 Supporting Services
  2200 Support Services—Instructional Staff
    2210 Improvement of Instruction Services
    2220 Educational Media Services
      2221 Service Area Direction
      2222 School Library Service
      2223 Audiovisual Services
      2224 Educational Television Services
      2225 Computer-Assisted Instruction Services
      2229 Other Educational Media Services
3000 Community Services
  3400 Public Library Service

D OPERATIONAL UNIT
001 XYZ Elementary School
501 ABC Middle School
701 DEF High School

E PROGRAM
1100 000 Regular Programs
  1110 000 Elementary Programs
    1111 001 Program No. 1–XYZ
          Elementary School

F SOURCE OF FUNDS
1 Local
3 State
4 Federal

G FISCAL YEAR
1 FY 1972-73
2 FY 1974-75
3 FY 1975-76

H INSTRUCTIONAL ORGANIZATION
10 Elementary School
20 Middle/Junior High School
30 High School

I JOB CLASSIFICATION ACTIVITY
100 Official/Administrative
200 Professional—Educational
400 Technical

J TERM
1 Fall Term—Day
2 Fall Term—Evening

K SPECIAL COST CENTERS

Fig. 8.2. Summary of expenditure accounts. Excerpted from Charles Roberts and Allen Lichtenberger, *Financial Accounting: Classifications and Standard Terminology for Local and State School Systems,* Handbook II, Revised (Washington, D.C.: U.S. Government Printing Office, 1973).

LMC budget that begins with this kind of interaction and is the end result of comprehensive planning has an excellent start.

Cost Estimates

Average costs for books in various subject areas are available in several publications. Dealing with commercial jobbers over a period of time also provides a fair gauge of costs, minus usual discounts for various types of books. For the inexperienced book buyer, the advertised or quoted discounts can be both confusing and disturbing. For example, advertised discounts may apply only to trade books in regular publishers' bindings. Library bindings are a special classification, as are "short discount" items. Encyclopedias usually do not have to be estimated, because quotations are readily available in most locales through area representatives. If a specific list of books has been developed, and if time is not a factor, most reputable jobbers will provide a quote on a given list and hold the quote firm for a specified period.

Cost estimates for many audiovisual media may be obtained in the same manner as estimates for books, using standard tools in the field. When time permits, one can request direct quotes from producers or jobbers. Large school district and state agencies may have contract discount agreements with equipment and other vendors, and prices are available through the district business office, the office of a district LMC director, or by direct contact with the contract vendors.

There are various estimates of replacement costs of audiovisual media and equipment. Such costs are estimated to be from 10 to 20 percent each year based on normal wear and tear, accidental damage, and the need for updating collections. In the absence of specific records for the individual school, which would be the most accurate way to determine replacement needs, it is probably safest to allow for a 15 percent replacement factor until accurate record-keeping procedures are initiated.

Estimates on the frequency of replacing audiovisual equipment in the school range from five to ten years. A fairly simple process would be to use ten years as the estimated life-span of equipment, compute the cost of the total equipment inventory, and use 10 percent as a replacement factor. Prices would be computed at current rates.

A thorough maintenance check should be given at the end of each year to all equipment that has been actively used. This can be accomplished at various other times, such as during vacation periods. If a qualified equipment technician is employed in the school, or if a district LMC staff assumes that responsibility, the head of the LMC has one less problem to contend with. However, in the absence of this service, it is usual to contract this service with a reputable commercial firm. Some audiovisual equipment vendors offer complete service facilities. Otherwise, most dealers will provide a cost-per-unit range for each type of equipment requiring annual maintenance. To arrive at an estimated total cost for annual maintenance, the cost-per-unit range is multiplied by the average number of units to be serviced.

Wherever possible, information should be available in tabular form both for record keeping and for presentation purposes. Figure 8.3 is an example of a form used for recording maintenance costs.

Item	Number To Be Serviced	Estimated Unit Cost Range	Estimated Total Cost Range
16mm projector Filmstrip projector Tape recorders etc.			

Fig. 8.3. Annual contracted maintenance costs.

If actual use figures are not available for supplies needed for media design and production, estimates of requirements must be provided. Types of equipment available for production purposes must be balanced against anticipated student and teacher demands. From a practical point of view, one must begin with a knowledge of the production capabilities of the LMC facility and staff.

The cost of renting films and videotapes varies widely, depending on both the instructional focus of the school and collections available in the district, public libraries, and regional education centers. Past performance records would be of assistance where estimates are required. If specialized instructional programs are developed around the film as a principal vehicle for motivation and learning, a major revision of planning is in order. One should be aware of new instructional methods involving extraordinary financial considerations.

It is frequently desirable to project a budget for a three- to five-year period. In this case, it is necessary to gather data relative to existing inventories of media and equipment, to establish terminal goals for attainment, and to secure cost estimates for each item to be included in the budget request. Figure 8.4 provides a tabular representation of estimates to reach projected goals in three years. The format presented is suitable for media and equipment and may be modified for other uses.

Item	Inventory Current	Quantity Needed	Estimated Total Cost	1/3 Budget Each of Three Years Year 1-Year 2-Year 3
Records Tapes etc. Replacement				

Fig. 8.4. Media required to meet stated goals (3 years).

BUDGETING SYSTEMS

Many school districts allow limited participation of LMC personnel in budget planning. A standard form is provided for an enumeration of anticipated requirements for the next fiscal year, and no written justification is requested. Central administrative personnel make whatever adjustments are deemed necessary in the figures and incorporate the information provided into the total budget package for the district. The superintendent of schools or an assistant provides an oral report to the school board and, if required, to other agencies that request clarification. This practice has caused confusion and misunderstanding and has precipitated a great deal of criticism of budgeting procedures.

The following are representative of types of budgeting systems used in school districts and libraries. Emphasis is focused on PPBS and ZBB because they are integrated systems and include planning, programming, and budgeting.

Line-Item Budgeting

The line-item budget, often called an "object of expenditure budget," is perhaps the most common system employed. Expenditures are divided into broad categories, such as materials, equipment, and salaries. In budget planning, the organization reviews what was spent in previous years and then adds the cost for new or expanded programs. This scheme, which focuses on input, is fairly easy to develop, understand, and control. In some cases, justification may be required for each recommendation made in the budget package. The budget request may also contain a summary form so the reader can see at a glance the previous year's allotment, the projected increase, the recommendation for the new fiscal year, and a projection for three to five years (see figure 8.5).

Category	Allotment Prior Year	Projected Increase Current	Recommendation Current	Projected Year 1-Year 2-Year 3
430 Library Books				
440 Periodicals				
etc.				

Fig. 8.5. LMC budget summary.

Formula Budgeting

In this system, funds are requested and allocated using a predetermined standard or formula related to such items as personnel, media, and services. Although not commonly used in schools, a formula budget, focused on input, can be devised using the recommendations of national guidelines.

Performance Budgeting

This form of budgeting is concerned with the performance of services and related activities. The approach focuses on the amount of work to be done, the cost of doing this work, and the benefits derived from doing the work. The system is very much oriented to the concept of accountability and work to be accomplished. This output-oriented system is considered the forerunner of program budgeting.

Program Budgeting

This approach focuses on the activities or programs of an organization rather than individual items of expenditure. The program budget relates resources to an organization's activities, output or programs, and is designed to achieve cost-effectiveness.

Planning, Programming, Budgeting System (PPBS)

When PPBS was initially implemented in the schools during the 1960s, it was widely acclaimed as a panacea for educational improvement because its approach to integrating essential elements would result in increased funding. Although it still enjoys popularity as a system, expectations for PPBS have been modified and processes improved.

PPBS is a comprehensive planning process that includes a program budget as its major component. As an integrated approach, it takes the essential elements of planning, programming, and budgeting and systematically coordinates these elements (see figure 8.6). The effort is designed to provide a decision-making procedure so that resources are efficiently allocated to achieve stated objectives.

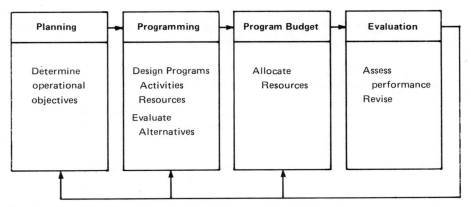

Fig. 8.6. PPBS process.

Some characteristics of PPBS are:

1. It is program oriented and relates input and output.

2. Objectives for the total system and each program are specified.

3. Evaluation can be accomplished since performance is related to objectives.

4. The process incorporates systems analysis procedures where appropriate.

5. Long-range fiscal planning, five years or longer, is deemed essential.

6. All relevant alternatives are considered.

7. Scarce resources may be allocated in the most efficient manner.

8. The approach is flexible and accommodates the needs of most organizations for internal programming and control.

9. The system does not require the replacement of an existing accounting system.

PPBS requires the preparation of a series of documents: the program structure and statement of objectives, program analyses (cost-effectiveness analyses) and memoranda, and the multiyear program and financial plan. In the preparation of these documents, PPBS requires:

1. Clarifying and specifying the ultimate goals or objectives of each activity for which a government budgets money.

2. Gathering contributing activities into comprehensive categories or programs to achieve the specified objectives.

3. Examining, as a continuous process, how well each activity or program has done—its effectiveness—as a final step toward improving or even eliminating it.

4. Analyzing proposed improvements or new program proposals to see how effective they may be in achieving program goals.

5. Projecting the entire costs of each proposal, not only for the first year, but for several subsequent years.

6. Formulating a plan, based in part on the analysis of program content and effectiveness, that leads to implementation through the budget.[3]

PPBS may be applied to all programs of a school district or may be focused on one element, such as the district LMC system or a single school LMC. The actual budget should be considered merely the climax of a chain of events. Comprehensive planning, using forms provided by the district or developed internally, can be used to generate the data needed for program analysis and review (see figure 8.7).

Under optimum conditions, the LMC program should be eliminated from consideration as an isolated entity in the budget, and the costs of this service should be assigned to other educational areas, that is, a cost factor should be added to each area of school service, including science, math, English or language arts, guidance, health, independent study programs, and so on. Distributing the costs for this program—media, personnel, facilities, services—would provide an overview of the relative contribution of the LMC system to each area of concern; through this assignment, the actual program costs in principal areas of study could be determined more accurately. If the LMC is to be budgeted as an operational entity, which is usually the case, the perspective cited above should receive due consideration. The LMC is for students and teachers, and not for the LMC staff. Program relationships must be clearly delineated to provide a picture of how, where, and when the instructional program is served.

LMC:	Code:
Program Title:	
Program No.:	Program Level:
Program Objectives:	
Program Description:	

Resources:
 	
   Personnel
 	
   Other
	Costs:

Fig. 8.7. PPBS generalized program data sheet.

PPBS requires the preparation of a document that includes not only dollar values, but also a narrative presentation of program relationships. Basic to the presentation is the development of LMC system goals that will incorporate the ideals of service to teachers and students in terms of the educational program of the school, the individual personal needs of students, and the professional needs of the faculty.

The next step in the procedure calls for a program description. This section should delineate the parameters of the LMC system for the school. A recitation of assets, activities, and intended achievements would be provided and the relationship between these elements clearly delineated.

The third ingredient, a system analysis and evaluation, is presented in narrative form and spells out how well the system serves students and teachers. Quantitative deficiencies must be related to qualitative factors. The fact that the book collection does not meet national standards is meaningless; a justification in terms of programming must be made. A deficiency exists only if a need is not being met under present conditions. Knowing how many students, during a given period of time, will require access to the resources provides quantitative data for use. If a knowledge of the range of students' abilities, such as reading scores, is added to this, an adequate statement of deficiency can be developed.

Step four of the project requires the development of long-range plans. This is a major strategy designed to bring about constructive, positive change. It requires an analysis of goals, program, and system evaluation in order to project where the LMC system will be in three to five years.

Zero Base Budgeting (ZBB)

Zero base shares many of the positive (and negative) aspects of PPBS, which was considered by many to be the forerunner of ZBB. The most apparent difference between ZBB and traditional budgeting processes or PPBS is the effort to engage in the process without reference to previous years. Rather than a panacea, ZBB is considered to be a rational, integrated system designed to relate the elements of planning, budgeting, and evaluation to programs (see figure 8.8).

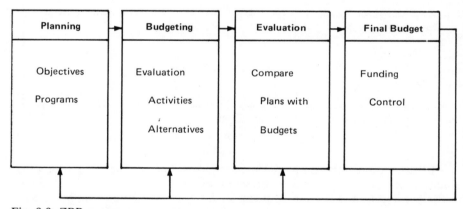

Fig. 8.8. ZBB process.

Some characteristics of ZBB are:

1. The system starts from "scratch," that is, with no carry over of programs or funding.

2. All activities must compete for limited resources.

3. The system is function or program oriented.

4. Alternative ways of achieving objectives and alternative levels of service are examined.

5. Objectives for the total system and each program are specified.

6. Decision packages for each decision unit (program) must be developed and ranked.

7. The system is flexible in terms of processes and forms, and can therefore accommodate the needs of a total organization or a single unit.

The ZBB procedure includes:

1. Establishing objectives (and obtaining the agreement of management).

2. Structuring an implementation strategy (designing decision units which are programs, functions, or activities).

3. Identifying data requirements (essential input).

4. Completing decision packages (documents clearly identifying an activity for evaluation).

5. Ranking all decision packages (decision making).

6. Approving and funding (those packages essential to achieve objectives).[4]

Fundamental concerns in the ZBB process are determining what it is one is trying to do (objectives), determining how it is to be done (implementation strategy), and determining what resources will be needed to do it (input).

Decision units may be described as programs or cost centers. In a school or district plan, the LMC system could be considered a decision unit. In the school LMC, elements such as technical services, media design and production, and other primary elements could also be considered decision units. Decision packages, related to these units, are designed as requests for an allocation of funds to support a specific activity (see figure 8.9).

A major premise of ZBB is that a budget is developed without reference to funding for previous years. In practice, the full process might be done every two or three years. During the interim, new packages would be developed to justify new programs or to revise old ones.

LMC	Package 1
Package Name:	Activity:

Activity Purpose (objectives)	Resource Requirements
	Prior Budget / Budget Period / Pro-jected
Activity Description (what is done)	Personnel
Activity Benefits (to users)	Media
	Equipment
Activity Alternatives Different ways considered Different levels considered	Supplies Other
Consequences If Not Approved	
Prepared By: Date:	Approval: Date:

Fig. 8.9. ZBB generalized decision package.

ADMINISTERING THE BUDGET

The budget finally allotted to the school LMC and district LMC system provides an operational plan for the year. Regardless of the dollar outcome, at least three basic factors are available for the library media specialist to work with: a service plan for the media system, an acquisitions plan, and a public relations vehicle.

As part of the public relations and service programs of the LMC, the head of the LMC has an obligation to provide teachers and administrators with a review of the LMC's budget and to recommend ways to adjust program expectations to reality. Such information may be presented through the committee structure of the school. The opinions of teachers should be considered before final judgment is made. If student participation is expected in the evaluation and selection of media, in the formulation of LMC policy and service programs, students should also be kept informed.

Generally, the budget of a school district allows flexibility in the handling of funds. Flexibility is provided so that the administration can meet emergency situations and can structure the most effective use of whatever funds become available. Instructional program changes make this flexibility desirable.

It is, then, legitimate to make judgments based on new evidence of need. For example, the amount to be spent for videocassettes can be decreased and the sum to be spent for microcomputer software can be increased, if necessary. However, using media funds for equipment, or vice versa, can rarely be justified. In the same way, it is rarely justifiable to use a book account for the purchase of large quantities of audiovisual media. The budget request represents a realistic appraisal of the needs of the LMC program, and the need for each item and each dollar requested has been justified. If transfer of funds *is* justifiable, however, approval can usually be obtained from school and district administrators, who likewise can recognize the necessity for transfer.

One possible way of avoiding the transfer problem is to gain the right of budget review prior to final approval and allocation of funds. This allows for the restructuring of funds in various accounts before allotments are put into final form. In other situations, priorities are set in advance.

The LMC is a many-faceted operation. It is, in part, a business organization responsible for the expenditure, in many cases, of thousands of dollars each year. One can expect that financial officers for the district will have accurate accounting procedures established for the control of funds. Monthly or periodic financial accounting statements are often issued to departments to provide information about the status of accounts up to that date. If this information is provided on a regular basis and is reasonably up-to-date, it can be of value. A simplified bookkeeping system should be employed in the LMC to monitor the status of all accounts.

SUMMARY

- The head of the LMC must be well-informed about the school and LMC, as well as budgeting procedures in the school district.

- The budget is a principal control mechanism of management.

- Two budgeting systems which have captured the interest and imagination of government, business, education, and libraries are PPBS (Planning, Programming, Budgeting System) and ZBB (Zero Base Budgeting). Both systems integrate and relate planning, programming, and budgeting. ZBB's unique approach is the effort to engage in the process without reference to previous years.

ACTIVITIES

1. Describe the relationship between school LMC and district LMC system budgets.

2. Analyze the budgetary process and administration of the budget in a selected school LMC. Complete the same process for a district LMC system.

3. Investigate the following topics: (1) PPBS and (2) ZBB.

NOTES

[1]American Association of School Librarians and Association for Educational Communications and Technology, *Media Programs: District and School* (Chicago and Washington, D.C.: American Library Association and Association for Educational Communications and Technology, 1975), 41.

[2]Charles T. Roberts and Allan Lichtenberger, *Financial Accounting: Classifications and Standard Terminology for Local and State School Systems*, Handbook II, rev (Washington, D.C.: Government Printing Office, 1973), 50.

[3]"What Is a Programming, Planning, Budgeting System?" *NEA Research Bulletin* (December 1968): 113.

[4]Logan Cheek, *Zero-Base Budgeting Comes of Age* (New York: Amacom, 1977), 20.

BIBLIOGRAPHY

American Association of School Librarians and Association for Educational Communications and Technology. *Media Programs: District and School.* Chicago and Washington, D.C.: American Library Association and Association for Educational Communications and Technology, 1975.

Chen, Ching-chih. *Zero-Base Budgeting in Library Management: A Manual for Librarians.* Phoenix, Ariz.: Oryx Press, 1980.

Hartley, Harry. *Educational Planning-Programming-Budgeting: A Systems Approach.* Englewood Cliffs, N.J.: Prentice-Hall, 1968.

Liesener, James. *A Systematic Process for Planning Media Programs.* Chicago: American Library Association, 1976.

National Education Association, Committee on Educational Finance. *Planning for Educational Development in a Planning, Programming, Budgeting System*. Washington, D.C.: National Education Association, 1968.

Quality Library Services K-12. Columbus, Ohio: Department of Education, 1986.

Recommended Standards for Educational Library Media Programs. Springfield, Ill.: State Board of Education, 1986.

Roberts, Charles T., and Allan Lichtenberger. *Financial Accounting: Classifications and Standard Terminology for Local and State School Systems*, Handbook II, rev., Washington, D.C.: Government Printing Office, 1973.

Appendix A

SCOPE AND SEQUENCE*

SCOPE AND SEQUENCE — Concept/Skill	PHASE I				PHASE II			PHASE III			PHASE IV		
	K	1	2	3	4	5	6	7	8	9	10	11	12
I. How to use the library/media center													
A. Orientation													
location within building	X	X	X	X	X	X	X	X	X	X	X	X	X
manners (library conduct)	X	X	X	X	X	X	X	X	X	X	X	X	X
library/media center rules	X	X	X	X	X	X	X	X	X	X	X	X	X
circulation procedures	X	X	X	X	X	X	X	X	X	X	X	X	X
names of personnel	X	X	X	X	X	X	X	X	X	X	X	X	X
other general information on use	X	X	X	X	X	X	X	X	X	X	X	X	X
B. Care of Materials													
print	X	X	X	X	X	X	X	X	X	X	X	X	X
nonprint	X	X	X	X	X	X	X	X	X	X	X	X	X
C. Location of Material													
"easy" books	X	X	X	X	X								
fiction and nonfiction	X	X	X	X	X	X	X	X	X	X	X	X	X
reference			X	X	X	X	X	X	X	X	X	X	X
location of Dewey categories				X	X	X	X	X	X	X	X	X	X
location of magazines	X	X	X	X	X	X	X	X	X	X	X	X	X
vertical file (pamphlets)				X	X	X	X	X	X	X	X	X	X
AV material and equipment	X	X	X	X	X	X	X	X	X	X	X	X	X
D. Card catalog													
method of indexing collection				X	X	X	X	X	X	X	X	X	X
alphabetical order					X	X	X	X	X	X	X	X	X
guide cards			X		X	X	X	X	X	X	X	X	X
call numbers				X	X	X	X	X	X	X	X	X	X
types of cards (author, title, subject)					X	X	X	X	X	X	X	X	X
nonprint material cards					X	X	X	X	X	X	X	X	X
subject headings (related topics)					X	X	X	X	X	X	X	X	X
cross references (see, see also)					X	X	X	X	X	X	X	X	X
analytics								X	X	X	X	X	X
filing rules								X	X				

*From *Information Skills for South Dakota Students* (Pierre, S.D.: South Dakota State Library, 1986). Reprinted by permission.

	PHASE I				PHASE II			PHASE III			PHASE IV		
---	K	1	2	3	4	5	6	7	8	9	10	11	12
E. Dewey Decimal Classification													
10 major categories				X	X	X	X	X	X	X	X	X	X
function of decimal point				X	X	X	X	X	X	X	X	X	X
Categories and subcategories				X	X	X	X	X	X	X	X	X	X
other classification systems (Library of Congress, etc.)					X			X	X	X	X	X	X
Cutter or author letters								X	X	X	X	X	X
II. Reference and Research													
A. Parts of books or nonprint materials													
cover	X	X	X	X	X	X	X	X	X	X	X	X	X
spine	X	X	X	X	X	X	X	X	X	X	X	X	X
check out card/pocket, date due slip	X	X	X	X	X	X	X	X	X	X	X	X	X
title page (author/title)		X	X	X	X	X	X	X	X	X	X	X	X
edition			X	X	X	X	X	X	X	X	X	X	X
copyright page, date		X	X	X	X	X	X	X	X	X	X	X	X
blurb	X	X		X	X	X	X	X	X	X	X	X	X
table of contents			X	X	X	X	X	X	X	X	X	X	X
publisher			X	X	X	X	X	X	X	X	X	X	X
preface				X	X	X	X	X	X	X	X	X	X
illustrations, plates, maps, charts	X	X	X	X	X	X	X	X	X	X	X	X	X
footnotes					X	X	X	X	X	X	X	X	X
glossary					X	X	X	X	X	X	X	X	X
index				X	X	X	X	X	X	X	X	X	X
appendix, addenda						X	X	X	X	X	X	X	X
bibliography						X	X	X	X	X	X	X	X
script, guide with nonprint material					X	X	X	X	X	X	X	X	X
B. Dictionaries													
alphabetical order		X	X	X	X	X	X	X	X	X	X	X	X
guide words				X	X	X	X	X	X	X	X	X	X
pronunciation guides				X	X	X	X	X	X	X	X	X	X
other guides/special helps					X	X	X	X	X	X	X	X	X
abridged vs. unabridged								X	X	X	X	X	X
special language dictionaries						X	X	X	X	X	X	X	X
special subject dictionaries						X	X	X	X	X	X	X	X

	PHASE I				PHASE II			PHASE III			PHASE IV		
	K	1	2	3	4	5	6	7	8	9	10	11	12
C. Encyclopedias													
scope of coverage						X	X	X	X	X	X	X	X
currentness (copyright date)						X	X	X	X	X	X	X	X
order of arrangement (alphabetical, other)					X	X	X	X	X	X	X	X	X
guide words					X	X	X	X	X	X	X	X	X
headings, subheadings					X	X	X	X	X	X	X	X	X
cross references					X	X	X	X	X	X	X	X	X
illustrations, maps, charts					X	X	X	X	X	X	X	X	X
index					X								
bibliographies and other study guides							X	X	X	X	X	X	X
D. Indexing services													
Readers' Guide (abridged, unabridged)					X	X	X	X	X	X	X	X	X
Children's Magazine Guide						X	X	X	X	X	X	X	X
Biography Index											X	X	X
Play Index											X	X	X
Poetry Index											X	X	X
Short Story Index											X	X	X
other special indexes											X	X	X
E. Other reference sources													
purpose and location						X	X	X	X	X	X	X	X
almanac						X	X	X	X	X	X	X	X
atlas, gazetteer						X	X	X	X	X	X	X	X
parliamentary procedure							X	X			X	X	X
quotation books											X	X	X
statistical sources									X	X	X	X	X
yearbooks, handbooks							X		X	X	X	X	X
book reviews								X	X	X	X	X	X
directories								X	X	X	X	X	X
government publications											X	X	X
biographical sources (subject arrangement)											X		X
on-line databases												X	X

	PHASE I				PHASE II			PHASE III			PHASE IV		
	K	1	2	3	4	5	6	7	8	9	10	11	12
F. Newspapers/magazines													
general periodicals						X	X	X	X	X	X	X	X
specialized subject periodicals							X	X	X	X	X	X	X
viewpoint and bias							X	X	X	X	X	X	X
editorials						X	X	X	X	X	X	X	X
microforms						X	X	X	X	X	X	X	X
G. Vertical file													
general content						X	X	X	X	X	X	X	X
maps							X	X	X	X	X	X	X
pictures						X	X	X	X	X	X	X	X
pamphlets						X	X	X	X	X	X	X	X
clippings						X	X	X	X	X	X	X	X
career information						X	X	X	X	X	X	X	X
viewpoint and bias							X	X	X	X	X	X	X
H. Research techniques													
authoritativeness, scope, bias of sources						X	X	X	X	X	X	X	X
primary vs. secondary sources							X	X	X	X	X	X	X
restate information in own words				X		X	X	X	X	X	X	X	X
note taking					X								X
locate information to support opinion						X	X	X	X	X	X	X	X
summarizing, annotating							X	X	X	X	X	X	X
draw inferences, make generaliza-tions, tentative conclusions						X	X	X	X	X	X	X	X
outlining					X	X	X	X	X	X	X	X	X
alphabetical order			X	X		X	X	X	X	X	X	X	X
footnotes					X		X	X	X	X	X	X	X
skimming for information					X	X	X	X	X	X	X	X	X
bibliography as a resource							X	X	X	X	X	X	X
prepare bibliography using standard format										X	X	X	X
online access to databases										X		X	X
I. Community resources						X	X	X	X	X	X	X	X

	K	1	2	3	4	5	6	7	8	9	10	11	12
J. Other libraries													
visit another library	X			X	X	X	X	X	X	X	X	X	X
use another library	X			X	X	X	X	X	X	X	X	X	X
use interlibrary loan							X	X	X	X	X	X	X
III. Production													
A. Equipment*													
how to handle, set up, use	X	X	X	X	X	X	X	X	X	X	X	X	X
how to care for after use	X	X	X	X	X	X	X	X	X	X	X	X	X
*may include:													
8mm projector				X	X	X	X	X	X	X	X	X	X
16mm projector				X	X	X	X	X	X	X	X	X	X
filmstrip projector	X	X	X	X	X	X	X	X	X	X	X	X	X
filmstrip viewer	X	X	X	X	X	X	X	X	X	X	X	X	X
record player	X	X	X	X	X	X	X	X	X	X	X	X	X
cassette player					X	X	X	X	X	X	X	X	X
slide projector					X	X	X	X	X	X	X	X	X
lettering devices							X	X	X	X	X	X	X
dry mount press							X	X	X	X	X	X	X
overhead projector				X	X	X	X	X	X	X	X	X	X
opaque projector				X	X	X	X	X	X	X	X	X	X
video player/recorder/camera				X	X	X	X	X	X	X	X	X	X
microfilm reader/printer										X	X	X	X
microcomputer	X			X	X	X	X	X	X	X	X	X	X
B. Producing materials													
illustrating stories	X	X	X	X	X	X	X	X	X	X	X	X	X
transparencies				X	X	X	X	X	X	X	X	X	X
writing poetry				X	X	X	X	X	X	X	X	X	X
filmstrips				X	X	X	X	X	X	X	X	X	X
slides				X	X	X	X	X	X	X	X	X	X
dry mount press								X	X	X	X	X	X
mounting pictures								X	X	X	X	X	X
lettering								X	X	X	X	X	X
cassette tapes								X	X	X	X	X	X
videotapes									X	X	X	X	X
film (8 or 16mm)										X	X	X	X
puppets	X			X	X	X	X	X	X	X	X	X	X

Column headers by phase: PHASE I (K, 1, 2, 3); PHASE II (4, 5, 6); PHASE III (7, 8, 9); PHASE IV (10, 11, 12)

	PHASE I				PHASE II			PHASE III			PHASE IV		
	K	1	2	3	4	5	6	7	8	9	10	11	12
realia						X	X	X	X	X	X	X	X
making a book						X	X	X	X	X	X	X	X
VI. Reading promotion													
Caldecott award books	X	X	X	X	X	X	X	X	X	X	X	X	X
picture books (wordless)		X	X	X	X	X	X	X	X	X	X	X	X
Newbery award books				X	X	X	X	X	X	X	X	X	X
"easy" books	X	X		X	X	X	X	X	X	X	X	X	X
poetry				X	X	X	X	X	X	X	X	X	X
biography/autobiography	X	X		X	X	X	X	X	X	X	X	X	X
fairy tales		X	X	X	X	X	X	X	X	X	X	X	X
tall tales				X	X	X	X	X	X	X	X	X	X
plays					X	X	X	X	X	X	X	X	X
mythology				X	X	X	X	X	X	X	X	X	X
short stories					X	X	X	X	X	X	X	X	X
types of fiction (historical, science, etc.)					X	X	X	X	X	X	X	X	X
best books about South Dakota				X		X	X	X	X	X	X	X	X
Jr. Great Books								X	X	X	X	X	X
best books for young adults								X	X	X	X	X	X
recommended adult books for young adults								X				X	X
choose material appropriate for reading level											X	X	X
reading for information				X	X	X	X	X	X	X	X	X	X
reading for pleasure			X	X	X	X	X	X	X	X	X	X	X
booktalks			X	X	X	X	X	X	X	X	X	X	X
history of books and printing		X		X	X	X	X	X	X	X	X	X	X
make up story endings		X		X	X	X	X	X	X	X	X	X	X
story writing		X	X	X	X	X	X	X	X	X	X	X	X
story sequence		X	X	X	X	X	X	X	X	X	X	X	X
story morals		X	X	X	X	X	X	X	X	X	X	X	X
story drama		X	X	X	X	X	X	X	X	X	X	X	X
book reports				X	X	X	X	X	X	X	X	X	X
puppet plays		X		X	X	X	X	X	X	X	X	X	X
recognize author's work					X	X	X	X	X	X	X	X	X
evaluate by reading reviews					X	X	X	X	X	X	X	X	X

Appendix B

USES OF COMPUTERS IN SUBJECT AREAS*

	K	1	2	3	4	5	6	7	8
Drill and Practice			Mathematics ———————————— Library Skills ————————→						
		Reading ———————————————————————————————→							
		Language Arts ————————————————————————————→							
		Music ——————————————————————————————→							
					Art ——————————————————————→				
Simulation						Historical, Economic ————————————→			
								Political ————→	
					Science and Environmental				
Tutorial				General Skills ————————————————————————→					
				Language Arts ———————————————————————→					
				Mathematics ———————————————————————→					
					Social Studies ————————————————————→				
					Science ————————————————————————→				
							Health and Nutrition ——————————→		
									Industrial Arts ——→
									Art ————→
						Safety ———————————————————→			
			Music ——————————————————————————————→						
Word Processing					Keyboarding ———————————— ————————→				
		Beginning Writing Composition ————————————————————————→							
				Creative Writing ——————————————————————→				
						Школ School Newspaper ————————→			
Data Bases						Simple Visicale-Type Programs			
							Historical and Scientific Data Bases		
						Local Information			
Tool									
Problem Solving						Spreadsheet Math ——————————————→			
Calculation					Music Composition ——————————————————→				

*From *A Guide to Computers in Education: Instruction* (Hartford, Conn.: State Department of Education, 1985), 35-37. Reprinted with permission of the Connecticut State Department of Education.

High School

	Drill and Practice	Simulation	Tutorial	Word Processing	Data Bases	Tool Problem Solving Calculation	Inter-facing
Arts	Music	Simulation of instruments	Music – History Rhythm Pitch Art	Musical notation processing	Music Inventory	Music Digital Synthesizers	
Business	Accounting	Accounting Basic Business	Language Arts Math	Typing Office Procedures Business English	Accounting Data Process-ing Office Prac-tice		
Foreign Language	Vocabulary Practice	Use of written language in games, other simulated situations	Various Instru-mental Schemes				
Health and Safety		Nutrition	Various aspects		Records		
Home Economics	Theory and Content	Content Areas	All Content Areas		Nutrition and Growth	Nutrition Analysis	
Industrial Arts		CADD, CAM, CNC Photo-typesetting	Tool Use	Photo-typesetting		CADD, CAM, CDC Microprocess-ing Analog	
Language Arts	Skill Review Grammar		Literature	Writing Process Journalism	Research		
Library Media	Library Media Skills				Searches		
Mathematics	Math Review	Trig Functions Graphing	Math Concepts			Electronic Spreadsheet Number Cruncher	
Physical Education	Game Rules	Games			Records Scores	Movement Analysis	
Science		Biology Genetics	Physics Biology Chemistry		General Data Base Programs	Laboratory Analysis	Laboratory Analysis
Social Studies	Skill Review	Historic Political Economic Events		Research Papers	History Data Bases	Quantitative Methods in History	

Appendix C

*JOB DESCRIPTION**

JOB DESCRIPTION OF THE DIRECTOR

REPORTS TO: Superintendent or Designee

SUPERVISES: Instructional and/or Support Personnel

PURPOSE: To provide leadership in the development, implementation and evaluation of a specific area for the benefit of the systems' total educational program.

DUTIES AND RESPONSIBILITIES:

A. MAJOR FUNCTION: *Program Management*

The Director provides effective leadership in developing comprehensive program plans and implementing and evaluating the planned programs.

B. MAJOR FUNCTION: *Fiscal Management*

The Director assists/prepares budgets, coordinates with other departments or agencies to assure maximum services, maintains records/reports/inventories in accordance with local/state/federal policies.

C. MAJOR FUNCTION: *Information Management*

The Director shares information about programs with various publics, serves as liaison between the school system and other agencies and assists in the development of inservice staff development. The Director accomplishes personal growth objectives and demonstrates professional ethics.

D. MAJOR FUNCTION: *Personnel Management*

The Director assists in selection and placement of personnel, delegates and supervises staff responsibilities and assists in evaluating staff.

---

*Adopted by the State Board of Education, July, 1983. From *Media Program Recommendations: Guidelines for School Media Programs* (Raleigh, N.C.: Department of Public Instruction, 1986), II-11. Reprinted by permission.

Appendix D

PERFORMANCE APPRAISAL INSTRUMENT*

MEDIA COORDINATOR PERFORMANCE APPRAISAL INSTRUMENT

Rating Scale
(Please Check)

	Superior	Well Above Standard	Above Standard	At Standard	Below Standard	Unsatisfactory

Media Coordinator Name _____

School _____

1. Major Function: Managing Instruction†   ☐ ☐ ☐ ☐ ☐ ☐

   1.1 Management of Instructional Time

   1.2 Management of Student Behavior

   1.3 Instructional Presentation

   1.4 Monitoring of Student Performance

   1.5 Instructional Feedback

   1.6 Facilitating Instruction

   1.7 Correlating Instruction

Comments _____

_____

_____

† Incorporates Major Functions 1-6 from TEACHER PERFORMANCE APPRAISAL
INSTRUMENT in evaluation of direct teaching activities.

June, 1987

*From *Media Program Recommendations: Guidelines for School Media Programs* (Raleigh, N.C.: Department of Public Instruction, 1986), F-1-4. Reprinted by permission.

231

Rating Scale
(Please Check)

Superior	Well Above Standard	Above Standard	At Standard	Below Standard	Unsatisfactory
☐	☐	☐	☐	☐	☐

2. Major   Function: <u>Managing Public Relations</u>

    2.1   Promotes positive staff relationships.

    2.2   Promotes positive student relationships.

    2.3   Maintains a good relationship between
        school and community.

Comments _____

_____

_____

☐	☐	☐	☐	☐	☐

3. Major   Function: <u>Planning for the Media</u>
   <u>Program</u>

    3.1   Develops annual and long-range plans
        for the media program based on periodic
        assessment.

    3.2   Plans with teachers to integrate media
        skills into the curriculum.

    3.3   Designs   motivational   activities   to
        promote reading.

    3.4   Plans a schedule that allows for both
        instruction and collection development
        within administrative guidelines.

Comments _____

_____

_____

Rating Scale
(Please Check)

	Superior	Well Above Standard	Above Standard	At Standard	Below Standard	Unsatisfactory

4. Major Function: <u>Managing Resources</u> □ □ □ □ □ □

    4.1 Provides leadership for the Media Advisory Committee.

    4.2 Analyzes the collection to determine needs.

    4.3 Uses standard selection tools and practices to evaluate and select all instructional materials.

    4.4 Coordinates the acquisitions process.

    4.5 Insures accessibility to resources.

    4.6 Offers a variety of instructional resources to meet curriculum objectives and learning styles.

    4.7 Administers the media program budget.

    4.8 Promotes the use of current technologies.

    4.9 Maintains media resources.

Comments _____

_____

_____

5. Major Function: <u>Managing the Facility</u> □ □ □ □ □ □

    5.1 Has organized media center so that areas are identifiable.

    5.2 Support areas are organized.

5.3 Provides an environment that reflects the multiple goals of the media program.

5.4 Considers health and safety regulations when arranging facility.

5.5 Facility organized for efficient circulation.

Comments _____

_____

_____

6. Major Function: <u>Professional Responsibilities</u> ☐ ☐ ☐ ☐ ☐ ☐

6.1 Upgrades professional knowledge and skills.

6.2 Provides growth opportunities for staff and students.

6.3 Carries out non-instructional duties as assigned and/or as need is perceived.

6.4 Adheres to established laws, policies, rules, and regulations.

6.5 Submits accurate reports promptly.

Comments _____

_____

_____

Appendix E

SCHOOL LIBRARY MEDIA CENTERS*

Evaluation Instrument

Check (✓) Degree of Effectiveness
(If answer is no, check column 0)

MEDIA SPECIALIST	Low 0	1	2	3	High 4
1. The media center is directed by a qualified professional knowledgeable in both print and non-print media.					
2. Adequate supportive staff is provided for the administration of the program.					
3. Services are provided to students for the required amount of time.					
4. The media staff are members of the professional organizations.					
5. The head of the media center has no nonlibrary related extracurricular duties.					
6. The head of the media center is employed for 10 or more months.					
7. Parent-volunteers are being used.					
8. There is a local library media supervisor employed by the district.					
PROGRAM					
9. The LMC (library media center) is open the required number of hours.					
10. There is a planned library media program.					
11. Student assistants are used.					
12. There is a library or media club.					
13. Flexible scheduling is being used.					

*From *Media Programs: An Evaluation Guide* (Columbia, S.C.: Department of Education, 1983), 14-16. Reprinted by permission.

	Low				High
	0	1	2	3	4
14. All students are allowed to take books home.					
15. Services are provided to kindergartens.					
16. Teachers accompany their classes when there is group use of the center.					
17. Study halls are not held in the LMC.					
18. Instruction in library skills is offered.					
19. Audiovisuals are being used by students as well as by teachers.					
20. ITV programs are used extensively in the school.					
21. Instructional radio programs are used extensively in the school.					
22. Materials are being produced locally.					
23. Teachers and administrators are involved in the selection of materials.					
24. The staff is involved in planning with teachers.					
25. The staff serves on curriculum study committees.					
26. The hours of the LMC have been extended to evenings and weekends.					
27. The community is involved with the LMC.					
28. There is a district materials center serving professional needs.					

MATERIALS

	Low				High
29. There is a written policy for the selection of materials.					
30. Print and nonprint materials are cataloged together in one catalog.					
31. All materials are arranged for easy accessibility.					
32. The print collection meets the State standards for quantity.					

		Low			High
	0	1	2	3	4
33. The print collection meets the American Library Association recommendations for quality.					
34. The audiovisual collection meets the accepted standards for quantity.					
35. The audiovisual collection meets the accepted standards for quality.					
36. The reference collection is adequate.					
37. The periodical collection is adequate.					
38. The collection of newspapers is adequate.					
39. The vertical file material is adequate.					
40. There are indexes to periodicals.					
41. There are professional materials for teachers.					
42. The collection includes locally produced materials.					
43. There is a human resource file.					
44. The LMC is not used for nonlibrary activities.					

FACILITIES

45. The physical facilities are adequate.					
46. The physical facilities are attractive.					
47. Necessary auxiliary rooms are provided.					
48. The furniture and equipment are satisfactory.					
49. Carrels or listening centers are in use.					

FINANCE

50. This LMC receives adequate financial support.					

	Low			High
	0	1	2	3	4
51. There is a separate budget for audio-visual equipment and maintenance.					
Total the number of checks in each column.					
Multiply		x1	x2	x3	x4
Add column totals together for Grand Total.		+	+	+	=

Grand Total

Scoring

1.   0-100 = Poor
2.   101-139 = Fair
3.   140-179 = Good
4.   180 & above = Excellent

Appendix F

SCHOOL LIBRARY BILL OF RIGHTS
for School Library Media Center Programs*

The American Association of School Librarians reaffirms its belief in the Library Bill of Rights of the American Library Association. Media personnel are concerned with generating understanding of American freedoms through the development of informed and responsible citizens. To this end the American Association of School Librarians asserts that the responsibility of the school library media center is:

To provide a comprehensive collection of instructional materials selected in compliance with basic written selection principles, and to provide maximum accessibility to these materials.

To provide materials that will support the curriculum, taking into consideration the individual's needs, and the varied interests, abilities, socioeconomic backgrounds, and maturity levels of the students served.

To provide materials for teachers and students that will encourage growth in knowledge, and that will develop literary, cultural and aesthetic appreciation, and ethical standards.

To provide materials which reflect the ideas and beliefs of religious, social, political, historical, and ethnic groups and their contribution to the American and world heritage and culture, thereby enabling students to develop an intellectual integrity in forming judgments.

To provide a written statement, approved by the local Boards of Education, of the procedures for meeting the challenge of censorship of materials in school library media centers.

To provide qualified professional personnel to serve teachers and students.

*Approved by American Association of School Librarians Board of Directors, Atlantic City, 1969. Reprinted with permission of the American Library Association.

ACCESS TO RESOURCES & SERVICES IN THE
SCHOOL LIBRARY MEDIA PROGRAM
AN INTERPRETATION OF THE LIBRARY BILL OF RIGHTS*

The School Library Media Program plays a unique role in promoting intellectual freedom. It serves as a point of voluntary access to information and ideas and as a Learning Laboratory for students as they acquire critical thinking and problem solving skills needed in a pluralistic society. Although the educational level and program of the school necessarily shape the resources and services of a school library media program, the principles of the LIBRARY BILL OF RIGHTS apply equally to all libraries, including school library media programs.

School library media professionals assume a leadership role in promoting the principles of intellectual freedom within the school by providing resources and services that create and sustain an atmosphere of free inquiry. School library media professionals work closely with teachers to integrate instructional activities in classroom units designed to equip students to locate, evaluate, and use a broad range of ideas effectively. Through resources, programming, and educational processes, students and teachers experience the free and robust debate characteristic of a democratic society.

School library media professionals cooperate with other individuals in building collections of resources appropriate to the developmental and maturity levels of students. These collections provide resources which support the curriculum and are consistent with the philosophy, goals, and objectives of the school district.

Resources in school library media collections represent diverse points of view and current as well as historic issues.

Members of the school community involved in the collection development process employ educational criteria to select resources unfettered by their personal, political, social, or religious views. Students and educators served by the school library media program have access to resources and services free of constraints resulting from personal, partisan, or doctrinal-disapproval. School library media professionals resist efforts by individuals to define what is appropriate for all students or teachers to read, view or hear.

Major barriers between students and resources include: imposing age or grade level restrictions on the use of resources, limiting the use on interlibrary loan and access to electronic information, charging fees for information in specific formats, requiring permissions from parents or teachers, establishing restricted shelves or closed collections, and labeling. Policies, procedures and rules related to the use of resources and services support free and open access to information.

*Reprinted with permission of the American Library Association.

The school board adopts policies that guarantee student access to a broad range of ideas. These include policies on collection development and procedures for the review of resources about which concerns have been raised. Such policies, developed by persons in the school community, provide for a timely and fair hearing and assure that procedures are applied equitably to all expressions of concern. School library media professionals implement district policies and procedures in the school.

Adopted June 26, 1986
AASL Directors Board

Adopted July 2, 1986
ALA Council

Appendix G

LIBRARY AND CLASSROOM USE OF COPYRIGHTED VIDEOTAPES AND COMPUTER SOFTWARE*

By Mary Hutchings Reed and Debra Stanek

Mary Hutchings Reed is a partner in the law firm of Sidley & Austin, Chicago, and counsel to the American Library Association. Debra Stanek will graduate in June from the University of Chicago Law School.

After receiving numerous queries regarding library use of copyrighted videotapes and computer programs, I asked ALA attorney Mary Hutchings Reed to prepare a paper that would address the issues that librarians had brought to my attention and offer some guidance. The result is the following which we've published as an insert so that it can be removed and posted for ready access. A longer, more detailed article by Debra Stanek, "Videotapes, Computer Programs and the Library," will appear in the March 1986 issue of *Information Technology and Libraries*. These papers express the opinion of ALA's legal counsel; individuals and institutions deeply involved in copyright matters should consult their own attorneys. *Donna Kitta, Administrator, ALA Office of Copyright, Rights & Permissions*

I. VIDEOTAPES

The Copyright Revision Act of 1976 clearly protects audiovisual works such as films and videotapes. The rights of copyright include the rights of reproduction, adaptation, distribution, public performance and display. All of these rights are subject, however, to "fair use," depending on the purpose of the use, the nature of the work, the amount of the work used and the effect the use has on the market for the copyrighted work.

Libraries purchase a wide range of educational and entertainment videotapes for in-library use and for lending to patrons. Since ownership of a physical object is different from ownership of the copyright therein, guidelines are necessary to define what libraries can do with the videotapes they own without infringing the copyrights they don't. If a particular use would be an infringement, permission can always be sought from the copyright owners.

---

*American Libraries (February 1986). Reprinted with permission of the American Library Association.

A. In-classroom Use In-classroom performance of a copyrighted videotape is permissible under the following conditions:

1. The performance must be by instructors (including guest lecturers) or by pupils; and

2. the performance is in connection with face-to-face teaching activities; and

3. the entire audience is involved in the teaching activity; and

4. the entire audience is in the same room or same general area;

5. the teaching activities are conducted by a non-profit education institution; and

6. the performance takes place in a classroom or similar place devoted to instruction, such as a school library, gym, auditorium or workshop;

7. the videotape is lawfully made; the person responsible had no reason to believe that the videotape was unlawfully made.

B. In-library Use in Public Libraries

1. Most performances of a videotape in a public room as part of an entertainment or cultural program, whether a fee is charged or not, would be infringing and a performance license is required from the copyright owner.

2. To the extent a videotape is used in an educational program conducted in a library's public room, the performance will not be infringing if the requirements for classroom use are met (See I.A.).

3. Libraries which allow groups to use or rent their public meeting rooms should, as part of their rental agreement, require the group to warrant that it will secure all necessary performance licenses and indemnify the library for any failure on their part to do so.

4. If patrons are allowed to view videotapes on library-owned equipment, they should be limited to private performances, i.e. one person, or no more than one family, at a time.

5. User charges for private viewings should be nominal and directly related to the cost of maintenance of the videotape.

6. Even if a videotape is labelled "For Home Use Only," private viewing in the library should be considered to be authorized by the vendor's sale to the library with imputed knowledge of the library's intended use of the videotape.

7. Notices may be posted on videorecorders or players used in the library to educate and warn patrons about the existence of the copyright laws, such as: MANY VIDEOTAPED MATERIALS ARE PROTECTED BY COPYRIGHT. 17 U.S.C. § 101. UNAUTHORIZED COPYING MAY BE PROHIBITED BY LAW.

C. Loan of Videotapes

1. Videotapes labelled "For Home Use Only" may be loaned to patrons for their personal use. They should not knowingly be loaned to groups for public performances.
2. Copyright notice as it appears on the label of a videotape should not be obscured.
3. Nominal user fees may be charged.
4. If a patron inquires about a planned performance of a videotape, he or she should be informed that only private uses of it are lawful.
5. Videorecorders may be loaned to a patron without fear of liability even if the patron uses the recorder to infringe a copyright. However, it may be a good idea to post notices on equipment which may be used for copying (even if an additional machine would be required) to assist copyright owners in preventing unauthorized reproduction. (See I.B.7)

D. Duplication of Videotapes

1. Under limited circumstances libraries may dupe a videotape or a part thereof, but the rules of § 108 of the Copyright Revision Act of 1976 which librarians routinely utilize with respect to photocopying, apply to the reproduction.

II. COMPUTER SOFTWARE

A. Purchase Conditions Generally

Most computer software purports to be licensed rather than sold. Frequently the package containing the software is wrapped in clear plastic through which legends similar to the following appear:

> You should carefully read the following terms and conditions before opening this diskette package. Opening this diskette package indicates your acceptance of these terms and conditions. If you do not agree with them you should promptly return the package unopened and your money will be refunded.

OR

> Read this agreement carefully. Use of this product constitutes your acceptance of the terms and conditions of this agreement.

OR

> This program is licensed on the condition that you agree to the terms and conditions of this license agreement. If you do not agree to them, return the package with the diskette still sealed and your purchase price will be refunded. Opening this diskette package indicates your acceptance of these terms and conditions.

While there is at present no caselaw concerning the validity of such agreements (which are unilaterally imposed by producers), in the absence of authority to the contrary, one should assume that such licenses are in fact binding contracts. Therefore by opening and using the software the library or classroom may become contractually bound by the terms of the agreement wholly apart from the rights granted the copyright owner under the copyright laws.

Following such legends are the terms and conditions of the license agreement. The terms vary greatly between software producers and sometimes between programs produced by the same producer. Many explicitly prohibit rental or lending; some limit the program to use on one identified computer or to one user's personal use.

B. Avoiding License Restrictions

Loans of software may violate the standard license terms imposed by the copyright owner. To avoid the inconsistencies between sale to a library and the standard license restriction, libraries should note on their purchase orders the intended use of software meant to circulate. Such a legend should read:

PURCHASE IS ORDERED FOR LIBRARY
CIRCULATION AND PATRON USE

Then, if the order is filled, the library is in a good position to argue that its terms, rather than the standard license restrictions, apply.

C. Loaning Software

1. Copyright notice placed on a software label should not be obscured.
2. License terms, if any, should be circulated with the software package.
3. An additional notice may be added by the library to assist copyright owners in preventing theft. It might read: SOFTWARE PROTECTED BY COPYRIGHT, 17 U.S.C. § 101. UNAUTHORIZED COPYING IS PROHIBITED BY LAW.
4. Libraries generally will not be liable for infringement committed by borrowers.

D. Archival Copies

1. Libraries may lawfully make one archival copy of a copyrighted program under the following conditions

   a) one copy is made;
   b) the archival copy is stored;
   c) if possession of the original ceases to be lawful, the archival copy must be destroyed or transferred along with the original program;
   d) copyright notice should appear on the copy.

2. The original may be kept for archival purposes and the "archival copy" circulated. Only one copy—either the original or the archival—may be used or circulated at any given time.

3. If the circulating copy is destroyed, another "archival" copy may be made.

4. If the circulating copy is stolen, the copyright owner should be consulted before circulating or using the "archival" copy.

E. In-library and In-classroom Use

1. License restrictions, if any, should be observed.
2. If only one program is owned under license, ordinarily it may only be used on one machine at a time.
3. Most licenses do not permit a single program to be loaded into a computer which can be accessed by several different terminals or into several computers for simultaneous use.
4. If the machine is capable of being used by a patron to make a copy of a program, a warning should be posted on the machine, such as: MANY COMPUTER PROGRAMS ARE PROTECTED BY COPYRIGHT, 17 U.S.C. § 101. UNAUTHORIZED COPYING MAY BE PROHIBITED BY LAW.

III. EXAMPLES

1. A high school English teacher wants to show a videotape of the film "The Grapes of Wrath" to her class. The videotape has a label which says "Home Use Only."

As long as the § 110 (I) requirements for the classroom exception apply, the class may watch the videotape.

2. Same situation as 1, but 4 classes are studying the book, may the videotape be shown in the school auditorium or gym?

Yes, as long as the auditorium and gym are actually used as classrooms for systematic instructional activities.

3. Several students miss the performance, may they watch the videotape at some other time in the school library?

Yes, if the library is actually used for systematic instructional activities the classroom exception applies. Most school libraries are probably used as such. If it is not, such a performance may be a fair use if the viewing is in a private place in the library.

4. May several students go to the public library and borrow the videotape to watch it at home?

Yes, the library may lend the videotape for in-home viewing by a student and a small group of friends.

5. May the student go to the public library and watch the videotape in a private room?

This normally would not be permitted because more than one person would be watching the videotape. However, such a use probably would be fair under § 107 because of its relationship to the classroom activities.

6. May an elementary school teacher show a videotape of the film "Star Wars" to his or her class on the last day of school?

Because a classroom is a place where a substantial number of persons outside of a family and friends are gathered, performances in them are public. Assuming that this performance is for entertainment rather than with systematic instruction, the classroom exception would not apply. It is unlikely that such a public performance would be a fair use.

7. A book discussion group meets in a classroom at the high school. May they watch a videotape of "The Grapes of Wrath"?

No, the discussion group is not made up of class members enrolled in a non-profit institution, nor is it engaged in instructional activities, therefore the classroom exception would not apply. Any such performance would be an infringing public performance because it is a place where a group of persons larger than a family and its social acquaintances are gathered. Permission of the copyright owner should be sought.

8. Same as 7, but the group meets at a public library.

The performance may be infringing because the library is open to the public and the audience would be a group larger than a family and friends outside of a non-profit instructional program.

9. A patron asks if he can charge his friends admission to watch videotapes at his home.

The library's duty in this situation is merely to state that the videotape is subject to the copyright laws. In fact, as long as the patron shows the videotape at home to family or social acquaintances the performance would not be a public one, and therefore not infringing even if they share the cost of the videotape rental.

10. A patron asks if he can charge admission to the general public and show the videotape at a public place.

The duty is the same as in the previous situation; however, the proposed use is an infringement of copyright.

11. A librarian learns that a patron is borrowing videotapes and using them for public performances.

Again, there is a duty to notify the patron that the material is subject to the copyright laws. There is room for a variety of approaches to this situation, but there is no legal reason to treat videotapes differently from any other copyrighted materials which are capable of performance. While there is no clear duty to refuse to lend, there is a point at which a library's continued lending with actual knowledge of infringement could possibly result in liability for contributory infringement.

12. A book about the Apple IIe computer contains a diskette with a program for the computer. May the software be loaned with the book?

If the software is not subject to a license agreement it may be freely loaned like any other copyrighted work. If it is licensed, the agreement may or may not prohibit lending. A careful reading of the license is in order. If the license appears to prohibit any ordinary library uses the software producer should be contacted, and the agreement amended in writing. If this is not possible, the library should be able to return the package for a refund, as the seller, by selling to a library, may be on notice of ordinary library uses.

13. A math teacher uses one diskette to load a computer program into several terminals for use by students.

This use would violate copyright laws as well as most license agreements. It violates § 117 of the Copyright Act, which authorizes the making of *one* copy if necessary in order to use the program, because it creates copies of the program in several terminals. Further, many license agreements prohibit use of the software on more than one terminal at a time, as well as prohibiting networking or any system which enables more than one person to use the software at a time.

14. A math teacher puts a copy of "Visicalc" on reserve in the school library. The disk bears no copyright notice. May the library circulate it?

The disk ought to bear the copyright notice, but whether it is the library's legal duty to require one or to affix it is unclear. Individual library reserve policies may govern this situation—it's probably a good idea to require that the appropriate notices be affixed prior to putting the copy on reserve. Further, the lack of copyright notices may put the library on notice that this is a copy rather than the original program. If the original is retained by the teacher as an archival copy (i.e., not used) there is no problem. If not, then the reserve copy is an unauthorized copy and its use would violate the copyright laws and most license agreements. While the library might not be legally liable in this situation it would be wise to establish a policy for placing materials on reserve which prevents this.

15. May the library make an archival copy of the "Visicalc" program on its reserve shelf?

Usually yes. Section 117 permits the owner of the software to make or authorize the making of one archival copy. If the teacher who put the program on reserve has not made one, she or he may permit the library to do so. Remember, most license agreements and the copyright laws permit the making of *one* archival copy.

16. Same as 15, except the reserve copy is damaged. May the library make another copy (assuming it has the archival copy) for circulation?

Yes, the purpose of an archival copy is for use as a back-up in case of damage or destruction. The library may then make another archival copy to store while circulating the other.

17. Same as 16, except the reserve copy is stolen.

Perhaps. It is not clear whether the purpose of a back-up copy includes replacement in the event of theft but arguably it does. However, § 108(c) permits reproduction of audiovisual works (which includes many computer programs) in the event of damage, loss, or theft *only* if a replacement may not be obtained at a fair price. Further, some license agreements require that archival copies be destroyed when possession (not ownership) of the original ceases. Therefore a replacement copy may need to be purchased. A safe course is to consult the software vendor.

18. When the teacher retrieves his or her copy of the program may the library retain the archival copy?

No. When possession of the orignal ceases, the archival copy must be transferred with the original or destroyed. If it is returned with the original, the teacher would not be permitted to make additional copies—he or she would have an original and the archival copy. Most license agreements contain similar provisions.

19. A librarian learns that a patron is copying copyrighted software on the library's public access computers.

There is a duty to notify the patron that the software is subject to the copyright laws. The computers should have notices similar to those on unsupervised photocopiers.

INDEX

AASL/AECT guidelines (national), 20, 29-30, 110-11, 128, 136, 146-47, 154, 172, 205

Access to Resources and Services in the School Library Media Program: An Interpretation of the Library Bill of Rights, 240-41

Accountability, 106

Accreditation: A Way Ahead, 13

Achievements, 33, 74-100, 184
  curriculum development and improvement, 33, 75, 96-100
  design and production of media, 33, 75, 95-96
  guidance and consulting services, 33, 74-80
  instruction and in-service, 33, 74, 80-95

Acoustical treatment, 160

Acquisitions, 196

Activities, management, 33-34, 43-70
  controlling, 33-34, 61-69
  leading, 33-34, 59-61
  organizing, 33-34, 54-58
  planning, 33-34, 46-54

Administering the budget, 218-19

Administration, 45

Administrative space, 154

Administrators, school, 104-6

Aides, 96, 125-26

Alliance for Excellence, 9-12

Alternatives in LMC facilities organization, 140-45
  centralized LMC divisional or resource center schemes, 142-43
  centralized LMC system, 141-42
  decentralized LMC system, 144-45
  school as LMC concept, 140-41

Appraisal, personnel, 131, 231-34

Architect, 138-40

Assembling resources, 58

Assets, 33-34, 104-31, 135-69, 172-200, 204-19
  budget, 33-34, 204-19
  facilities, 33-34, 135-69
  media, 33-34, 172-200
  personnel, 33-34, 104-31

Assumptions/attributes, 46

Attributes, schools, 6, 46

Audio, 168, 181
  equipment, 181
  media, 181
  storage, 168

Authority, 54-56

Behavioral Requirements Analysis Checklist, 115

Bennett, William J., 5

Block diagram, 64-65

Bowie, Melvin, 26

BRS, 37

Budget, 33-34, 204-19
  administering, 218-19
  preparation, 204-11
    background information, 204-9
    cost estimates, 209-10
  systems, 211-18
    formula, 212
    line-item, 211-12
    performance, 212
    PPBS, 213-16
    ZBB, 216-18

Card catalog, 164
Career ladder, 128-29
Carrels, 161-63
Caudill, William, 148-49
Ceilings, 159
Centralized LMC divisional or resource
   center schemes, 142-43
Centralized LMC system, 141-42
Certification, 115-16
Chairs, 164
Chapman, Edward, 33
Circulation/distribution, 150-51, 153-54,
   164, 196-98
Clerks, 125-26
Collection building, 185-86
*College: The Undergraduate Experience
   in America*, 4
Communication, 61, 78-79
   defined, 61
   one-way, 61
   students, 78
   teachers, 79
   two-way, 61
Community groups, media selection, 190
Competencies, 115-20
Comprehensive planning, 47-53
Computer software, copyright, 244-46,
   248
Computers, 36-37, 84-86, 151-52, 228-29
   assessment, 84-85
   databases, 37
   instruction, 85-86
   learning laboratory, 151-52
   uses in subject areas, 228-29
Conference rooms, 151, 154-55
Connecticut guidelines, 84-86, 115-16,
   228-29
Consulting services for teachers, 78-80
   communication, 79
   information retrieval and utilization, 79
   professional services, 80
Controlling, 33-34, 61-69, 204-19
   budget, 64, 204-19
   defined, 61
   effectiveness, 62-63
   efficiency, 64
   evaluation, 68-69

feedback loop, 62
   flow charting, 64-66
   public relations, 66-67
   publicity, 66
   reports, 66
Coordination, 61
Coordinator, LMC, 121-22
Copyright, 242-48
   computer software, 244-46, 248
   videotapes, 242-44, 247
Cost estimates, 209-10
   audiovisual media, 209-10
   equipment replacement, 209
Criteria, 6, 97-98, 192-95
   media and equipment, 192-95
   quality of schools, 6
   subject matter selection, 97-98
Criticism, 2-7, 13-15
   education, 2-7
   library education, 13-15
Cross media, 181
Curriculum development and improvement, 33, 35, 96-100
   development, 97-98
   implementation, 99-100
   independent study, 28, 98-99
   individualization, 28, 98-99
   inquiry, 28, 98-99
   subject matter selection, 97-98

Darkroom and recording studio,
   152-53
Databases, 37
Decentralized facilities, 144-45
Decentralized LMC system, 144-45
Decision making, 53-54
   defined, 53
   optimizing, 53
   process, 53
   satisficing, 53
   strategies, 53
   values, 54
Decision packages, 217-18
Departmentation, 54-55
Deployment of personnel, 127-28

Design and production of media, 33, 35,
  95-96, 100, 185
  aides, 96
  defined, 95-96
  design, 95-96
  library media specialist, 95
  production, 96, 185
  students, 96
  teachers, 96
  technicians, 96
Diagnostic standards, 68
Dialog, 37
District director, job description,
  230
District LMC system, 35-36
Drucker, Peter, 44, 63

Education, 2-13
  *College: The Undergraduate Experience
    in America*, 4
  Elementary School Recognition
    Program, 5-6
  *Nation at Risk: The Imperative for
    Educational Reform*, 2-3
  portrait, successful secondary schools,
    7
  quality criteria, 6
  quality indicators, 6
  reform, 2-13
  Schools of the Future, 5
  *Search for Successful Secondary
    Schools*, 6-7
  *Tomorrow's Teachers: A Report of the
    Holmes Group*, 4
Educational specifications, 136-38
Effectiveness, 62-63
Efficiency, 64
Elementary and Secondary Education
  Act, 20
Elementary School Recognition Program,
  5-6
Ellsworth, Ralph, 157-58
Employee development, 58
Entrance, coatroom, lounge, 153-54
Equipment, 172-200, 209
  audio, 181

criteria, 194-95
  Illinois, 176-78
  Ohio, 174-75
media production, 185
microcomputers, 183-84
motion pictures, 180
replacement, 209
still pictures, 179-180
television, 182-83
Evaluation, 68-69, 100, 192
  defined, 68
  diagnostic standards, 68
  media and equipment, 192
  projective standards, 68
  qualitative, 68-69
  quantitative, 68
Evaluative Criteria, 69
Extracurricular programs, 78

Facilities, 135-61
  centralized, 141-43, 149-61
    internal physical environment, 158-60
    primary space, 150-53
    security, 160
    support space, 153-57
    traffic patterns, 157-58
  factors in planning, 135-45
    alternatives in organization, 140-45
    architect, 138-40
    rationale for space, 135-36
    role of head of LMC, 137-38
  location, 145-49
    flexibility, 148-49
    relating space to program,
      146-48
Feedback loop, 62
Field experience, 184
Flexibility, 148-49
Flooring, 160
Flow charting, 64-66
  block diagram, 64-65
  decision flow chart, 65
  template, 64
Forecasting, 58
Formal instruction, 80-86
Formula budget, 212

Furniture, 161-69
  card catalog, 164
  carrels, 161-63
  chairs, 164
  circulation desk, 164
  open stacks, 165
  seating, 161-64
  shelving, 165-69
  storing media, 164-69
    audio cassettes, 168
    books, 165-67
    8mm films, 168
    filmstrips, 168
    kits, 168
    microforms, 168
    pamphlets, 168
    periodicals, 167
    records, 167
    16mm films, 168
    slides, 168
    transparencies, 168
  tables, 163
  vertical files, 168
  workstations, 161-62

General function area, 151
Graphics, 184
Gross, Ronald, 148
Group projects and research, 151
Guidance and consulting services, 33-35,
    74-80
  consulting services for teachers, 78-80
    communication, 79
    information retrieval and utilization,
        79
    professional services, 80
  guidance services for students,
      74-80
    communication, 78
    extracurricular programs, 78
    information retrieval and utilization,
        76-77
    reading guidance, 77-78
Guidance services for students, 74-80
  communication, 78
  extracurricular programs, 78
    information retrieval and utilization,
        76-77
    reading guidance, 77-78
Guidelines
  AASL/AECT (national), 20, 29-30, 110-
      11, 128, 136, 146-47, 154, 172, 205
  Connecticut, 84-86, 115-16, 228-29
  Illinois, 113, 176-78, 207
  Mississippi, 118-20
  Nevada, 112
  North Carolina, 28-29, 82, 121-26,
      230-34
  Ohio, 114, 174-75, 205
  South Carolina, 105-6, 235-38
  South Dakota, 83, 222-27
  Virginia, 81-82
Guidesheets, 90

Ho, May Lein, 26

Illinois guidelines, 113, 176-78, 207
Independent study, 28, 98-99
Individualization, 28, 98-99
"Information Age," 1
Information retrieval and utilization,
    76-77, 79
  students, 76-77
  teachers, 79
Information technology, 8
Inquiry, 28, 98-99
In-service, 33, 74, 92-95. See also Instruc-
    tion and in-service; Personnel
  library media specialists, 94-95
  LMC-initiated in-service, 93-94
Instruction, 33, 74, 80-82
  applications of technology, 92
  Connecticut, 84, 228-29
  formal programs, 80-86
  guidesheets, 90
  instructional systems, 87-89
  North Carolina, 82
  pathfinders, 91
  scope and sequence, 222-27
  small groups, 89-90
  South Dakota, 83, 222-27
  use of computers, 84-86, 228-29
  Virginia, 81-82

Instruction and in-service, 33, 35, 74, 80-95
  in-service, 33, 74, 92-95
    library media specialists, 94-95
    LMC-initiated in-service, 93-94
  instruction, 33, 74, 80-92
    application of technology, 92
    formal programs, 80-86
    guidesheets, 90
    instructional systems, 87-89
    pathfinders, 91
    small groups, 89-90
Instructional kits, 184
Instructional planning, 152
Instructional system components, 95
Instructional systems, 87-89
Internal physical environment (LMC), 158-60
  acoustical treatment, 160
  ceilings, 159
  flooring, 160
  lighting, 159
  temperature control, 158
  wall treatment, 160
Inventory, 200

Job analysis, 58
Job descriptions, 107-8, 121-26, 230
  aide, 125-26
  coordinator, 121-22
  director, 230
  library media specialist, 121-22
  technician, 123-24

Khadem, Riaz, 66
Knapp Foundation, 20

Leadership, 60-61
Leading, 33-34, 59-61
  communication, 61
  coordination, 61
  leadership, 60-61
  motivation, 59-60
Learning activity packages, 87-89

Library cooperatives, 36
Library education, criticism of, 13-15
Library media center, 25-29, 33-37, 235-38
  defined, 28-29, 33-37
  evaluation instrument, 235-38
  research, 25-28
Library media specialist, 115-23, 231-34
  certification, 115-16
  competencies, 115-20
  job description, 121-22
  performance appraisal, 231-34
  personality, 122-23
Liesener, James, 51-52
Lighting, 159
Line and staff organization, 54-55, 57
Line-item budget, 211-12
Line organization, 54-56
LMC-initiated in-service, 93-94
Location of LMC, 145-49
Loertscher, David V., 26
Lorber, Robert, 66

Maintenance and repair, 156
Maintenance of media and equipment, 199-200, 209
Management
  activities, 33-34, 43-70
    controlling, 33-34, 61-69
    leading, 33-34, 59-61
    organizing, 33-34, 54-58
    planning, 33-34, 46-54
  communication, 61
  coordination, 61
  current ideas, 43-46
  defined, 43
  effectiveness, 62-63
  efficiency, 64
  evaluation, 68-69, 100
  leadership, 60-61
  microcomputer use, 184
  motivation, 59-60
  7S framework, 44
  style, 45, 60-61
Management by Objectives (MBO), 48-51, 62, 131

Manager, 43
  middle, 43
  supervisory, 43
  top, 43
Matrix organization, 54-55, 57
Mazlow, Abraham, 59
Media and equipment, 33, 98, 172-200
  building media collections, 185-88
    balance, 187
    new schools, 185-86
    resource sharing, 187-88
    school closings, 187
  defined, 172
  Illinois, 176-78
  Ohio, 174-75
  selection, 188-95
    criteria, 192-95
    direct evaluation, 192
    district-level coordination, 191
    media policy, 188-89
    organizing for selection, 191
    who selects, 189-91
  technical services, 195-200
    acquisitions, 196
    circulation/distribution, 196-99
    inventory/weeding, 200
    maintenance, 199-200
    preparation and organization, 196
  types of media and equipment, 179-85
    audio, 181
    field experience, 184
    graphics, 184
    instruction kits, 185
    microcomputers, 183-84
    motion pictures, 180
    realia, 185
    still pictures, 179-80
    television, 182-83
    three-dimensional media, 185
Media center. *See* Library media center
Media production, 96, 152-53, 185
Media selection policy, 188-89
Media specialist. *See* Library media
  specialist
Microcomputers, 36-37, 84-86, 151-52,
  184, 228-29
  assessment, 84-85

  instruction, 85-86
  learning laboratory, 151-52
  management use, 184
  uses in subject areas, 228-29
Mississippi guidelines, 118-20
Motivation, 59
  Mazlow, Abraham, 59
  Nierenberg, Gerard, 59

Naisbitt, John, 1
*Nation at Risk: The Imperative for
  Educational Reform*, 2-3
National Task Force on Educational
  Technology, 7-9
NELINET, 36-37
Networks, 35-37
Nevada guidelines, 112
*New Directions in Library and Informa-
  tion Education*, 15, 116-18
Nierenberg, Gerard, 59
North Carolina guidelines, 28-29, 82,
  121-26, 230-34

OCLC, 36
Odiorne, George, 45
Ohio guidelines, 114, 174-75, 205
Online networks, 36
Open stacks, 165
Optimizing, 53
Organization charts, 55-57
Organizing 33-34, 54-58
  assembling resources, 58
  authority, 54-56
  defined, 54
  departmentation, 54-55
  line and staff organization, 54-55, 57
  line organization, 54-56
  matrix organization, 54-55, 57
  staffing positions, 57

Parents, media selection, 190
Pathfinders, 9
Performance appraisal, 231-34
Performance budget, 212

Personality, library media specialist, 122-23
Personnel, 33-34, 57-58, 104-31, 231-34
  accountability, 106
  appraisal, 131, 231-34
  considerations, 106-10
    job descriptions, 107-8
    position classification, 108-9
    selection, 109-10
  planning process, 57-58
  school level considerations, 104-6
    school administrators, 104-6
    service approaches, 106
  staffing, 57-58, 110-31
    career ladder, 128-29
    deployment of personnel, 127-28
    Illinois, 113
    library media specialists, 115-23
    Mississippi, 118-20
    Nevada, 112
    Ohio, 114
    reality staffing, 127
    supervision, 129-31
    support staff, 123-27
Peters, Thomas, 2
Planning, 33-34, 46-54
  comprehensive, 47-54
  decision making, 53-54
  defined, 46-47
  objectives, 47
  performance standards, 49-51
Planning process, personnel, 57-58
Planning, Programming, Budgeting
    System (PPBS), 48, 213-16
Planning systems
  Management by Objectives (MBO),
    48-51, 62, 131
  Planning, Programming, Budgeting
    (PPBS), 48, 213-16
  Zero Base Budgeting, 48, 216-18
Policy, media selection, 188-89
Portrait, successful secondary schools, 7
Position classification, 108-9
Preparation and organization, media,
  196
Primary space (LMC), 150-53
  circulation/distribution, keys, 150-51

computerized learning laboratory,
  151-52
conference rooms, 151, 154-55
darkroom and recording studio, 152-53
general function area, 151
group projects and research, 151
instructional planning, 152
media production, 152-53
professional collections, 152
small group listening and viewing, 151
Production of media, 33, 35, 95-96, 100,
  185
  aides, 96
  defined, 95-96
  design, 95-96
  library media specialist, 95
  students, 96
  teachers, 96
  technicians, 96
Professional services, 78-80
Projective standards, 68
Promotion, 58
Public relations, 66-67

Qualitative standards, 68-69
Quality, 6-7
  criteria, 6-7
  indicators, 6
Quantitative standards, 68

Radio. *See* Television and radio
Reading guidance, 77-78
Realia, 185
Realities, 12
Recording studio, 152-53
Recruitment, 58
Reddin, William, 48
Reform, 2-15
  education, 2-13
  library education, 13-15
Relating LMC space to program, 146-48
Reports, 66
Research, 25-28, 122-23
  library media center, 25-28
  library media specialist, 122-23
Resource sharing, 187-88

Satisficing, 53
School administrators, 104-6
School as LMC concept, 140-41
School closings, 187
School financial accounting guide, 207-8
School level considerations, 104-6
  school administrators, 104-6
  service approaches, 106
School Library Bill of Rights, 189, 239-41
Schools, 2-13. *See also* Education
  criteria of quality, 6-7
  indicators of quality, 6
  reform, 2-13
  themes, 7
Schools of the Future, 5
Scope and sequence, instruction, 222-27
Search for Successful Secondary Schools,
  6-7
Seating, 161-64
Secretary of Education, 5
Security, facilities, 160
Selection, 97-99, 109-10, 192-95
  equipment, 194-95
  media, 192-94
  personnel, 109-10
  subject matter, 97-98
Separation, 58
Service approaches, LMC, 106
7S framework, 44
Shelving, 165-69
Skills inventory, 58
Small group instruction, 89-90
Small group listening and viewing, 151
Software, copyright, 244-46, 248
South Carolina guidelines, 105-6, 235-38
South Dakota guidelines, 83, 222-27
Stacks, open, 165
Staff convenience center, 156
Staffing, 57, 110-31
Standards, 49-51, 68-69. *See also*
  Guidelines
  defined, 68
  diagnostic, 68
  performance, 49-51
  projective, 68
  qualitative, 68-69
  quantitative, 68

Still pictures, 179
Storage space, 155
Storing media, 164-69
  audio cassettes, 168
  books, 165-67
  8mm films, 168
  kits, 168
  microforms, 168
  pamphlets, 168
  periodicals, 167
  records, 167
  slides, 168
  transparencies, 168
Strategies, 53-54
Student assistants, 127
Students, 31-33, 76-78, 96, 194
  communication, 78
  design and production, 96
  extracurricular programs, 78
  formal instruction, 80-86
  guidance services, 76-78
  information retrieval and utilization,
    76-77
  media selection, 194
  needs, 31-33
  reading guidance, 77-78
Style, management, 45, 60-61
Subject matter selection, 97-98
Successful schools, 5-7
Supervision, 129-31
Support space (LMC), 153-57
  administrative space, 154
  entrance, coatroom, lounge, 153-54
  maintenance and repair, 156
  staff convenience center, 156
  storage spaces, 155
  technical services, 154
  television and radio, 155-56
Support staff, 123-27
  aides, 125
  student assistants, 127
  technicians, 123
  volunteers, 127

Tables, 163
Teachers, 30-31, 78-80, 96, 194

communication, 79
consulting services, 78-80
design and production of media, 96
information retrieval and utilization,
    79
media selection, 194
needs, 30-31
professional services, 80
Technical services, 153-54, 195-200
acquisitions, 196
circulation/distribution, 196-99
facility, 153-54
inventory/weeding, 200
maintenance, 199-200
preparation and organization, 196
Technicians, 96, 123-24
Television and radio, 36, 155-56, 182
Temperature control, 158
Third Wave, 1
3A system, 33-35, 43-69, 74-100, 104-31,
    135-69, 172-200, 204-19
achievements, 33, 35, 74-100, 184
activities, 33, 34, 43-69
assets, 33-34, 104-31, 135-69, 172-200,
    204-19
Three-dimensional media, 185
Three *I*s, 28, 98-99
independent study, 28, 98-99
individualization, 28, 98-99
inquiry, 28, 98-99
Toffler, Alvin, 1
*Tomorrow's Teachers: A Report of the
Holmes Group*, 4

Traffic patterns, 157-58
Training and development, 130-31
Transfer, 58
Transforming American Education, 7
Triple A, 33-35, 43-69, 74-100, 104-31,
    135-69, 172-200, 204-19
achievements, 33-35, 74-100, 184
activities, 33-34, 43-69
assets, 33-34, 104-31, 135-69, 172-200,
    204-19

U.S. Department of Education, 5-7
Elementary School Recognition
    Program, 5-6
*Search for Successful Secondary
    Schools*, 6-7

Vertical files, 168
Videotapes, copyright, 242-44, 247
Virginia guidelines, 81-82
Volunteers, 127

Wall treatment, 160
Waterman, Robert, 2
Weeding, 200
Workstations, 161-62

Zero Base Budgeting (ZBB), 48, 216-18